Collaboration thr~

Edited by Amanda Ravetz, ~tle
and Helen Felcey

B L O O M S B U R Y
LONDON • NEW DELHI • NEW YORK • SYDNEY

Bloomsbury Academic

An imprint of Bloomsbury Publishing Plc

50 Bedford Square
London
WC1B 3DP
UK

1385 Broadway
New York
NY 10018
USA

www.bloomsbury.com

First published 2013

British Library Cataloguing-in-Publication Data
A catalogue record for this book is available from the British Library.

ISBN: HB: 978-0-8578-5391-2
PB: 978-0-8578-5392-9

Library of Congress Cataloging-in-Publication Data
A catalog record for this book is available from the Library of Congress.

Typeset by Apex CoVantage, LLC, Madison, WI, USA.
Printed and bound in India

Contents

List of Illustrations   ix

Acknowledgments   xi

Contributors   xiii

Introduction: Collaboration through Craft   1
Amanda Ravetz, Alice Kettle and Helen Felcey

PART I: EXPERIENCING COLLABORATION THROUGH CRAFT

Introduction   19
Alice Kettle, Helen Felcey and Amanda Ravetz

1. Collaboration: A Creative Journey or a Means to an End?   22
Lesley Millar

2. Moving Things around . . . Collaboration and Dynamic Change   31
Helen Carnac

3. Triangulation: Working towards a Practice of Collaboration   45
David Gates, Alice Kettle and Jane Webb

4. The Creation of a Collective Voice   59
Brass Art: Chara Lewis, Kristin Mojsiewicz and Anneké Pettican

PART II: THE GENERATIVE POWER OF CRAFT

Introduction   73
Helen Felcey, Alice Kettle and Amanda Ravetz

5. Catalytic Clothing and Tactility Factory:
Crafted Collaborative Connections   77
Trish Belford

6. The Aesthetic of Waste: Exploring the Creative Potential of Recycled Ceramic Waste 88

David Binns

7. Designing Collaboration: Evoking Dr Johnson through Craft and Interdisciplinarity 100

Jason Cleverly and Tim Shear

8. sKINship: An Exchange of Material Understanding between Plastic Surgery and Pattern Cutting 114

Rhian Solomon

PART III: INSTITUTIONAL COLLABORATIONS

Introduction 127

Helen Felcey, Alice Kettle and Amanda Ravetz

9. Department 21: The Craft of Discomfort 130

Stephen Knott

10. Skills in the Making 142

Simon Taylor and Rachel Payne

11. Project Dialogue: Promoting a Transdisciplinary Approach to Postgraduate Arts Pedagogy 157

Barbara Hawkins and Brett Wilson

12. A Question of Value: Rethinking the Mary Greg Collection 170

Sharon Blakey and Liz Mitchell

PART IV: COLLABORATION IN AN EMERGING WORLD: ANOTHER WAY OF BEING?

Introduction 189

Alice Kettle, Helen Felcey and Amanda Ravetz

13. Expanded Battlefields: Craft as a Different Sort of Reenactment 193

Allison Smith

14. Crafts and the Contemporary in South Asia— A Collaborative Journey 206

Barney Hare Duke and Jeremy Theophilus

15. Circling Back into That Thing We Cast Forward:
A Closing Read on *Gestures of Resistance*   219

Judith Leemann and Shannon Stratton

16. Expanded Craft, Dispersed Creativity: A South Asian Residency   233

Cj O'Neill and Amanda Ravetz

EPILOGUE

A Response: The Limits of Collaboration   247

Glenn Adamson

Index   251

Illustrations

FIGURES

1.1. *Souvenir Line: Nomadic Memory*, 2004.   25

1.2. Kiyonori Shimada and Gabriella Göranssen in Shimada's outside installation for Cultex at Gallery F15, 2009.   28

2.1. Walking, Talking, Making, Berlin, 2011.   36

2.2. Intelligent Trouble: Process shot, 2010.   39

2.3. Intelligent Trouble at the Institute of Making, 2011.   40

3.1. Notes and sketches for Pairings project, 2009.   50

3.2. Triangulation Theory Workshop, 2010.   54

3.3. *Pairings* exhibition, Triangulation Theory Collection, 2010.   56

4.1. *Still Life No. 1*, 2011.   61

4.2. *Moments of Death and Revival*, 2008.   64

5.1. Helen Storey and Trish Belford adding final touches to *Herself*, 2010.   81

5.2. Printing the velvet for concrete wall panel, 2011.   85

6.1. Waste bone china tableware, 2010.   93

6.2. Cast tile, 2010.   96

6.3. Prototype cast tiles, 2010.   96

7.1. Dr Johnson's House, 17 Gough Square, London, 2009.   101

7.2. *Interactive Table and Escritoire*, 2009.   102

7.3. Pro Forma, 2009.   103

9.1. The vacated painting studios, 2010.   131

9.2. Department 21 chairs made during the opening of *Take a Seat in Department 21*, 2010.   135

9.3. Paint-by-number workshop, 2010.   138

9.4. Discussion on the deck, 2010.   138

10.1. Drawing in three dimensions, 2009.   143

12.1. Tray of Noah's Ark animals, about 1840.   172

12.2. Broken spoon, brass, probably made about 1680. 179

12.3. Chatelaine, steel and silver, 1880. 180

13.1. *Hobby Horse*, 2006. 199

13.2. *By the by and by and by*, 2007. 200

13.3. *Fancy Work (Crazy Quilting)*, 2010. 202

14.1. Arts Reverie, 2011. 208

14.2. *Painted Bedford Truck*, 2011. 215

15.1. Ehren Tool, *Occupation*, 2010. 221

15.2. *Gestures of Resistance*, 2010. 223

16.1. Neet/Community, 2010. 235

16.2. The Pol Project, 2010. 236

COLOUR PLATES

1. *Untitled* (detail), 2004.

2. *Pairings* exhibition, 2010.

3. *The Myth of Origins, Proteiform 3*, 2008.

4. 'Child's own tutor' alphabet fan, c. 1920.

5. Ceramic flower bicycle, Ahmedabad, India, 2011.

6. Sara leading, day 7; John listening, day 7, 2010.

7. *The Muster (Troops Drilling at Fort Jay),* 2005.

8. Diagram of connections, The Pol Project, 2010.

Acknowledgements

The present volume has its origins in the Pairings project, led by Alice Kettle at Manchester Metropolitan University (MMU). The setting of an institution with its different territories and conversations provoked a desire to exchange ideas across the seemingly discrete and designated territories of art and design. The questions Pairings posed were far-reaching and sometimes controversial, examining aspects of thinking and making fundamental to the manifestation of craft in an institutional context. It is a testament to the rich learning and experimental environment of Manchester School of Art and MIRIAD (Manchester Institute for Research and Innovation in Art and Design) that Pairings came into being. We would especially like to thank Alex McErlain, former senior lecturer at MMU, who initiated and nourished the project; Stephanie Boydell, curator in the Special Collections Gallery (MMU), who facilitated the exhibition and tour; and Alke Gröppel-Wegener, who provided analysis, commentary and editorship for the first *Pairings* catalogue.

Through the simple device of bringing people, materials and organizations together and seeing what happened, the Pairings project extended beyond MMU to become a broad practice-based, research-focused forum. In particular, the international conference Pairings: Conversations, Collaborations, Materials held at MMU in 2011, provided the foundations for this volume. We thank all the individuals, institutions and organizations who were part of that conference and those who continue to be involved in this ongoing project, for their insightful contributions.

Beyond the contributors to this volume, we would like to thank a number of people who read and commented upon or otherwise contributed to this book: Beccy Kennedy at MIRIAD, MMU; Bill Lucas at the Centre for Real World Learning University of Winchester; Anne Douglas at Gray's School of Art, Robert Gordon University; Jessica Hemmings, at Edinburgh College of Art; Anna Grimshaw at Emory University; and Glenn Adamson at the Victoria and Albert Museum and the MAP Consortium. Last but not least, we thank our postgraduate students at MIRIAD and students on the Manchester School of Art MA Design programme for their generous contributions to our thinking about collaboration and craft.

We are very grateful for financial support provided by MIRIAD, Manchester School of Art, MMU for the initial Pairings project and for continued and varied forms of support up to the publication of this book. Finally, we acknowledge all those who have been generous enough to allow us to use the images to which they hold the permissions. Every effort has been made to contact all copyright holders. The publishers will be pleased to make good in future editions any errors or omissions brought to their attention.

Contributors

Glenn Adamson is head of research at the Victoria and Albert Museum. He is co-editor of the *Journal of Modern Craft*, the author of *Thinking through Craft* (Berg Publishers/V&A Publications, 2007), *The Craft Reader* (Berg, 2010) and *Invention of Craft* (Berg, 2012). He is co-editor of *Global Design History* (Routledge, 2011) and *Surface Tensions* (Manchester University Press, 2012). His most recent project is a major exhibition and publication for the V&A entitled *Postmodernism: Style and Subversion, 1970 to 1990*.

Trish Belford founded Belford Prints Ltd, a small, unique textile business. In 2004, she became senior research fellow at the University of Ulster, developing projects such as Tactility Factory with architect professor Ruth Morrow (QUB) (www.tactilityfactory.com), Wonderland & Catalytic Clothing with Professor Helen Storey (LCF) (http://www.helenstoreyfoundation.org/), and *Shadow Tissues*, a Leverhulme-funded project with Dr Philip Sykas (MMU) assisted by research assistant Beth Milligan. In 2009 she was awarded the Society of Dyers and Colourist silver medal.

David Binns is reader in contemporary ceramics at the University of Central Lancashire, Preston, UK. He is a member of the UNESCO International Academy of Ceramics (Geneva) and a fellow of the UK Crafts Potters Association. His ceramic work is in collections, including the Museum of Arts & Design, New York, and the World Ceramic Museum, Fuping, China. His current research involves exploring how recycled ceramic, glass and mineral waste can be developed as a unique new 'eco-material'.

Sharon Blakey is senior lecturer and joint programme leader for BA (Hons) Three-dimensional Design at Manchester School of Art, MMU. She exhibits her work in the United Kingdom and abroad and has lectured at conferences nationally and has published in a number of academic and professional journals and catalogues. She is currently researching the Mary Greg Collection held at Manchester Art Gallery and is working on creative projects in collaboration with weaver Ismini Samanidou, jeweller Jenny Walker and graphic designer Jonathan Hitchin.

Brass Art is the collaborative practice of Chara Lewis, senior lecturer, Manchester School of Art, MMU; Dr Kristin Mojsiewicz, lecturer, Edinburgh College of Art/Edinburgh University; and Anneké Pettican, senior lecturer, University of Huddersfield. Recent exhibitions include *Flights of Fancy*, Tatton Park Biennial (2012); *Dark Matters*, Whitworth Art Gallery, Manchester (2011); *Skyscraping*, Yorkshire Sculpture Park (2008); and *The Jerwood Drawing Prize*, The Jerwood Space, London (2008). Recent papers include *From Wunderkammern to Kinect—The Creation of Shadow Worlds*, Siggraph, Los Angeles (2012); *Wonder and the Digital Double*, the 2nd International Conference on 3D Body Scanning Technologies, Lugano, Switzerland (2011); and *Digital Doubles* ISEA, Dortmund (2010; www.brassart.org.uk).

Helen Carnac is an artist, maker and curator. She is a founding member of Intelligent Trouble and a fellow of the Royal Society of Arts. Projects include co-chair, UK Contemporary Jewellery's conference Carry the Can (2006); Cultural Leadership Fellowship (UK, 2009); curator of *Taking Time: Craft and the Slow Revolution* (2009); guest professor (KHB, Berlin, 2011); Walking, Talking, Making (UK, 2010); *Marking Place* (Sint Lucas, Antwerp, 2011); *Intelligent Trouble* (King's College London, 2011); *The Tool at Hand* (Milwaukee Art Museum, 2011–12); *Drawing, Permanence and Place* (Kunstverein, Coburg 2012); and Side by Side (Siobhan Davies Dance, London, 2012).

Jason Cleverly is course leader for contemporary crafts at University College Falmouth. He has developed a series of situational, interpretive sculptural craftworks for museums and art galleries. Many of these projects have been developed in close collaboration with social scientists at King's College London. He is a PhD student undertaking a critical evaluation of this situated design practice.

Helen Felcey is a practicing artist working in ceramics and exhibiting internationally. She is programme leader for the MA Design programme at Manchester School of Art, MMU. Helen's research interests are in collaborative, social craft and design practices, which inform education, research and local community. She co-curated the Pairings: Conversations, Collaborations, Materials (2012) international conference. Since 2008, Helen has been chair of the National Association for Ceramics in Higher Education (NACHE). During this time, NACHE has worked with the British Ceramics Biennial on FRESH, which profiles graduates of higher education ceramics programmes in the United Kingdom.

David Gates designs and makes furniture. His PhD research at King's College London examines the narratives and discourses of workshop practice. Awarded the Jerwood Prize for Contemporary Makers 2010 and the Wesley

Barrell Prize 2011, he jointly founded Intelligent Trouble. Recent exhibitions include *Taking Time; Craft and the Slow Revolution* (2009–11), *Intelligent Trouble* at Contemporary Applied Arts (2010), *Jerwood Contemporary Makers* (2010–11), *Starting Points* at the Siobhan Davies Studios (2010), *Host*, San Francisco (2011) and *The Tool at Hand*, Milwaukee Art Museum (2011–12).

Barney Hare Duke specializes in contemporary crafts as an artist, teacher, manager, Arts Council England development officer, independent arts consultant, curator and project manager. He is a co-director of A Fine Line: Cultural Practice with Jeremy Theophilus. A Fine Line programme includes The British Ceramics Biennial, Stoke-on-Trent, 2009–14; Material Response, international artists residencies and curatorial initiatives; and Craft Who Cares research project. A Fine Line holds a visiting fellowship with MIRIAD, Manchester Metropolitan University, United Kingdom.

Barbara Hawkins is an arts educator, researcher and practitioner in the Faculty of Creative Arts at the University of the West of England, Bristol, United Kingdom. Previously the head of the faculty's graduate school, her work has been strongly focused on issues concerning postgraduate practice-led arts study. She co-founded the transdisciplinary teaching and research group Project Dialogue six years ago to promote innovative approaches to arts-doctorate research training. Currently, she is the departmental research degrees coordinator with special responsibility for practice-led research, contributes to faculty doctoral research governance and continues to supervise arts-practice doctoral students.

Alice Kettle is senior research fellow at Manchester School of Art, MMU and has been visiting professor at the Centre for Real World Learning, University of Winchester since 2010. Her artistic practice is in stitched textile with work in international collections, including Whitworth Art Gallery, Manchester; MIAA Turin, Italy; and Crafts Council, London. Commissions include National Library of Australia; National Maritime Museum, London; and Winchester Discovery Centre UK. She co-authored *Machine Stitch Perspectives* (2010) and *Hand Stitch Perspectives* (2012) and is co-founder and curator of the *Pairings* project.

Stephen Knott was the third holder of the AHRC-funded Modern Craft: History, Theory and Practice Collaborative Doctoral Award at the Royal College of Art/Victoria and Albert Museum. His recently completed PhD, 'Amateur Craft as a Differential Practice', explores the historical evidence and theoretical richness of this marginalized phenomenon. His broad research interests are reflected in publications, which include an article about railway modelling enthusiasts in *Design and Culture*, the recent history of the producing consumer (or 'prosumer') for the same journal, a chapter on paint-by-number kits in an edited volume entitled *Surface Tensions* (Manchester University Press, forthcoming), and written work as managing editor for the *Journal of Modern Craft*.

Judith Leemann is assistant professor in Fine Arts 3D/Fibers at the Massachusetts College of Art and Design. She was assistant editor of *The Object of Labor: Art, Cloth, and Cultural Production* (School of the Art Institute of Chicago and MIT Press, 2007). Recently published work includes articles in *Journal of Curriculum and Pedagogy*, *Frakcija*, *Textile: A Journal of Cloth and Culture* and *LTTR*. With Shannon Stratton she co-curated *Gestures of Resistance* at the Museum of Contemporary Craft in Portland, Oregon (2010). Since 2009 she has produced an annual distributed audio project, reading aloud.

Lesley Millar is professor of textile culture and director of the Anglo-Japanese Textile Research Centre at the University for the Creative Arts, UK. She curated *Revelation* (1996–98), Textural Space (2001), *Through the Surface* (2003–05), *21:21—the textile vision of Reiko Sudo and NUNO* (2005–7), *Cloth & Culture NOW* (2008), *Cultex: textiles as a cross-cultural language* (2009–11) and *Lost in Lace* (2011–12). She is currently leading an EU project entitled Transparent Boundaries (2012–13). In 2008 she received the Japan Society Award and in 2011 was appointed MBE.

Liz Mitchell is a freelance curator and writer. She previously worked for Manchester Art Gallery as interpretation development manager and decorative art curator and has specialist interests in historic and contemporary craft and visitor engagement in museums and galleries. Liz has presented at conferences nationally and is published across a range of academic and professional journals and catalogues. She is researching a PhD on the Mary Greg Collection at Manchester Art Gallery, MIRIAD, MMU.

Cj O'Neill is an artist trained in design with a specialism in ceramics. She is senior lecturer on craft route of the MA Design Lab and programme leader, creative business development, Manchester School of Art, MMU. She is currently studying for her PhD at MIRIAD. Cj is interested in the building of memories through objects and surface pattern, and her work is exhibited internationally, including the *Art of the Industrial Ceramics*, the Gardiner Museum, Toronto, the MAD Museum New York, and the British Ceramics Biennale, Stoke. She is interested in the reuse of materials and engaging communities with craft/design. Her work has included a number of projects which have a social dimension, the Wesley Project in Manchester, UK, an organization that supplies furniture, household goods and clothing to those in need in Manchester at the lowest possible prices.

Rachel Payne is a senior lecturer in education at Oxford Brookes University and is currently studying an educational doctorate at the University of Bristol.

She taught the secondary PGCE art/design programme at Oxford Brookes from 2004 to 2012 and runs the artist teacher scheme master's programme in collaboration with Modern Art Oxford. Current research focuses on analysing how Year Seven pupils learn when working with an artist in a contemporary art gallery.

Amanda Ravetz is a senior research fellow at the Manchester Institute for Research and Innovation in Art and Design at MMU. She studied fine art at the Central School of Art and Design and has a PhD in social anthropology with visual media from the University of Manchester. In 2001 she became a lecturer in visual anthropology at the University of Manchester, followed by an Arts and Humanities Research Council Fellowship at Manchester Metropolitan University in 2004. She has made a number of films and written catalogue essays and books, including *Observational Cinema*, co-authored with Anna Grimshaw (Indiana University Press, 2009).

Tim Shear is a learning technologist in the Technology Enhanced Learning unit and part of the Academy for Innovation and Research at University College Falmouth. His technical explorations are a blend of: open-source frameworks, collaborative Web sites, prototyping locative games, augmented craftworks and tangible interfaces for museums. A recent locative work 'Landscapecutter' formed part of an international touring exhibition *Inside Out: Sculpture in the Digital Age*, launched at 'Object' Australian Centre for Design, Sydney (2010).

Allison Smith's artistic practice investigates the material culture of historical reenactment and the role of craft in constructions of national and gender identities. Artist-led participatory projects include *The Muster* (2004–06), *Notion Nanny* (2005–07), *SMITHS* (2008–) and *Arts & Skills Service* (2010–). Smith received a BA in psychology from the New School for Social Research, a BFA in sculpture from Parsons School of Design, and an MFA from the Yale University School of Art. She is chair of the sculpture program at California College of the Arts.

Rhian Solomon completed a BA in materials practice at Brighton University in 2005. As an artist and researcher she has exhibited and lectured at various UK colleges on her interests in collaborative thinking and working. Solomon is the director and founder of the sKINship research project that seeks to promote collaboration between plastic surgery and pattern cutting professions.

Shannon Stratton's practice is in the studio, art history, theory and criticism. She teaches in art history, theory and criticism and fiber and material studies at The School of the Art Institute of Chicago and is critical studies fellow at The Cranbrook Academy of Art in Michigan. She is co-founder and executive and creative director of threewalls Chicago, a not-for-profit residency and exhibition space. Through threewalls she has published and co-edited three editions of *PHONEBOOK*, a guide to artist-run projects in the United States; organized the Hand-in-Glove Conference and founded the Propeller Fund with Gallery 400. With Judith Leemann, she curated *Gestures of Resistance* at the Museum of Contemporary Craft in Portland, Oregon (2010).

Simon Taylor became head of learning at Ikon Gallery, Birmingham, in 2011. He was formally education manager for The Making, a crafts development agency. His background is in contemporary ceramics, and he taught in colleges in the South East, working with a wide range of students, including children with special needs, prisoners and young offenders. Simon has a MA in museums and galleries in education from the Institute of Education (University of London) and a BA honours degree in three-dimensional design from the University of Brighton.

Jeremy Theophilus is a co-partner of A Fine Line: Cultural Practice. He is a writer, curator and project manager with a focus on craft. He was a gallery director and worked for Arts Council England. He is a visiting research fellow at MIRIAD, MMU. He is writing a monograph on the Egyptian artist/calligrapher Ahmed Moustafa, and his work with the weaving studio Ateliers Pinton in Aubusson (2013). He curated *Signs for Sounds* on contemporary letterform and calligraphy (2011, 2013). He is co-director with Barney Hare Duke of the British Ceramics Biennial in Stoke-on-Trent, and with Anupa Mehta, they own a haveli in Ahmedabad, India, for artists' residencies.

Jane Webb specializes in the relationships between theory and practice. She is senior lecturer in art history at Manchester School of Art, MMU, specializing in material culture. Her own freelance critical writing and making practice occurs alongside research interests in the relationships between the history of ideas and place. She is writing a series of books to be published by Bloomsbury, under the title of *Fashion Perspectives*, concerning the dress collection at Platt Hall, Manchester.

Brett Wilson is a retired scientist (professor of communications) and co-founder of Project Dialogue in the Faculty of Creative Arts at the University of the West of England, Bristol, UK, where he has been scientist in residence for the past six years. Project Dialogue explores underlying commonalities across research in the arts and sciences and promotes a transdisciplinary postgraduate teaching programme for practice-led arts research students. Project Dialogue's journal and conference publications extend from transdisciplinary teaching methodologies to Bayesian constructs in epistemologies of science.

Introduction: Collaboration through Craft

Amanda Ravetz, Alice Kettle and Helen Felcey

This book is about collaboration through craft—workmanship-like exchanges between individuals and across disciplinary boundaries that are freely entered into, and that through joint endeavour leave one or both sides significantly changed. In using the term 'craft' we include both 'the crafts'—those 'genres' that have in the past been distinguished by different materials whether metal, wood, ceramics, textiles or glass (Greenhalgh 2002: 1)—*and* the workmanship of which Pye writes (1995) that can occur in any field at all, but crucially involves risk and contingency, so that craft is about using skilled attention to enter life's generative, relational, temporal and improvisatory flow (Hallam and Ingold 2007).

Our aim in putting this collection together is to insert craft into the growing contemporary debate about what it means to work with others—with the political and cultural ramifications this brings—while also questioning where craft stops and other territories begin. Our intended readership are those who identify explicitly with craft—makers, craft artists, those who write about craft and who enjoy craft—but also those in allied fields who are interested in the relevance of the workmanship of risk and improvisation to debates about expertise. Collaboration through craft, we argue, is linked to new forms of collaborative expertise that rather than transmitting pre-existing content, involves opening situations up to the 'rule-finding' capabilities and the plural skills of willing participants.

Our privileging of accounts by practitioners—those with direct experience of craft collaborations—reflects the idea voiced long ago by Ruskin that skilled making and skilled thinking are not distinct activities nor should their separation be encouraged. As editors we believe that the turn towards explicit collaboration through craft currently being witnessed demands 'reports from the field' (Grimshaw et al. 2010: 147)—first-hand critical accounts that allow the generative practices of art and design to affect and inform craft theory. Such critical reflections from within practice are increasingly recognized as central to artistic research (Coessens et al. 2009).

Collaboration loosens many of the conceptual limitations placed on craft by a fundamental and mistaken opposition between innovation (creativity) and tradition (improvisation) (Hallam and Ingold 2007: 1–24). Once this opposition is overturned, it becomes possible to see craft as something that is wide-reaching, forward-facing, flexible, relational, pedagogically up to date, technologically innovative, socially engaged and politically charged. Collaboration extends the parameters of craft. Whether across materials and techniques, or the borders between craft and other defined areas of practice, the cross-fertilization of materials, processes and concepts questions what craft is, providing makers and others with opportunities for *un*learning, opening craft up to alternative ways of thinking about itself.

COLLABORATION AND THE SOCIALITY OF CRAFT

Craft as an idea, something to ponder, debate and analyse, emerged during the early nineteenth century at a moment when artisanal labour was separated out from other related processes and products. The term 'craft' was established and defined through its perceived difference from industrial, technological and fine art modes of production (Adamson 2009: 5). Yet craft's association with practical knowledge has always lent it a significance that goes beyond this apparently bounded self.[1]

Writing in 2002, Paul Greenhalgh suggested that the various genres that make up the crafts were combining, melting and dissembling into a healthier state than ever before, vibrant and poised for radical change. The crafts, he explained, had come together for a variety of artistic, political and institutional reasons, but despite having no intrinsic cohesion and being a somewhat arbitrary consortium, they had held together and at times 'successfully protected themselves as a collective' (Greenhalgh 2002: 1).

More recently Glenn Adamson reminded his readers that although in the twentieth century the idea of craft had remained largely identified with *the* crafts, the post-disciplinary spirit of the 1990s and beyond had begun to seriously challenge the conflation of the crafts and craft. He offered a metaphor for negotiating this situation, imagining the crafts as an archipelago of islands and craft as a constellation of stars. Where the first is a territory that some, but not all, inhabit, the second is a collection of much-debated and contested properties that together might offer a means by which to navigate (2007: 6). Reflecting on how craft transcends disciplines, Adamson also noted that while 'scholars are beginning to view craft practice from the standpoint of social history, anthropology and economics, practitioners of various kinds are exploring the problematics of craft through increasingly diverse means' (2007: 6).

Anthropologists and archaeologists have long assumed that many of the properties associated with craft—materials, tools, techniques of the body, practical skill—are highly social and open to shared working. In the anthropological cannon, making and shared human labour cannot easily be prised apart. Objects, people and institutions are understood to be intimately interconnected, networked or 'meshworked' (Ingold 2011: 63).[2] Furthermore these properties are understood by some social scientists to be the means by which human beings and their environments are co-created and coexist.

For media sociologist David Gauntlett, all making involves the connecting of materials, people and ideas. In a view that chimes with that of the anthropologist Tim Ingold, Gauntlett suggests that acts of creativity have an inherently social dimension, as making and sharing things increases makers' engagements with their social and physical environments (2011: 2). But although Ingold similarly emphasizes the fundamental sociality of making, for him the world is not connected only through human agency, but is a meshwork of already 'entangled lines of life, growth and movement' (2011: 63). As part of this entanglement, materials draw the maker into a profound dialogue with the forces of decay and growth.

The collaborative implications of such dialogue are touched upon by Donald Schön in an article from the 1980s that discusses the problematic division between research and practice in the teaching of professional knowledge (1984: 5). Schön proposes that one aspect of tacit knowledge is 'reflective conversation with the materials of a situation'. He uses the example of a 'desk-crit' between an architectural student and a studio master to show how conversations between materials and people can lead to the generation of new and unexpected ideas. In conversation with the student the studio master's talking and drawing around various design problems allows the situation itself to 'speak back', offering the designers the chance to accept or reject the implications of this back-chat (Schön 1984: 5).

Schön's analysis of material conversations is deeply relevant to craft. For as the architect-cum-teacher explores and extends his past repertoire of situations, exemplars and images through drawing and talking, so craft conversations must remain open to past experience without reducing the new situation to 'features that conform to a set of familiar rules' (Schön 1984: 5). The openness of craft to the contingent and the unknown—the maker's ability to respond to the interwoven lines of the meshwork of which they are part—is an important key to craft's social character and its collaborative potential.

Craft's sociality—its permeability and malleability—can however make it vulnerable to manipulation and capable of being manipulative. Sennett, whose definition of craft is very wide, uses the story of the atom bomb to illustrate how the craftsperson can, through the pride taken in their work, be blinded to the social or political consequences of what they make (2008: 4–5, 295). While extreme, this example serves to highlight the dangers inherent in any job done to high standards 'for its own sake'. The well-crafted job can be a burden in other ways too. Herzfeld (2004), and Venkatesan (2009), focus, respectively, on the situations of craftspeople in Crete and India where artisans are simultaneously marginalized and venerated. Craft is respected as a repository of ancient skills and traditions yet used to denigrate artisans and deny them the fruits of modernity (Herzfeld 2004: 5). Such examples remind us of the problematics of thinking through craft cross-culturally where to be understood on their own terms, making processes and crafted objects might require different analytical concepts from one's own (Henare et al. 2007). The sociality of craft then does not prevent craftspeople or craft objects from being undervalued or misunderstood.

But if the sociality of skill, tools, technologies and material culture have long been studied in these fields, the explicit linking of these scholarly debates to contemporary understandings of craft has only recently begun to take shape. It is not that the material voice has been silent historically in areas where collaboration and shared working are a potent force. On the contrary, craft has readily engaged with questions of feminism, labour, amateurism and the domestic, popular culture, everyday histories and manufacturing. One thinks of the popularity of knitting, embroidery and quilting groups as clear examples of craft's social power. In recent times craftivism with its stated purpose of engendering active change and community engagement provides an obvious example of craft's collaborative capacity. Added to this, increasing numbers of artists are using craft materials collaboratively. To give just one example, Anne Wilson's work *Wind/Rewind/Weave* links materials, community, manufacturing, textile production and social history (Wilson 2011). But despite growing numbers of explicit and intentional collaborations being initiated by craft artists, craft collaboration has not yet been systematically debated or written about.

How do collaborations between craft artists—along with social readings of craft like those above—illuminate craft's fluid and vocal character in ways instructive to craft and to other professions and fields? Adamson's metaphor of craft as a constellation of properties provides a helpful starting point for addressing this question, for by examining the *collaborative* aspects of this constellation we might better grasp craft's wider potential power and reach.[3]

COLLABORATION THROUGH CRAFT

While theories that circulate around craft can sometimes seem to reduce materials to something inert, makers know that materials have their own lives, active qualities and movements. Tim Ingold invites us to take a stone, wet it and place it on the desk before us. Seeing the stone dry directs our attention to a world of materials that is in constant flux and transformation (2011: 16). In Ingold's words materials 'circulate, mix with one another, solidify and dissolve in the formation of more or less enduring things' (Ingold 2011: 16).

We might ask where one material begins and another ends? For Sennett, the tenacity of craft (also noted by Greenhalgh 2002), is explained by its flux and metamorphosis and by the human compulsion towards materials which arouse the mind, drawing associations with the magic of the unforeseen and unknown, and with the alchemy of material and making (Sennett 2008: 123).

The transformative ability of materials is a powerful starting point for many of the collaborations in this volume. The necessary conditions for collaboration through craft is often a mutual and visceral attraction to 'stuff', although paradoxically, working closely with others may require a willingness to temporarily give up possessiveness towards materials, objects and associated skills. This surrender can be a way to collectively hold open 'potential space' for others.

The drama and magnetic qualities of materials are heightened as they meet through collaboration with new sensory experiences that characterize the material dialogue between maker and material. As the late Peter Dormer noted, 'In making with real materials one comes up against gravity and physics. One comes up against the unexpected in materials themselves' (1997: 147). As is so often true of collaboration, this can become a question of negotiation—and of how this negotiation must be crafted as an integral part of the making process.

The outcome of focusing collaborative working through materials can be new substances, techniques, processes and forms, with the ability to beguile or indeed conflict and destroy each other. If the material world is part of everyday life, the materials of collaboration can serve to focus and heighten these sensuous exchanges.

Many materials have a discernible place of origin which can motivate makers to pool knowledge, skills and resources in ways that challenge, extend or retain this provenance. Materials are valued depending on how and by whom they have been transformed. The discarded, the everyday can become the medium through which makers share their ideas and imaginings. Suggestively citational—referencing and articulating identity, provenance, status—materials can lead to the transformation of people, engineering new kinds of social relations. But such transformation frequently demands advanced material knowledge and precision. Attempts to undertake material collaborations can unsettle or discomfort participants, leaving them aware of what they do not know and cannot do.

With materials come the actions of craft. How do these operate? David Pye contrasts the workmanship of certainty to that of risk. The former relates to work that is predetermined, having a predictable and certain outcome. The latter is 'not predetermined, but depends on the judgment, dexterity and care' which can be 'habitual and unconscious' (1995: 20). The unconscious element of skill, which is a central aspect of tacit knowledge, is acquired through experience and example (Dormer 1997: 147–8). Collaboration through craft underlines and sometimes undermines the balance between certitude and risk. Too much uncertainty can result in poor-quality work but too little can precipitate an entropic restriction of ideas and forms. Similarly, in collaborative partnerships, not enough disruption leaves the status quo intact and too much can produce failure, or expose the collaborator to accusations of being a dilettante. The knowledge brought to bear by makers in these different scenarios has to do with the transposing of risk and care to an arena involving relationships not usually dealt with, involving friction that may go beyond the maker's existing skill set.

Dormer argues that craft knowledge is distributed through people and institutions working together in numerous ways and has the potential to adapt and change and be open-ended (1997: 149). Such change is often slow and sometimes imperceptible. The chapters in this volume evidence how craft works with what is already there, it is responsive and reflective, it acts like a mirror. We see differing skill sets emerging, navigated as a result of collaborative partnerships and foregrounding the habit of care by producing a different order of risk.

The nuances of the handmade are highly valued in the crafts and these can be increased when processes from different disciplines are blended together, but like risk, variation has to be controlled. In pattern cutting and plastic surgery, we see the extent to which variation is linked with identity—matching being important to both fields but meaning something quite different in each. Collaborating with those who hold different political and moral views might also be compelling for the transformative possibilities it suggests, putting the friction with which makers are familiar to new use, creating a forum where new degrees of transformation might conceivably take place.

Questions of materials and craft knowledge underline craft's relational reach. Through its connecting impulses craft draws us attentively, physically and imaginatively deeper into the connective tissue of a world we already inhabit. But such connective power can also be detected in more politically charged contexts than the romance of connection suggests, seen for example in craft's implication in national-building projects. As Adamson (2007: 78) and Venkatesan (2009: 247–8) point out, understandings of skill that avoid the categorization of a certain work or product are incomplete without an equal understanding of the social, political and cultural investment involved in skilled workmanship. Craft skill is a way of achieving cultural authority which is then open to being contested (Adamson 2007: 78). Craft collaborations can be part of this authority or they can be used to challenge such authority with differing political results.

Our contributors show how the potential for collaboration gathers around the challenges of territory and deterritorialization—the joining with others of similar mind to confirm, ironize or defy boundaries constructed from difference. A number encounter the fault lines between the urban and the pastoral, the professional and the amateur in their encounters with craft. Collaboration across political and geographical divides can invoke explosive, cathartic or simmering emotions, fuelled by uneven craft economies and craft languages. Added to this, not all our contributors identify themselves primarily with the crafts, and we see the supplemental properties of craft in some accounts— how craft provides props for art through its ability to deliver the well made and the handmade. It is through collaboration that these and other craft identities can be strengthened, unravelled or remade.

But if materials, skill and identity have collaborative potential, other properties which are less often noted by those who write about craft also appear and reappear throughout the chapters. Movement can be crucial to collaboration just as collaboration can reveal the centrality of movement to craft. Ingold tells us that the concentration needed to bring together the movements that occur inside and outside the body 'reaches out into the environment along multiple paths of sensory participation' (2011: 18). If awareness is needed to move along paths of sensory participation, then intentionally shared movements can open up a deeper awareness of materials and places. This sensory participation might then be extended to the visitors at an exhibition, the comparative movements of cloth and skin, the slow movement of light and shadow over objects or the movement that animates meaningful craft gestures. Movements in each case convey life and aliveness and become a way for the maker to reach beyond the singular person into a shared environment. Collaboration might then involve choreographing the movements inherent in practical skill, revealing the counterpoints to them or developing the resistance within and between them. A focus on movement challenges the emphasis on the static product, the noun, the object.

Linked with movement is the taking and investing of time, which is implicit in most making. It is experienced differently according to the material ingredients and can be elongated, cut short or interrupted through the mechanics of process. Duration might refer here to the natural cycle, the waiting times in between drying time, kiln time, of repetitious action. A statistic now familiar to many, to be a world-class expert takes 10,000 hours (Gladwell 2008). Sennett sees the temporality of craft as 'one way to separate craft and art: craft practice is stretched out' (2008: 123). Extended duration can also communicate a sense of 'truthfulness' to ones peers and employers (Gladwell 2008: 62). According to Dormer making single objects takes much longer than the non-maker understands (1997: 149).

One manifestation of the time of craft can be seen in the slow craft movement, which emerged in association with the slow movements in food. Craft with its closeness to the principles of hand making and material eloquence, is well placed to slow processes further and thereby induce increased reflection, whether of the object, the properties or the processes. In the chapters that follow, craft, together with other modes of production, contributes to the bespoke, the carefully crafted one off object. The obverse is the experience of speed, the compression of processes that can occur through collaboration, where the perfection of an object may be of less consequence. Shared making can offer the possibility of increased productivity. Developments in technology have replaced the skilled artisan and lent a different temporality from that of the past. The hand now needs to imagine the process of making without the necessity to make. The shared digital languages of disciplines now convene with a fluidity of time, allowing recycling, reproduction and reinvention of ideas and of craft itself.

Finally, to consider collaboration through craft is to recognize that making crucially involves dialogue, what Risatti sees as an integration of conception and execution 'so that a subtle feedback system occurs when physical properties of materials encounter conceptual form and conceptual form encounters physical material' (2007: 169). As this happens 'a truly dialectical and dialogical process takes place. It is this process of mutual conditioning and modifying that occurs during making that is at the heart of the creative act of craftsmanship' (Risatti 2007). According to Risatti this dialogical process involves a different worlding experience to that, say, of fine art. It requires respect for material realities which in and of itself 'expands the craftsman's imaginative horizon of possibilities by offering a process of experiencing while the work is imaginatively formed into an actual, real entity' (Risatti 2007: 202).

This give and take between idea, form and matter, if it usually ends with an object, may, through collaboration, be extended, dilated or stretched to include others—other people, ideas, materials and forms. The fact that craft is socially and culturally situated, performative and involves proximity makes it a potent force and one that seems highly able to adapt. We need to understand craft expertise as something that can be amended, transformed and reconstituted.

COLLABORATIVE CRAFT EXPERTISE

The expert is an important part of craft discourse and the master craftsperson stands as an early example of this expertise. A common anxiety about collaboration is that certain kinds of joint working can lead to the loss of specific specialist knowledge through dilution or contamination. Debates on expertise include discussions as to whether collaborations of the kinds explored in this book will eventually dilute the skills transmitted from teacher to learner, master to apprentice.

Scott Lash helps us see concerns about the loss of skill as part of a broader sociological shift that has taken place in modernity—the contemporary individual has become nonlinear and reflexive, no longer relying on rule following, but needing to become competent in rule finding instead (2002).

In the past, professional expertise was constituted and owned by professional experts who were socially licensed to practice and disseminate. Diversity tended to be othered and devalued and expertise was generalizable and involved a contextual production of theory which could be applied in a deductive way. Practice models tended to emphasize this unified model. Now more emphasis is placed on innovation, intentionality has replaced objectivity and chaos and risk have taken the place of determinate rules and judgement. Expertise is in this sense is now less about end—result driven processes and more about *engaging* in a process.

These shifts in expertise provide the context for the kinds of knowledge unveiled in the many collaborations through craft in this book. Collaboration through craft produces insights that are contingent and generative rather than transmitting preexisting content. But as a dialogical practice, collaboration through craft goes further than this, increasing sensitivity to how our bodies feel, relate and produce meaning. The collaborations described here involve a reciprocal modelling of material and making that depends, in Grant Kester's words, on 'new modes of aesthetic experience and new frameworks for thinking about identity through the haptic and verbal exchanges that unfold in the process of collaborative interaction' (2011: 113).

Kester believes that artists working with a dialogical aesthetic have demonstrated through their experiments and practice, ways around the 'conative drive of possessive individualism', the part of the modern subject that depends for a sense of self on the possession of both property and of inherent faculties and powers (2011: 113). While it has been enshrined in European thought since the seventeenth century that it is rational to pursue one's own advantage, Kester points out there is an instability in the modern bourgeois subject because when status depends on possession, it can be lost as well as expanded. The modern subject who is dependent on possession is paradoxically also dependent on others for their self-constitution. The bourgeois identity is marked by ambiguity—a colonizing expansion of the self which at the same time requires an opening out to otherness.

Collaborative working impinges on the expressive powers of the individual because of how it opens to the fluidity and relationality of the bourgeois identity. Collaboration through craft suggests a form of expertise which takes the ambivalent permeability, relationality and contingency that is part of the modern subject, and 'develop[s] the skills necessary to mitigate violence and objectification in our ongoing encounters with difference' (Kester 2011: 107). Kester is careful to note that dialogical art practice does not sidestep or 'cure' modern subjectivity but instigates an oscillation between critical distance and engagement, autonomy and dialogue. The possessiveness of the modern subject is not purged so much as mitigated. According to Kester, collaborative art practice involves durational modes of making and thinking which allow for the continual modification of expression, enunciation and reception. Such modes of making are dependent 'on somatic, aesthetic forms of knowledge: the exchange of gesture and expression, the complex relationship to habitus and habit, and the way in which conflict, reconciliation and solidarity are registered in and through the body' (Kester 2011: 111–12).

Collaboration occurs by reflecting the present but also by encountering challenges which open other territories to the reservoir of material. As a frame, collaboration can be expansive in its vision, absorbed back into practice and made real with action repeatedly constituted and reconstituted. By working with others we can encounter a process by which agency is left deliberately unguarded while retaining its ability to reframe a given reality. Thus, the virtual and imagined become material. The material also becomes the maker, as making creates productive confusion between other and self. These elements are in constant flux, their magnetism both drawing together relationships and pushing them apart. Given this, a collaborative method 'locates creative praxis within a different set of coordinates [from avant-garde specular models] and in so doing, raises a series of ethical questions' (Kester 2011: 115). These questions, Kester states, while different, are neither more nor less compelling than those encountered in other forms of art practice.

A COLLABORATIVE VOLUME

This book challenges ideas of craft as self absorbed, uncritical, solitary or bounded by tradition. The contributions underscore the dynamism of craft, its generative power, capacity for drama, improvisation, performativity and poetics in the negotiated 'between' spaces of contemporary craft environments. The contributors share an interest in the *problematics* of collaboration—how working with others can blur identities, challenge notions of individual authorship, test skills, subvert territorial divisions between supposedly discrete or antithetical fields, produce ideas that would not have been reached alone, demand improvisation on the basis of existing skills and expand horizons. While for some collaboration is a deliberate intentional act, for others craft's seeping into unfamiliar areas is less self-conscious. Yet all the contributors understand craft's capacities to be relational, adaptable and influential in modes of cross-fertilization, questioning the intentions and the impact of craft connections within and as part of other modes of thinking and practice.

What are some of the personal experiences of collaboration and how does collaboration between different makers happen? David Gates, Alice Kettle and Jane Webb's emerging dialogue is driven by material exchanges of wood, textile and the written word. Shifts and contradictions of aesthetics and knowledge are played out in a repositioning and temporary relinquishing of each maker's sense of ownership of 'their' distinct material. This is aided by a process of 'triangulation'—the holding open by three of potential space for one another. Helen Carnac emphasizes the importance of conversation and movement to collaborative making and connecting. Walking puts things into motion and can speed up the exchange of ideas; but this movement can also expose the tensions and frictions that are liable to be occluded once a finished craft object goes out into the world. Lesley Millar similarly notes the tensions of collaboration. There is the difficulty of managing the different languages: of making, management, identity, education and museum interpretation. A collaboration that goes beyond teamwork however, involves more than linguistic fluency. Millar stipulates it must deliver mutuality of benefit to all partners from the point of process to the point of outcome. As collaborators who have already secured long-term mutuality, Brass Art: Chara Lewis, Anneké Pettican and Kristin Mojsiewicz use playful explorations of doubles, hybrids and phantasms to loosen the boundaries between their separate identities. Their collective sensibility conjures up experiences of the uncanny, of temporary dissolutions of selves, and of transformation, making use of craft in its supplemental capacity. Together these chapters underline the material, sensual and tacit experiences of craft collaborations. With a strong bias towards the experiential, these authors evoke what joint working feels, looks and sounds like.

Collaboration reveals craft to be an explicitly generative activity. Across the sites of fashion, medicine, new technology and exhibition spaces, collaborations by makers show how important shared working and knowledge exchange is to the creation of new materials and surfaces. Trish Belford discusses a selection of projects where knowledge of textiles works together with science to create thought-provoking solutions to contemporary design questions. David Binns describes a research project which fuses recycled glass, ceramic and mineral waste to create a new composite 'eco-material' with a range of unique aesthetic properties. Developed in collaboration with material scientists, chemists and industrial partners, these collaborations offer alternatives to existing products, while also provoking interest in environmental issues from consumers and audiences.

The *affect* of craft can be demonstrated and enhanced through collaboration. Cleverly and Shear describe how interdisciplinary partnership can help works of craft to create and encourage co-participation and collaboration. Their *Interactive Table and Escritoire*, created for the *House of Words* exhibition at Dr Johnson's House in 2009, engendered new analogue and digital forms of visitor engagement. For Rhian Solomon the potency of craft's affect lies in the contrasting yet comparable material surfaces of fabric and skin. Questioning the potential for cross disciplinary practices between plastic surgery and pattern cutting for fashion, Solomon outlines new methods for pattern cutting and garment design that have been informed by surgical technique using adaptations from the surgeon A. A. Limberg's flap designs. In both chapters the authors demonstrate how craft can be a willing partner in new thinking about pressing technological, aesthetic and environmental questions.

The collaborations outlined in this book might well become the new imperative for how institutions involved in craft need to work, although as a number of the chapters show, this is likely to take different forms in different institutional contexts. Stephen Knott gives a participant-observer's account of Department 21, a ground-up initiative at the Royal College of Art devised by postgraduate students to combat the persistence of discrete art and design territories in a post-disciplinary age. Craft appears here as the interloper, never quite named but keenly present. Barbara Hawkins and Brett Wilson consider the historical and cultural factors that have traditionally worked against collaborative and integrated curriculum developments in postgraduate education. Addressing art and design education where students experience the accelerating influence of research and debate over direct teaching, they ask how curriculum options and their teaching strategies can develop a broader more inclusive approach. Simon Taylor and Rachel Payne provide a practical response to the recent UK report that found that craft and design were poorly taught in many schools. The programme they initiated in a collaboration with Oxford Brookes University provided master classes in contemporary crafts practice to PGCE trainees and explored new approaches to visual research. Also interested in curriculum change, this time for undergraduate art and design students, Sharon Blakey and Liz Mitchell uncover the Mary Greg collection at Manchester City Art Gallery and show how it catalyzed an investigation into the various divergent and shared agendas of gallery and museum staff, educationalists and craft makers. Their collaborative partnership aimed to reconsider the way in which we, as individuals and institutions, value our material culture heritage and use it as source for inspired thinking in making and practice.

In contrast to the image of craft as a field that is backward looking, necessarily analogue-based and conceptually hidebound, collaboration highlights the fluidity of craft as it moves across cultural and temporal borders. Craft here can be understood as a form of prospective knowledge, leading us to question our understanding of the past, our cultural interactions and our emergent futures.

Allison Smith explores craft as a vessel for radical ideas. Using examples of her recent work, she reflects on the power of craft to expose conflicting ideas about civic culture and to foreground conditions of dissensus and diversity. Craft here is seen as an intimate and direct mode of engagement, an object facilitating an occasion and an occasion lending value to an object. The exchange between object and occasion is also a strong theme in the curatorial practice of Judith Leemann and Shannon Stratton who examine the promise and challenge of curating emergent craft practices in and for institutional settings. Through a twinned reading of the material manifestations of an unfolding exhibition and the critical engagements of its artists and curators, they focus on the potential and turbulence evident at the growing edge of collaboration, on the demands 'performative craft' makes on its lay and professional audiences, and on the moments when craft, in its particular way, becomes a fulcrum across which to imagine and articulate new forms of relationship within communities. Barney Hare Duke and Jeremy Theophilus advocate that it is creative practitioners who are the essential navigators and shapers of how we understand, share and value culture. Their organization A Fine Line: Cultural Practice brings together craft practitioners from divergent cultures to explore the contexts and attitudes inherent in craft culture. Issues inevitably arise in these exchanges around those whose economic sustainability is dependent on craft and those whose choice it is to make. Their cultural exchanges shed light on the variety of approaches of craft practice and on how knowledge and methods of making might be equitably shared. Cj O'Neill and Amanda Ravetz ask the simple question: What is it we so value about the opportunity to collaborate? Taking up anthropologist James Leach's idea of 'dispersed creativity', they discuss two different ways of assigning value to a residency they collaborated on in India. The first celebrates the outcomes of the residency and the second celebrates the forms of creativity that remain dispersed between agents. The appeal of the latter they conclude is in the way it underscores the way work done by one person registers in the changes and growth of another.

CONCLUSION—THE VALUE OF COLLABORATION THROUGH CRAFT

In their work on creativity and cultural improvisation Hallam and Ingold argue that there is no script for social and cultural life; rather all practices are improvised, and in being improvised are generative, relational and temporal (2007: 1). Their point is that much academic knowledge is retrospective—it is knowledge made after the event that fails to respond to the needs and reality of a 'crescent world'. The current collection shows craft to be a field of knowledge and a social and cultural concept delicately poised between the freedoms and constraints that are so crucial to improvisation, giving those involved in craft access to a number of crucial tools when it comes to challenging retrospective and static forms of knowledge.

For many, collaboration is a temporary excursion and the learning that results from collaboration is something to be used back within their established practice. But whether temporary of not, the language of friction, risk and care gains added depth through extension into new areas. The language of craft is enriched by articulating ideas and processes in different ways. Seeing that craft flows out into other areas encourages increasingly open-ended and engaged processes. These new discourses are changing the field and the previous rigidity of craft genres. In collaboration with and through craft, we recognize craft's fundamentally social and relational character. Acts of collaboration highlight properties of craft in their widest sense. Collaboration opens up the core principles of craft to deeper examination, creating another stage of craft exploring its own craftsmanship and of makers demonstrating the relevance of craft beyond 'the crafts'.

NOTES

The editing of this book has also been a journey of collaboration. One of us is a visual anthropologist and filmmaker (Amanda Ravetz); the other two are researchers, educationalists and craft practitioners (Alice Kettle and Helen Felcey). Collaboration has challenged and changed our understanding and our own discourses. We have attempted to weave our voices together without losing differences of timbre and tone or erasing our divergent interpretations. We have discovered much about the fluid and fundamental character of craft in the process.

1. See Sennett (2008: 70–72) for an historical account of craft's fluctuating social status.
2. For Ingold skilled practices enmesh us in the lifeweb as for example with drawing which can improvise and trace 'a path that runs not from an image in the mind of a maker to its expression in the material world' (Ingold 2011: 218).
3. While there is vigorous debate about which properties should and should not be part of this constellation, a long list might look something like this: material, skill, technique, tacit knowledge, handwork, risk, pastoral, supplemental meaning and amateur.

REFERENCES

Adamson, G. (2007), *Thinking through Craft,* Oxford: Berg.

Adamson, G. (2009), *The Craft Reader*, Oxford: Berg.

Coessens, K., Crispin, D., and Douglas, A. (2010), *The Artistic Turn: A Manifesto*, Leuven: Leuven University Press.

Dormer, P. (1997), 'Craft and the Turing Test for Practical Thinking', in Peter Dormer (ed.), *The Culture of Craft: Status and Future*, Manchester: Manchester University Press, 137–57.

Gauntlett, D. (2011), *Making Is Connecting*, Cambridge: Polity Press.

Gladwell, M. (2008), *Outliers: The Story of Success*, New York: Little, Brown and Company.

Greenhalgh, P. (2002), 'Introduction: Craft in a Changing World', in Paul Greenhalgh (ed.), *The Persistence of Craft: The Applied Arts Today*, London: A and C Black, 1–17.

Grimshaw, A., Owen, E., and Ravetz, A. (2010), 'Making Do: The Materials of Art and Anthropology', in Arnd Schneider and Chris Wright (eds), *Between Art and Anthropology: Contemporary Ethnographic Practice*, Oxford: Berg, 147–62.

Hallam, E., and Ingold, T. (eds) (2007), *Creativity and Cultural Improvisation*, Oxford: Berghahn.

Henare, A., Holbraad, M., and Wastell, S. (eds) (2007), *Thinking Through Things: Theorising Artefacts Ethnographically*, London: Routledge.

Herzfeld, M. (2004), *The Body Impolitic: Artisans and Artifice in the Global Hierarchy of Value*, Chicago: University of Chicago Press.

Ingold, T. (2011), *Being Alive*, London: Routledge.

Kester, G. (2011), *The One and the Many: Contemporary Collaborative Art in a Global Context*, Durham, NC: Duke University Press.

Lash, S. (2002), 'Foreword: Individualization in a Non-Linear Mode', in Ulrich Beck and Elisabeth Beck-Gernsheim (eds), *Individualization: Institutionalized Individualism and Its Social and Political Consequences*, London: Sage, vii–xiii.

Pye, D. (1995), *The Nature and Art of Workmanship*, London: Herbert Press.

Risatti, H. (2007), *A Theory of Craft*, Chapel Hill: University of North Carolina Press.

Schön, D. A. (1984), 'The Architectural Studio as an Exemplar of Education for Reflection-in-Action', *Journal of Architectural Education*, 38/1: 2–9.

Sennett, R. (2008), *The Craftsman*, London: Allen Lane.

Venkatesan, S. (2009), *Craft Matters,* New Delhi: Orient Blackswan Private Ltd.

Wilson, A. (2011), *Wind/Rewind/Weave*, Knoxville, TN: Knoxville Museum of Art.

PART I

EXPERIENCING COLLABORATION THROUGH CRAFT

Introduction

Alice Kettle, Helen Felcey and Amanda Ravetz

This section explores experiences of collaboration tempered by the maker's wish to depart from a centred place. The authors give us accounts of the generative tensions and spaces opened up by collaboration seen from intimate and situated points of view. The emphasis is on hearing from those who write and talk about something they know through doing, rather than on those who can 'write vivid descriptions without being able to enact those descriptions for real' (Dormer 1997: 147).

The reasons for collaboration are complex. The zeitgeist may be directed towards collaboration; it may be in fashion to demonstrate craft's application and integration into a community. The impetus and catalyst for collaboration can come from a philanthropic sense of social sharing, a desire for engagement, or a more inward existential questioning of identity. The singularity and drive towards certainties of personal identity, the knowing who you are by what you do, is often caught up with materials, and allied with the marketplace. The authors here speak of the certainty of uncertainty, which is the currency of the times. No longer can economic assumptions be made. It is a fluid being, thinking and working, which is required.

Collaboration could come about through a desire within the present economic climate for self-reflection and prudence to 'invoke social cohesion', as Carnac suggests, a personally directed response to the 'austerity' politics of a bankrupt society through the search for genuine mutual, cooperative support. Millar talks of 'changes in expectation . . . and the current tensions within the sector . . . moving the walls of certainty and creating spaces for occupation.' At the same time, the institutional encouragement towards collaboration can lead to scepticism on the part of makers as to whether their own and others' motives are genuinely about a search for mechanisms of shared working or are driven through economic pragmatism.

In these chapters, the specialized material practice of craft is evident alongside the qualities and frictions of inviting collaboration with another material or artist/maker. The progression through this section is from Millar's injunction—collaborate! to Carnac's investigation of necessary friction, tension and movement in craft collaborations; to Kettle's, Gates's and Webb's exploration of the creative potential of the between positions set up amongst different practices; to Brass Art's well-established joint practice in which there is fluid yet rigorous blurring between individual and collective selves.

A perceived certainty of the crafts has been the 'singular vision' (Millar) and the following of process through the conviction of 'origination, struggle, final outcome'. The chapters divert from this fixed point of destination, choosing to explore methods of engagement, process, established assumptions and life. They offer a variety of reasons to work with others which are formal, political and conceptual—craft is outward looking and bold. Millar suggests that through collaboration artists gain more control over what is presented in the public domain; Carnac speaks of a way to give 'a different account of motivations such as those not fully allied to an art market or their representation by others'; for Gates, Kettle and Webb, it is a way to reinvigorate/expand craft and for Brass Art to develop narrative and explore identities and gender.

Inevitably, to leave the certainty of the crafts as an established set of practices and materials produces a 'fluid set of practices, propositions and positions that shift and develop' (Greenhalgh 2002: 1). With such a shift comes mess, chaos and 'impossibility' (Carnac, quoting Lind 2007: 29). What is gained through collaboration may be risk, 'disaster' (Carnac) or new potential and 'freedom and vitality' (Gates, Kettle, Webb). It is a messiness of unpredictable process 'and a tangle of interconnected thinking [which] articulates something of knowing' (Carnac) and is occupied by tension and friction. But tension can create an opening through which something new can come. Gates, Kettle and Webb see a 'constant state of tension in difference', a tautness of constructive potential where the invitation to share practice requires constant repositioning. It is through 'ongoing negotiation along a continuum of chaos and order . . . [that] we come together and move apart'.

Millar describes movement through the opening of imaginative spaces, through shifts in thinking, territories of practice, workshops and material identities. Different temporalities are invoked; a different perception of time from that which we become used to in singular work—sometimes (although not always) a slowing down. Three of the chapters centre on workshop or gallery domains, which are interpreted from different material vantage points, with thresholds crossed and mixtures of making present and potent. Brass Art make in the between spaces which allow creative mistakes, transformation and 'conjuring' and which belong to no one, yet are inhabited by everyone. For Gates, Kettle and Webb the places of shared making occur as a new potential space 'for action that no one person possessed'. These territories of creative collaboration allow improvisation and play to enter and material understanding to be tested. In Millar's view, approaching collaboration in a field dominated by sensory and tacit knowledge requires understanding the role of materials and means, something that equally applies to Brass Art, who emphasize the well made. Improvisation 'emerges from and through established practices and traditions' (Gates, Kettle and Webb) making us think of the necessary presence of both in what Frayling calls the 'deep play of craft of everyday life' (Frayling 2011: 10), an intermingling of intuition and inspiration, and the tacit knowledge and skill that Sennett (2008: 50) speaks of which is acquired through the constancy of making.

The de-centring and change of identity can be experienced as loss of self or authorship, of compromise or 'what might be at stake by allowing someone else to continue with our work' (Carnac). Millar posits that collaboration affords individuality, with 'ideas . . . tested in a forum—ideally, emerging tempered and strengthened'. The register of different languages varies. For some makers, identities are tied in with materials so that 'making appeared to be the common language of living and of seeing the world' (Gates, Kettle and Webb). It is with Brass Art that the poesis of collective identity and imagination are fully formed with 'collaborative practice as an indivisible whole that amounts to more than the summation of its parts'.

All agree that collaboration is likely to produce something that could not have been achieved alone. But if collaboration is to do, to make and to discover something that cannot be achieved alone, then this only happens by changing and opening up practices of makers and of audiences, by shifting expectations about what craft is, what it does, where and why it belongs in our lives. The impact of these collaborations can affect the inner world of thought, dialogue and identity, and the outer material world to 'alter the very environment' (Millar). The conflict contained within the intra personal and the intra material go hand in hand with the freedom to participate and the imposed requirement to do so. Maybe there is no retreat from a sense of responsibility to occupy a shared world even if the consequence of collaboration can be destabilizing and filled with the discomfort of change and uncertainty. Gates Kettle and Webb tell us that for better or worse 'each one of us was changed by the other, perhaps for good'.

REFERENCES

Dormer, P. (1997), 'Craft and the Turing Test for Practical Thinking', in Peter Dormer (ed.), *The Culture of Craft*, Manchester: Manchester University Press.

Frayling, C. (2011), *On Craftsmanship*, London: Oberon Masters.

Greenhalgh, P. (2002), *The Persistence of Craft*, London: A&C Black.

Lind, M. (2007) 'The Collaborative Turn', in *Taking The Matter into Common Hands, on Contemporary Art and Collaborative Practice*, London: Black Dog.

Sennett, R. (2008), *The Craftsman*, London: Allen Lane.

−1−

Collaboration: A Creative Journey or a Means to an End?

Lesley Millar

INTRODUCTION

It could be said that by merely entering into a creative collaboration we are challenging the orthodoxy of individual achievement which, for more than one hundred years, has been the emphasis for practitioners in the arts. The origination, the struggle, the outcome are all realized through a single and singular vision, culminating with the 'dominant market mechanism for which value is based is on the authorship of the artistic genius' (What, How & for Whom [WHW] Collective 2005: 15). I propose that collaborative practice, particularly with reference to exhibition curation, can provide a dynamic model of resistance to the cult (and pressure) of individual achievement.

As one of a growing constituency of curators who have emerged from studio practice, I am determined to increase the profile of contemporary textiles. The appearance of the artist-curator is a response to established modes of practice within museums and galleries, auction houses and collecting, categorized as prioritizing the visibility of particular kinds of art—what we are shown and what we are not shown—and the concomitant public perception of value. The independent artist-curator, standing outside the establishment, and with a vested interest in taking a different approach, may exercise a freedom not easily available to those within. I will consider the role of collaboration in imposing alternative themes and modes of curation on established methods of practice.

In my role of textile practitioner/turned curator of textile exhibitions, when I am developing an exhibition, I inevitably draw on my knowledge and understanding built up over the many years of making textiles. I use what Antony Gormley calls 'the intuition of the "un-thought known"' (Gormley 2007: 118) and what Richard Sennett describes as 'the conversion of information and practices into tacit knowledge' (Sennet 2008: 50). However, to create a successful exhibition, such an approach needs the practical support of a team comprising many different skills. This is not necessarily collaborative practice, but it can become so. In this chapter I describe an example of a practical collaboration from my own experience to demonstrate the development from teamwork to collaboration.

WHY COLLABORATE?

There are many questions to consider when embarking on a collaboration: What form might the collaboration take? Does it have to have a material outcome? For the artist/maker whose normal practice is undertaken alone in the studio, is the collaboration more concerned with the process of collaboration than the outcome?

If the intention is to create a collaborative work, should the collaborators work together to develop a particular idea and then create their works individually? Or will they work together to produce a single work? All are valid approaches, and these questions should be asked to analyse and to understand collaborative working structures. However, the fundamental point is that the collaboration should, in the end, result in an outcome that could not be achieved alone by individuals (Nollert 2005: 26).

Artist Trish Bould has said, 'In my experience a good collaboration is very much a process, and amongst the most interesting things about collaboration are the outcomes which are not about the product at the end of the day, but about the knowledge gained about your own process and about the discipline.'[1] Artist Duro Seder takes the notion to an even further extreme. He saw such activities as a never-finalized process, as exemplified by his comments about Croatian artist collective Gorgona: 'The Collective Work cannot be foreseen as a form, only as an effort. The final appearance of the work is of no consequence at all' (WHW Collective 2005: 15).

Collaboration affords the opportunity for an accumulation of determination, sense of purpose, knowledge, skills and resources; ideas are tested in a forum—ideally, emerging tempered and strengthened. However, the word 'collaboration' carries both positive and negative meaning,[2] suggesting risk for those involved: a pooling of resources with the potential loss of control and compromise. What implications might this dual meaning and the notion of risk have on the kind of collaborations decided on?

Any collaboration is a matter of risk taking, of taking part in a discourse in which existing positions may be reinforced and extended or changed in ways none of the collaborators would have originally envisaged. Collaboration also provides that critical edge, that series of questions, of other views—some of which may be wholly contrary but all of which can stimulate useful investigation into new pathways. As the relationship develops, it can be seen as described by artist Trish Bould: 'sometimes together, sometimes parallel, sometimes moving apart but always flowing in the same direction'.[3] So it seems that, for a successful collaboration, there must be elements of mutuality as well as a willingness to be flexible and responsive and the confidence to allow each partner, on occasion, to move away from the centre.

TEAMWORK AND COLLABORATION

Pragmatically, within some projects, the journey, the search, the critical investigation requires a raft of different skills. Methods and ideas can be too large and complex for any one person to tackle, with the result that one or more partners are absolutely necessary to realize progress in a particular field. For those whose practice is based in the studio, embarking on a project that requires some element of working together with others, particularly from outside the creative process, can appear to be a series of amorphous stages. Those working in another field, for example project management, may be vital to the realization of a research project—there are only so many hats one person can wear.

When discussing exhibition curation and organization, it is important to remember that it will involve multidisciplinary and trans-sector participation. There will be not just one language but many: the language of making, of management, of public relations, of funding, of presentation and identity, of education and of museum/gallery practice and interpretation. Each sphere has its own language and its own terminology which reflect both its core activities and its concerns. It is important that each is given appropriate weight. In reality, these relationships are often examples of teamwork rather than collaboration. They are the pragmatic working relationships with those who have the necessary skills to facilitate the smooth running and success of the exhibition, working together under the leadership of the curator. A true collaboration requires a different approach based on mutuality of benefit from the process and the outcome; a willingness to 'let go' of ownership and to share and act on one another's ideas. However, relationships can change over time, and a fellow team member may become a collaborator. As an example of such a transition, I will discuss my working relationship with my designer Gerry Diebel, director of Direct Design, which I believe fulfils all the criteria of creative collaboration rather than teamwork (Figure 1.1).

The root of our fifteen-year relationship was very pragmatic—he had the graphic skills I needed to produce high-quality support material. Over the years, we have worked more closely together. He is a commercial designer, highly focused on the needs of his clients within their given marketplace. His interpretive skills in 'branding' my ideas have become crucial in my understanding of what I want to do and how it will develop. I need the sharp sensibility he brings, asking me to define the essence of a project in ways that

Fig. 1.1. *Souvenir Line: Nomadic Memory*. Jeanette Appleton and Naoko Yoshimoto. Commissioned for *Through the Surface*. 2004. Photograph: Damian Chapman and Ian Forsyth

can be translated into a visual tool of communication. To achieve this, I must continually refine my ideas. Once we have identified these visual tools, I reach the clarity of vision I can apply to the development of the project.

Together we decide on the title and the associated visual development through signs and symbols or typography. This takes a long time. Examples are the mentoring collaboration project Through the Surface, which incorporates the symbol of wavy lines, and Textural Space, which relies on the perfect marriage between typography and a graphic device to create the feeling of space. Both were award winners. Our collaboration has had a significant effect on how we work. It is organic, creative, pragmatic, institutional and mutually supportive, and it could only be possible through the slow accumulation of trust and respect.

Collaboration at its best relies on the best qualities of all parties to offer the potential for mutual development. This doesn't mean it is without conflict and edge. Every project produces challenge and tension, particularly when resolving the different requirements of our two disciplines, and the resolution is the better for it. As Paul Carter has pointed out when writing about collaboration between multidisciplinary art forms: 'The important work is done at the surfaces between adjacent disciplines' (Carter 2004: 178). I would add that, while the interface between disciplines can cause the friction that sparks the fire, it is the contemplative space between those surfaces from which

the work emerges. In terms of building relations and developing collaborations between the sectors, perhaps listening to and learning each other's languages is an important starting point. Indeed, Carter goes on to say that 'it is
the discourse between these [disciplines] that animates, amplifies and creates
the place of the work' (Carter 2004: 178).

CURATORIAL COLLABORATION

With this injunction in mind, I should like now to think about creative curatorial
collaboration between artist and curator or between artist and artist. If we are
taking the view that the organization of an exhibition is a creative act, and one
that would be best achieved as a collaboration, then the starting point should
be the role of the curator. The curator's role has changed over the past 150
years, moving from scholarly caring for a collection to interpreting objects to
provide a particular curatorial view.

International Power Listings[4] indicate that the curator is no longer anonymous but now has power and influence and operates as the entrepreneurial
celebrity interpreter—characterized by Gillian Howard as the 'curator-auteur'.
As Angelika Nollert described in her essay 'Art Is Life and Life Is Art', 'The
methodology and possibilities of curatorial activity are wide ranging. Over the
last years a change has taken place [...], with curatorial activity moving into
the foreground. The focus is on the process of curating and not the curator's
functions, and so the term curator has been replaced by curating' (2005: 28).
The creative freedom opened up through broadening the activity offers radical
and exciting possibilities for reading the work. However, in this climate, if the
collaboration is between curator and artist, questions may be raised concerning authorship; the imposition of self-conscious, personal interpretation creates a blurring of the threshold between the art and its presentation. In 'The
Museum Effect', Valerie Casey points out that 'while the notion of museum
interpretation was introduced to explain art and artefacts, the role of the interpreter has become so central in museums that the object that is being interpreted has been overshadowed by the performance' (Casey 2003).

An interesting example of blurring boundaries and the ambiguity of the
outcome was demonstrated at the fifty-fourth Biennale di Venezia (2011).
Here Bice Curiger, curator of the ILLuminations section, shifted the interpretive role of the curator one step further. Large-scale paintings by Tintoretto
were moved from their homes at the Gallerie dell'Accademia and San Giorgio
Maggiore Basilica to the Central Pavilion in the Giardini and exhibited alongside the selection of contemporary works. The rationale was to demonstrate
that the works of Tintoretto as 'one of the most experimental artists in the
history of Italian art, exert a special appeal today [and] will play a prominent
role in establishing an artistic, historical and emotional relationship to the

local context'.[5] Whether this continuum was established or not, for the viewer the effect of entering the Tintoretto area was one of entering an installation/intervention. In a 'turnaround' from the usual placing of contemporary works within the museum setting, the museum pieces were set within the most contemporary work of the day. In contrast to the rest of the biennale, the room resembled a museum, with uniformed guards in attendance, which differed keenly with, say, the Mike Nelson installation in which the attendants were students who sat outside the entrance. The atmosphere was a different kind of value—an economic one. The curatorial interpretation and the artistic performance became one.

THE ARTIST-CURATOR

I have described this shift from curator to curating, from noun to verb—from naming to doing—in some detail in order to think about what this shift might offer the artist and what the artist can offer and gain in return and to consider devising strategies for survival and advancement. What do we, the practitioners, think about the role of curator as interpreter? Is this what we want? As creators of exhibits, do we want to also take part in, or even orchestrate, the performance? If so, what do we bring to that performance? Are there different qualities of perception that a practitioner can offer in the interpretation? The answer for the last question is a resounding affirmative. We bring a context created through our haptic knowledge accrued through a lifetime of making. Through our individual practice, we draw on the knowledge of those who have gone before, and this in its own way is a kind of collaboration. The 'performance' of the exhibition is that very haptic knowledge of the maker/curator that enables us to employ our hidden alchemist and to play the magician. As Paul Carter says:

> Craft is associated with a gift for ambiguity. It is a skill in loosening positions that have been fixed. It naturally disrupts hierarchies [...] It dissipates powerful oppositions, and creates opportunities. But it's also a gift for putting things back together in a different way. Invention and re-membering, [...] are two aspects of a single intellectual process. The capacity to perform these sleights of hand—craft is traditionally associated with the magic arts—depends, though, on an advanced material knowledge. (Carter 2004: 179)

Whilst she would not claim to be a magician, textile designer Masayo Ave is someone who exploits her learned relationship, developing our intuitive relationship with the 'feel' of surface under our fingers, while translating it first into tangible and then into intangible material outcomes. Masayo Ave has been working with groups of children and adults to identify and describe

Fig. 1.2. Kiyonori Shimada and Gabriella Göranssen in Shimada's outside installation for Cultex at Gallery F15, Norway. 2009. Photograph: Lesley Millar

textures through mutually agreed, invented onomatopoeic descriptors: the sound of the surface. From these sounds she has gone on to design and develop objects and surfaces that, in turn, describe the sounds, thus completing the circle of communication, which she then begins again by exhibiting the objects and inviting the visitor to touch the surfaces. In this she uses the 'knowledge gained in the hand through touch and movement' (Sennett 2008: 35).

CONCLUSION

So, as artists we have knowledge and we have power but can we best demonstrate that knowledge and power as individuals or in collaboration with others? At a time when arts organizations, museums and galleries in a number of nation-states are dealing with funding cuts of an unprecedented savageness it is becoming increasingly apparent that a new model is inevitable. The changes in expectation of curatorial practice and the current tensions within the sector are moving the walls of certainty and creating spaces for occupation, within which common points of focus for collaborative activities may emerge and grow. There is now the opportunity for artists, makers, designers, to be proactive and to tackle potential competition for funding and 'gloved' plays for power by embracing new approaches and by helping to shape them from the bottom up.

I have described creative collaboration earlier as a discourse and the potential such working relationships may have in providing new models of practice. Gillian Howard has noted that 'in order to challenge and subvert the established structures that exist within the institutional gallery frame, onus for genuine collaboration ultimately lies with the curator' (Park 2008). I would like to propose a proactive approach to collaboration in which models are created that resist the pressure for specialization and individualism. Instead, by working collaboratively, we might pass 'the shuttle of creative vision back and forth, in a way that advances or changes the pattern [of] community in terms of affiliation, rather than filiation. It is a technique for making sense of gaps, interruptions and unpredictable crossovers' (Carter 2004: 5). Emerging from the spaces between disciplines, such an approach can only benefit from creative collaboration.

When we truly collaborate we are opening ourselves to other influences; the way we think, the way we approach our work, the outcomes, all will be affected. Our existing creative interactions in a collaborative relationship become multidirectional and open to unpredictable dynamics. The crossovers, the spaces between the surfaces, are the spaces within which 'we imagine the realization of our potentialities' (WHW 2005: 15).

Writer and poet Paul Auster describes such collaboration as similar to the alteration of the reality of each of 'two physical objects, [which] when brought into proximity of each other, give off electromagnetic forces that not only effect the molecular structure of each but the space between them as well, altering, as it were, the very environment' (Auster 2003: 138). The transference of such energy to the intersection between art practice and curatorial practice can potentially challenge perceptions and 'alter the very environment' in which exhibitions take place.

NOTES

1. Comments from Trish Bould were made during the seminar series Context and Collaboration, an AHRC-funded research project (principal investigator Lesley Millar), final report published online at <www.contextandcollabora tion.com> accessed 23 August 2012.
2. During war situations a 'collaborator' is understood to be working with the enemy, possibly covertly, and punished severely.
3. Comments from artist Trish Bould were made during the seminar series Context and Collaboration, an AHRC-funded research project (principal investigator Lesley Millar), final report published online at <www.contextandcollabo ration.com> accessed 23 August 2012.

4. *ArtReview* magazine produces an annual listing of the 100 most powerful people in the art world. Museum and gallery curators consistently occupy the top places. In 2011 for the first time, an artist, Ai Weiwei, took the premier position. Otherwise, in the top 10, positions 2, 3, 4, 6, 8, 9 and 10 were occupied by curators.
5. Curator's statement: <http://www.labiennale.org/en/art/news/news-54.html> accessed 12 January 2011.

REFERENCES

Auster, P. (2003), 'The Invention of Solitude, 1980–81', in *Collected Prose*, London: Faber and Faber.

Carter, P. (2004), *Material Thinking: The Theory and Practice of Creative Research*, Carlton, Victoria: Melbourne University Publishing.

Casey, V. (2003), 'The Museum Effect', Paper presented at the Louvre, at ICHIM 03: The Seventh International Cultural Heritage Informatics Meeting, Paris, France, September, <http://www.valcasey.com/thesis/thesis_effect.html> accessed 17 December 2011.

Gormley, A. (2007), 'Thinking about Naoto Fukasawa', in F. Naoto (ed.), *Naoto Fukasawa*, London: Phaidon.

Park, G. (2008), 'A Space to Talk: Curator, Artist, Collaborauteur', *Axis* [online journal] (May–July), <http://www.axisweb.org/dlFull.aspx?ESSAYID=122> accessed 5 October 2009.

Sennett, R. (2008), *The Craftsman*, London: Allen Lane.

What, How & for Whom Collective (2005), *Collective Creativity*, ed. R. Block and A. Nollert, Kassel: Kunsthalle Friedericianum.

–2–

Moving Things around . . . Collaboration and Dynamic Change

Helen Carnac

INTRODUCTION

My views in this chapter have been formed as a maker who works with materials such as metal, enamel, paper and found objects and one who draws, manipulates, collects and collates. I studied silversmithing, jewellery and allied crafts in higher education, spending a year as an intern, working for, amongst others, the goldsmith Jocelyn Burton and the designer Tom Dixon who both always had large teams working alongside them. I set up my first studio in 1994 in London, and after five years of working predominantly alone at my jeweller's bench, with my eye on the bench peg, I decided I needed to look in other directions and work in different ways. I wanted to work with and alongside other makers, and I suspect that this is where my interest in collaborative projects began.

In 1999, I co-founded a project called Dialogue,[1] exchanging work and making with a group of staff and recent graduates from London Guildhall University and Alchimia Jewellery School in Florence. Dialogue was both a collaboration in making and a conversation. It initiated a long period in my work when I actively chose to work with others, often in preference to working alone. I had also begun to think that the importance of my work did not only lie in a finished artefact but also was about a more open-ended and expansive process of putting things together and taking them apart, exploring the nuts and bolts of making.

Collaboration is a concept that can cover a multitude of working practices, and it is currently much used in contemporary art and making circles. One only has to look at the current Arts Council Web site and put 'collaboration' into its search window[2] (which today turns up 1,190 results) to see that it is a key term of reference. Given this, it could be dismissed by sceptics as evidence of a broader central government policy to promote or invoke social cohesion in contrast to the postwar period in which studio crafts have arguably been understood and presented as a field of individual producers selling to individual consumers.

But I have long suspected some missing elements within the well-worn narratives around the crafts and making of the kind précised above: firstly, the voices and words of makers who may give a different account of motivations not fully allied to an art market or their representation by others; and, secondly, a discourse capable of opening up what the crafts have to offer beyond an end product. The collaborations I write about here are an attempt to actively think about these issues in, around and through acts of making.

I often think about the context of working alone and what this means in our society today–is it relevant to work somewhat in isolation with only internal dialogue to sustain oneself? At points I have found, especially early in my career, that being cut off and unable to generate thought with others can produce a sense of dislocation that can be very profound and almost debilitating. So I understand working with others as a necessity for my practice and for maintaining what I do in solo mode. More recently, I have considered whether collaborative working has in fact become my standard mode. I am specifically interested in the actual act of collaborating physically with ideas and making, rather than focusing only on support systems, and in the discussion and doing that affects the physical output of the work.

Collaborating is a means for me to critically engage with others whilst making, to think about the daily reality of what I do as a maker and to concentrate on my subject through doing. But I do not think that collaboration is right in all circumstances. The real benefits of collaborative practice can be overlooked when there is pressure to act together because the funding or grant body demands this as an outcome. Working with others still needs to be done from choice.

Choice is important to acknowledge, alongside the working conditions or context in which the collaboration might take place, and knowing why you want to work together. Many of the projects that I will cite in this chapter have been funded by the artists themselves with no institutional remit or explicit links to cultural policy. The imperative to work together and to explore certain questions has been established by the artists through organic means such as conversations, and this has reflected the critical perspectives of their practices at that time.

SUBJECT AND SOURCES

This chapter focuses on different types of creative practitioners who all refer in some way to their work as a way of making. These practices have all been established for upwards of fifteen years—although I will also briefly touch on a project jointly established with a group of students. I have interviewed several key people along the way and will occasionally quote from these sources.

To begin with I draw on the thoughts and comments of Siobhan Davies,[3] the choreographer I recorded during a conversation we had. Davies, who frequently works with artists from different disciplines, talks about a process of making which has a clear resonance with my own standpoint. Reflecting on how she 'normally works . . . with another', Davies describes this as 'without compromise but ideally in such a way that their practice would move on having had this experience'.[4]

In line with Davies's sentiments, a key theme that has emerged in all the experiences of collaboration I will refer to here is that the artists described have not completely jettisoned their own practice when working with others. There is a clear maintenance or even extension of individual identity within a group dynamic. With this in mind I will also discuss a number of projects that I have personally been involved in over the past twelve years, particularly the collaborative group Intelligent Trouble.[5]

SHIFTING LANDSCAPES

Over the last decade I suggest there has been something of a change in contemporary craft practice. We are now more likely to see makers working together and to be able to see and engage with the process behind their making practice. In the UK national touring exhibition *Taking Time: Craft and the Slow Revolution*,[6] which I curated with Andy Horn and which opened in 2009, with an aim to explore the relationship between slow philosophies and making and crafts practices, many of the objects shown were open-ended and unfinished. Works such as Shane Waltener's *Garland 21* were participatory and evolving, the audience being invited to actively add to the artwork as an act of social making. The exhibition also had various forms of idea generation and methods for audiences to be involved in a thinking process with examples such as the *Making a Slow Revolution* blog and Amy Houghton's *One Centimetre Is Little Less than Half an Inch*, where visitors could type and leave their stories and memories of making. Besides this there were several artists in the exhibition working in tandem, for example Paul Scott and Ann Linnemann and the slow design partnership Boom-Weymeyer.

Aside from special exhibitions such as these, and on a more practical day-to-day level, what are the motivations to work with others? On the most prosaic level for anyone who works alone for long periods, it provides an opportunity to spend time with others working, talking, thinking and bringing different vocabularies together. Precise reasons for working in collaboration are often only reflected on with hindsight, but in the projects described here, motivations have included a wish to be thrown into different or unexpected modes of thinking; the need to experience a friction or difference in practice; the desire to share a vision or to think about the singular within the group; an interest in maintaining or showing difference through working together; the chance to have a space to talk about current issues; the search for a personal sense of well being and creativity; and in some cases, to just get things done.

In her 2007 essay 'The Collaborative Turn', Maria Lind ends by talking about the curatorial collective What, How & for Whom, mentioning that its 'motivation to collaborate is that it has to result in something that would otherwise not take place; it simply has to make possible that which is otherwise impossible'. Working with this 'impossibility' (Lind 2007: 29) and engaging in unknown scenarios which may offer new insight appear to be common reasons for artists and makers to collaborate. 'Mostly I enjoy being knocked off a perception that I have had about something because that jolt is so energising . . . ,' says Davies.[7]

ALWAYS BECOMING

Lind suggests that 'collaboration becomes an umbrella term for the diverse working methods that require more than one participant' (Lind 2007: 17). In this chapter I want to avoid using collaboration as a catch-all term and look in some detail at situations where the collaboration becomes a material process—a process that unravels through the doing of something in real time and perhaps in ways we might liken to a conversation.

The suggestion that learning 'is kinetic self exploration'[8] and that rather than placing information into our bodies and then working out what to do with it, we move through materiality as living material beings is important to consider here too, if we are to understand collaboration in terms of materials and movement. Ingold says, 'We are not embodied', meaning our experience of life is not an abstraction that happens to us, but a reality of us generating forms as we go along. 'To be, I would now say, is not to be in a place but to be along paths. The path and not the place, is the primary condition of being or rather of becoming' (Ingold 2011: 12). Working together we traverse paths in order to find something, where to know more of something we need to handle it, touch it and respond to it, and as Ingold also says, 'In order to observe we need to participate'.[9]

MAKING WALKING, TALKING AND TRACTION

In 2010 Russell Martin, Paul Harper and I convened a small invited symposium called Walking, Talking, Making.[10] In terms of collaboration we have worked together on several occasions over the past six years. Our common interest is in talk as an active component or process of creative practice. 'Our thinking behind the event came out of a growing dissatisfaction with more formal fora such as academic conferences and panel discussions. We felt that even the most successful of these was never quite as sustaining, or agreeable, as the conversation around the kitchen table'.[11]

Our aim was to bring together a group of people to make, talk and walk. But we had not thought fully about individual rationales for being together—of constituting a group that would collaborate in a conversation of various kinds—and this caused friction between members of the group, not being able to find traction or focus it seemed—that was until we walked. Walking offered an in-action opportunity to move through ideas and talk openly. But in the end, coming away from this two-day event, my enduring memory was a feeling of friction. As one of the participants, David Gates, reflected:

> For me the questions raised always come to the fore rather than the answers found . . . a group of people can come together to try and clarify and cohere some strands of thinking relating to a subject that we all come to or are involved in from different places. This inevitably draws on and relies upon disparate points of view and tension creates traction.[12]

What does this tension do, and how important is it? It seems that it may be closely aligned to making and friction, tension that occurs when making work, yet is often occluded in the way that work goes out into the world. Often all we see is the finished artefact—none of the messiness or conversation from along the way. 'But', as Ann Galloway says, 'what if messiness, disjuncture or tension were not considered enemies to collaboration? What if these seams (or scars) were things we did not try to hide, avoid or overcome?' (Galloway 2007: 154).

CO-CONFUSION

Some of this tension has led me to consider the conditions for collaboration and assumptions we make about putting things and people together—that they will naturally gel or perhaps a fear that they may not. In a more recent project in Berlin, as a guest professor in 2011, I ran a new Walking, Talking, Making project called Stitching Together Ideas in Time[13] that involved working with students over four months to think about place through the lenses of singularity and collaboration by walking. In Berlin, despite preconceived ideas about more collaborative social practices there, I found an emphasis on singularity in the environment that I was exposed to. Taking the students out and walking with them worked in terms of finding an alternative to this overdetermined institutional space. Being out and looking, observing and watching meant that we could operate together, outside the confines of the classroom—moving through ideas. Ultimately, the students worked together at different levels, supported one another and thought as a group. The students wrote the following together:

> Berlin is our first connection point to each other. We have used the city to explore our way. We are walking a way to explore Berlin . . . We are here in Berlin from eight different countries. We speak eight different languages. We have sixteen eyes and sixteen legs and we all have a different view on the city . . . We walked

together to find out about the nature of a place, its material, its stories and its pace. On these journeys we talked and got to know each other: about our different interests; experiences; cultures and origins. Initiating this process we asked ourselves questions and followed them to places in Berlin. We saw how these questions change in the process of walking, talking and thinking deeply . . .[14]

However, what this writing does not allude to is another word they constructed whilst mapping this out—'co-confusion'. Co-confusion seemed to perfectly describe a state of being faced with the unknown that the group was initially placed in. In this case the students did not necessarily have the experience to deal with this alone and relied on me and on one another to sustain movement at the beginning of the process. What they were left with at the end of four months was an ability to go into the unknown alone, while also knowing how to find ways of working with others to spur things along, sharing on a level grounding. Ultimately, the students produced projects about the environment both as a group and as individuals—the individual works being co-constitutive of the larger walking project (Figure 2.1). The project was about walking the city, collecting data and making observations. The students generated bodies of work that reflected their activities and processes of recording,

Fig. 2.1.   Walking, Talking, Making, Berlin. 2011. Photograph: Helen Carnac

collecting and synthesizing environmental data found as they traversed and lived in the city. 'With each new creation or collaboration we arrange and re-arrange different risks and responsibilities. The resulting assemblages can be so messy that it can be difficult to figure out how one is accountable to, and for, these arrangements' (Galloway 2007: 155).

KNOWING AND NOT (YET) KNOWING

Galloway's suggestion of messiness and a tangle of interconnected thinking articulates something of knowing and not yet knowing and the making and not yet made of process. In a conversation between me and Siobhan Davies, we talked about this at length.

HC: it's really intriguing then how something then grows, how you're develop-ing in a sense quite consciously with some of those things coming in and out . . . knowing but not knowing . . . bringing some knowing in.

SD: some knowing in is great and so knowing out is also useful . . . even though you might circle back and pick it up later . . . you drop something by the wayside so that it doesn't weigh you down and on a return journey you can pick it up to take it somewhere else.

In emphasizing this contingent nature of process, doing, handling mate-rial and working together, Intelligent Trouble (IT), a London-based collective of makers has sought to explore the possibilities of working together whilst 'shift[ing], change[ing] and remain[ing] the same'. IT began when a group of four makers, including me, decided that we wanted to work together, with no particular outcome but as a response to showing works together during the exhibition *In Transit* in 2009 in Munich, which was installed in a working foundry. During its four-day duration we responded to one another and our works, (re)positioning pieces, toying with juxtapositions and modifying works. 'Three days in there bored . . . for 35 hours and out of that came the conver-sation that gave rise to this'.[15]

Consequently, IT's first project began in August 2009 with a walk and a boat ride in London. It was there that we decided that each of us would make an edi-tion of four small works or assemblages of materials that we felt represented an aspect of our own practices to exchange with one another. These were, a month later, simultaneously exchanged, retaining one for reference, and work-ing on or responding to the others by the other members of the group.

> . . . going into our diaries and committing a certain amount of days to working together and so we had 6 days together in the workshop . . . you give yourself a framework and the blank paper for something like this to come out of and I firmly

believe that you can't do this [. . .] quite intense work by email from other ends of the country . . .[16]

This simple act started a network of exchange that, as it became more informal, became more intense. Notions of authorship, object-hood, trust, risk and dialogue became themes around which our conversations turned. We found ourselves wondering where one pair of hands ended and another began and what might be at stake by allowing someone else to continue with our work. Talk became a key part of the process and an important tool, but making and materiality were the themes on which everything turned. We worked individually but also came together at our studios to work, talk and eat during time we had set aside. We all agreed that face-to-face time and physical making together were key aspects.

The intention was that each starting point would pass through each of our hands. In the event some did and some did not, others galvanized tangential paths of making. Even though there was no initial intention to exhibit the outcome of this original exchange, the offer came and the project was exhibited at Contemporary Applied Arts in London in January 2010, virtually unedited, and curated by the group. It was met with differing receptions— from those who were refreshed and engaged in the open nature of a process that was so speculative, to those who wanted more structure and to be able to understand exactly what they were seeing. Throughout the duration of the six-week exhibition, a series of talks were held that were informal and conversational. The extract below is from one such event titled 'Dialogue and Conversation'.

What we were doing—having a kind of conversation . . . a bit like . . . an extended conversation around the table in a pub—sometimes two people are talking together, other times people are 'semi-eavesdropping' or over-hearing, a bit of picking up on it and chipping in with their own thoughts . . . it really did illustrate how even though we had a methodology for how we were going to produce this work and then . . . to set it out and introduce a sort of system of display it really was quite complex.[17]

In another extract of the text, another member of the group uses the familiar analogy to walking when describing a point when the group decided to make dovetails and the conversation was far more didactic. 'Doing something, comes easier, it's a bit like walking and conversation—everything is going in motion. When we were doing the dovetails my hands were busy, my mind was busy and it felt easier to converse'.[18]

Beyond the activities of making and working together, we felt that we needed to respond to the outside world and show the work in contexts both familiar and unfamiliar in our own individual practices. Some were conventional galleries and other informal spaces. Some of the more formal spaces were not necessarily familiar with the type of works we were producing and had to deal with expectations of visitors wanting, in some cases, to see the solo works of a named individual.

In the next exhibition *Under the Counter*[19] in September 2010, we exhibited an edited 'conversation' of works that had passed between us earlier that year when we gave each other 'permission to (re)-interpret, continue or dismiss any given passage'. The activity of 'selecting' took place back in the studio in August 2010 before the exhibition's installation. Unpacking the work, for the first time since the de-installing of the last show, we quickly decided which works would stay and which would go.

This activity was a telling evocation of how the project had happened. There were some interesting moments remembered and held in the work—a piece of oak passed to another, burnt, passed on in soot, mixed jointly into an ink, used to make marks by another and prints made with the soot, by pressing through the rolling mill, another finding a similar but different process to make prints with iron and oak (Figure 2.2). Reflecting on the process we surmised that 'during the editing of this work we found, that like many conversations, there were forgotten phrases, mistakes and repairs but also

Fig. 2.2. Intelligent Trouble: Process shot, with the work of Roseanne Bartley in background. 2010. Photograph: David Gates

Fig. 2.3. Intelligent Trouble at the Institute of Making. An installation at the Festival of Materials and Making, King's College London, November 2011. Photograph: David Gates

memorable excerpts, discoveries and jokes . . . we feel that the pieces shown here speak most eloquently of our interactions'.[20]

Since then IT has worked in several formations. Members stepping in and out of projects along the way as a loose network. Most recently, four of the group worked together at the Institute of Making,[21] King's College, London (2011), on a large durational installation in a 100-foot stairwell (Figure 2.3). In this version of events, what seemed most important was the making of a project together where the work became another conversation in an ongoing process, although at times it also seemed easier to work alone. What came to the fore was the engagement in a single material—jute twine—and our different ways of manipulating and exploring space from our own perspectives. 'As a group of makers we have explored the possibilities of working together and what new things could be done. Without jettisoning our own identities, opening our selves to the actions and provocations of others. Trying to find out a little about how each of us works and thinks, locating the overlaps in approaches'.[22]

Through each of the IT projects, the group has held public, audience-inclusive conversations, and we have written about and documented our works. Having begun by using a 'washing line' to install works during *In Transit*, the line has reappeared and been used as a form of communication in all our ongoing projects. From a line we installed at the promenade at Chelsea College of Art (at the Craft Council's Inaugural Craft Rally)[23] to exchange objects and ideas to our ongoing storyline project, through which we are able to collect stories of making from the audience. Perhaps we might think of these lines as a place that we hang ideas from.

CONVERSATION

It is this verbal and nonverbal conversation that is a part of the doing and making of work that seems to offer, a working 'in the now' (Gates 2013: 55). In his essay 'History in the Making; the Use of Talk Inter-disciplinary Collaborative Craft Practice', David Gates, a maker and current PhD student, writes: 'The fluidity of talk-in-interaction mirrors and captures the ongoing, contingent processes of making-in-interaction. Unfinished passages of talk, making and repairing in the now, making sense of enough to get to the next now, a parallel to making as a continuously unfinished process, doing enough to get to the next step. Talking and making are active, present verbs, the -ing implies the ongoing character of now—of becoming' (Gates 2013: 63).

Gates's 'making-in-interaction' is important to consider here. His words describe very well the process of collaborative working and its likeness to conversation. It is often difficult to pin precise words to actions after the event and live conversation perhaps holds more trace of what happens in a moment. 'Your language gets challenged and then your language gets enriched and then you challenge somebody else's language . . . needing to bring something in from your periphery . . . going out to the outer edge to find something and finding the memory at the edge . . . remembered'.[24]

REMEMBERING

There may be some perception that something will get lost from an individual's voice in collaborative practice, but perhaps if there is a loss, it can leave room for something new.

For me, collaboration has become easier over the years as I have gained experience and knowledge in my own practice, and I am less fearful of letting go of control, of working in the unknown, of unpicking process and sharing. I do wonder whether some assume that this improvisatory practice means that you are doing something without knowledge when in fact through your experience you are working from a position of knowledge and improvising and making adjustments in the moment. As Ingold acknowledges, 'In order to move with precision you have to improvise'.[25]

So are we reaching a period where improvisatory collaborative projects that build from individual sites of practice and knowledge can grow into something more profound? Can we accept that it takes a depth and breadth of knowledge to work in this way, but in order for practice to develop, we may need to open up to something new and unknown? Collaboration 'is as unusual as arranged marriages, initiated by people who are forced to get married, as rare as successful blind dates. Instead of formal mergers, temporary collaborations within self-determined activities may frequently be observed, but these rarely entail the literal merging of categories' (Lind 2007: 19).

But what are these categories to which Lind alludes, and if 'making' is a category, how many other categories does it embrace? My reason for talking to Siobhan Davies was not because she is from a discipline outside of the crafts but because when talking about her own work she speaks of making and materiality, about the body, about movement and about being, all of which I see as being connected to my own practice and the collaborations that I work in.

Ultimately, for me, collaboration is about thinking anew, taking risks and extending oneself with others. Through working in this way and understanding my working practice from differing perspectives, I now feel confident in not sitting within a given category but can move and think through ideas from different sites. The projects cited in this essay say something of the nature of ideas moving and shifting: the conversations made, the objects and materials worked on and passed around and walking that enables thinking—all are moving.

Shortly after writing this, I will be undertaking a residency with the dancer and choreographer Laïla Diallo, developed by Siobhan Davies Dance.[26] It will be the first time that I will work with someone unknown to me, not chosen by me and from an ostensibly different discipline. I am curious to see what happens. At once I imagine a scene from the film *Kitchen Stories* (Hamer 2003) where a scientific observer's job of watching a single man's kitchen habits for long periods of time, under instruction of silence, ultimately breaks as both want to share more than they can by only watching each other. Perhaps by moving ideas and things around physically we will be able to shift perspectives and move territory.

NOTES

1. Dialogue was founded in 1999 by Helen Carnac, Mikala Djørup and Alumni of Sir John Cass, London Guildhall University and The Alchimia Jewellery School, Florence, Italy.
2. <www.artscouncil.org.uk/google-search/?q=collaboration> accessed 18 July 2012.
3. Siobhan Davies CBE (born 1950) danced with the London Contemporary Dance Theatre during the 1970s, becoming one of its leading choreographers before founding her own company.
4. S. Davies, personal communication with H. Carnac, 2 December 2011.
5. Intelligent Trouble was conceived in Munich in 2009 by the makers Helen Carnac, David Clarke, Lin Cheung and David Gates. Other members include Katy Hackney, Shane Waltener and David Littler.
6. *Taking Time: Craft and the Slow Revolution* was curated by Helen Carnac and Andy Horn for the UK organization Craftspace. The exhibition toured eight UK venues between 2009 and 2011.
7. S. Davies, personal communication with H Carnac, 2 December 2011.
8. Quote noted by the author at a seminar at PAL: Movement and Meaning Lab held at Siobhan Davies Studios, 15 November 2011.
9. Ibid.
10. Walking, Talking, Making was a project organized by Paul Harper, Helen Carnac and Russell Martin for the organizations Artquest, London and Alias and was supported by the Artists Professional Development network.
11. P. Harper, email correspondence to participants in Walking, Talking, Making, 10th March 2010.
12. D. Gates, email communication with Walking, Talking, Making participants, 30th March 2010.
13. Stitching Together Ideas in Time was a project run by guest professor Helen Carnac and initiated by Greenlab, KHB, Berlin in 2011.
14. Students at Kunsthochschule Weißensee, Berlin, A Shared View: Stitching Together Ideas in Time. First draft made in June 2011, later re-written and published in Carnac (2012).
15. Excerpts from gallery conversation at Intelligent Trouble, London, March 2010.
16. Ibid.
17. Ibid.
18. Ibid.
19. *Under the Counter* was an exhibition curated by Intelligent Trouble for Smiths Row, Bury St Edmunds in 2010. The artists Roseanne Bartley, Elizabeth Callinicos, Intelligent Trouble, James Evans, Benjamin Lignel and Timothy Information Ltd were shown in the exhibition.

20. Excerpts from gallery conversation at Intelligent Trouble.
21. The Institute of Making is a multidisciplinary research club for those interested in the made world: from makers of molecules to makers of buildings, synthetic skin to spacecraft, soup to clothes, furniture to cities. Originally based at King's College, London, it moved to University College London, in 2012.
22. D. Gates, email correspondence to Walking, Talking, Making participants, 30 March 2011.
23. The Inaugural Craft Rally, Part 1, was an event curated by Artquest, Helen Carnac and Yorkshire Art Space for the UK Crafts Council in March 2010.
24. S. Davies, personal communication with H Carnac, 2 December 2011.
25. Quote noted by the author at a seminar at PAL: Movement and Meaning Lab held at Siobhan Davies Studios, 15 November 2011.
26. Side by Side is a residency developed by the Siobhan Davies Dance Company in 2012, which has investigated the act and process of making with dance artist Laïla Diallo and craft artist Helen Carnac. See http://www.siobhandavies.com/sidebyside/.

    Laïla Diallo is a dancer and choreographer born in Canada and now living in Bristol, UK. An associate artist at the Royal Opera House between 2009 and 2012 and the recipient in 2006 of a Rayne Fellowship for Choreographers, Laïla came to prominence as a performer with Wayne McGregor's Random Dance, where she danced from 1998 to 2005.

REFERENCES

Carnac, H. (2012), *A Shared View-Stitching Together Ideas in Time*, Berlin: Greenlab.

Galloway, A. (2007), 'Seams and Scars, or How to Locate Accountability in Collaborative Work', in C. Brickwood, B. Ferran, D. Garcia and T. Putnam (eds), *(Un)Common Ground. Creative Encounters across Sectors and Disciplines*, Amsterdam: BIS Publishers.

Gates, D. (2013), 'History in the Making; the Use of Talk in Interdisciplinary Collaborative Craft Practice', in L. Sandino and M. Partington (eds), *Oral History in the Visual Arts*, London: Bloomsbury, 55–63.

Hamer, B. (2007), *Kitchen Stories*, Svenska Filminstitutet, Bulbul Films, BOB Film Sweden.

Ingold, T. (2011), B*eing Alive: Essays on Movement, Knowledge and Description*, London: Routledge.

Lind, M. (2007), 'The Collaborative Turn', in *Taking the Matter into Common Hands, on Contemporary Art and Collaborative Practice*, London: Black Dog.

–3–

Triangulation: Working towards a Practice of Collaboration

David Gates, Alice Kettle and Jane Webb

INTRODUCTION

This chapter was written by three authors, the furniture maker David Gates, the textile artist Alice Kettle and material culture historian Jane Webb. Our individual work comes out of a range of disciplines and is aesthetically and materially different. David's work encompasses both traditional and contemporary furniture. He explores traditional skills and tools whilst considering the social role of furniture today and its relationship to three-dimensional space and sculptural form. Alice works mainly on a large scale, using gestural machine embroidery to create two-dimensional painterly and often figurative narratives with a rich surface quality of diverse threads and yarns. Like David, she is interested in exploring the relationship between traditional techniques and new technologies or contexts. Jane is primarily an academic and writes on the history of material culture with a particular emphasis on the place of textiles within social history. She is also theoretically interested in making but has done little practical work, though she has begun to produce objects and images as part of her own critical writing.

We first worked together on *Pairings* initiated by the Manchester School of Art, an undertaking designed to offer collaborative opportunities to makers from different disciplines, and to showcase the outcomes in a touring exhibition around the United Kingdom.[1] The project was part of the general fascination with collaborative practice in the art, design and craft world where 'seeing what happens' when different disciplines come together to provide new contexts for practice has almost become the norm. With an awareness of these previous initiatives, we were keen to genuinely work together, having witnessed what we all considered at times to be a superficial interchange and a subcontracting of skills.

This chapter examines how we worked together in what we understood to be a 'deep' collaboration and considers both the practical difficulties and genuine excitement experienced in maintaining the required openness and lack of possessiveness around skills and materials. This process was not a linear one, and we have tried to evoke this through the use of three voices. These are not our distinct voices but the methods of communication and levels of thinking that we have had to engage in. We have indicated them as follows: in normal text is the narrative of our meetings written and remembered by us in hindsight; in italics are our theoretical reflections; and in indented text are the email correspondences from our communications during the project.

In outlining our collaborative practice in this way, we hope to convey and examine the critical tension when three people work together. By tension, we do not mean tension in the negative, but rather as a tensile architectural structure, where a physical friction aids the maintenance of space between supports. We found that we came to visualize our collaboration of three in this way and that indeed three was crucial to creating a 'holding space' between us, offering each a continuous potential place for action that no one person possessed. We also discovered that at moments we took on different roles in maintaining this structure and that we had often thought of our positions in these spatial terms at the time. It is therefore this practice of being three that we will explore in the chapter, with the aid of theories concerning collaboration, spectatorship and liminal space.

CONVERSATION BEGINS

The underlying rationale of the *Pairings* project was that previously unknown makers from around the country should meet and exchange ideas and skills to produce something. This outcome was then to be exhibited as a statement of a new collaboration. In essence, then, the brief provided a framework but left the methodology open with no guide to the collaborative process. Thus, throughout the project, different configurations and methods took place to make working and producing collaboratively happen.

For us, the choreography of physical proximity and separation in working together became one of the fundamental ingredients. Much time was spent in the coordination of meetings and the negotiation of geographical location, while the moments of meeting up signified intense conversation or making which framed the in-between times where work continued separately, informed through email dialogue. On writing this chapter, the remembering of these sequences, causes and happenings invoked an analogy with the travelling and dis-/re-locating that all three of us experienced. This analogy allowed for collective and alternative memories, a psychological repositioning as well as a physical one, so that even when the location was on 'home turf', what was usually familiar seemed different. Whenever and wherever the meeting took place it became a new space in which we could all participate, allowing us to share and explore a novel set of ideas or practices. This relationship between physical placement and work will therefore provide a mechanism through which to reflect on four particular meetings: Alice's and David's studios, the British Library and Museum, Birmingham Museum and Art Gallery and firstly the gardens outside Manchester School of Art (All Saints Park).

> I do feel I am emerging into a new space. It makes me feel I want other things, more books, more fun! Just enjoying life and not doing what I should do! I feel as though there is so much to learn.

ALL SAINTS PARK

The coming together as three was unexpected (and unusual within the Pairings remit) as, until then, Jane had been assigned the role of critical writer, and it was intended that she would analyse and interpret the Pairings project. However, during the presentations Jane and David found an affinity in their joint interests in the role of discourse in and around practice, so during the day, Jane repositioned herself as a making participant assigned to one partnership, that of Alice Kettle and David Gates.

Previously, Alice had invited David to join her in collaboration since his research seemed to have a thematic link to the underlying theme of Pairings. David's research[2] focuses on the interaction and communicative practices in collaborative crafts. But as this was the first time David and Alice had come together in the context of Pairings, Jane joined them at the project's inception. In effect, then, we were always three.

> A triangle of practices seems to carry so much potential, especially using the openness of conversation as the starting point. With three possible pairs in dialogue, there are also three 'L' shapes, with each of us in turn at the angle or turning point of the 'L'. We might all meet anywhere in the area of the triangle. It's a horribly mechanistic image I know, one that reminds me of the diagrams and models in books on how to be a designer. No-one really works likes this, and I don't want to, but it does serve as a useful thought to perhaps forget quite quickly in such a rigid format.

Our first meeting took place after the official Pairings launch outside on the grass in All Saints Park. Looking back it seemed an ideal place, as it is a transitory space that allows for pausing, resting and changing direction. The early conversation centred on the role of text in recording and disseminating crafts practice. Jane and David spoke of making and its positioning in relation to craft history and theory, the establishing of affiliations with creative tradition, current ideas, and the difference of 'doing' craft, to the writing and talking 'about' craft. Alice felt outside of this emerging partnership and suggested that she should leave the group, but David and Jane convinced her not to.

> Here are some suggestions of what we could do, all of which can be ignored.
>   Go for a walk.
>   Go and look at something with art in it.
>   Talk about a piece of writing.
>   Play with Alice's sewing machines.

On the train back to London, David wrote about the first meeting, and these notes show a relational plotting. David found himself somewhere between Jane's text and theory and Alice's making practices and thus was instinctively pegging-out an immediate topography of identities and practices. Alice and Jane were quite unaware of David finding this place, 'between'.

> For myself I am very happy to be sitting between and alongside a site of practice and a site of theory, the opportunity to work with the ideas of materials and the ideas of words, and the crossing points between them.

THE BRITISH LIBRARY

The next meeting was at the British Library and the British Museum. In the library, we sat in the café and discussed our family histories and lives. Looking back to these conversations, none of us foregrounded our identities as makers, it was through the channels of family history that our connections to materiality surfaced. We all feel that our identities as individuals coming together were not made from the materially and disciplinary singular categories set out by institutions but rather from the more general, everyday immersion of encountering materials, of being in a made world and of the acts of doing. As such, making appeared to be the common language of living and of seeing the world, which provided the fixed and shared points of connection and the potential for collaboration.

The shift from a 'pairing' to a grouping of three has some precedent as noted by Anna Grimshaw, Elspeth Owen and Amanda Ravetz (2010) who highlight the work of Paul Ryan in defining a 'three person solution' or a 'threeing'. They note that rather than 'reifying established positions' that can often happen with a collaborative pairing, three '. . . results in a dislodging of categories that can otherwise seem self-evident and allows for identities to be constituted in and through the collaborative process itself' (Grimshaw, Owen and Ravetz 2010: 148). In a study of theatre and its relationship to cultural models of social engagement, Kirsten Hastrup (2004) identifies that, for communication to occur between individuals, the model of the Shakespearean actor and their audience is crucial in that for any two actors, the audience formed a 'third point'. The 'third point' is not that of a passive 'eavesdropper' but is that of an equal participant (Hastrup 2004: 225). However, this position is a 'third point', one that is not the same as the other two and forms a position of reflection, a mediatory role, an observer, a commentator, a practitioner, or even a devil's advocate.

Umm, I like the circular movement this is forming . . .

I'm liking the idea of implied movement and demountability/re-makability.

And flip books with something hidden in each layer . . . There is something very poetic about all these materials . . . but I need more drawings and text from you . . . I am hanging onto this idea of the cave, with a hidden interior. But I'm now getting carried away . . .

We are all busy, getting three together is hard!

I am happy for you to go ahead, as I can prepare things for you to do things with.

BIRMINGHAM CITY MUSEUM

A pivotal meeting at the Birmingham City Museum followed some months later. As a location, it was a geographical centre point. This centrality of place was combined with another transitional space, another café with people meandering around a series of exhibits. This was a coming together in an environment that belonged to none of us but had a long history and connection to making.

I agree that we really do seem to bounce off each other (okay, now I've got an image of us in big inflatable suits on a bouncy castle, but you know what I mean). Do we think it is a totally unrealistic idea that we could work together for at least say four days? I mean, we'd have to be somewhere that had all, or at least some of the equipment we each use, so we could all contribute to the making but . . . what do you think? Somewhere . . .

Critiquing theorists thinking about the concept of 'between', Metcalfe and Game argue that those theorists 'maintain a Euclidian logic by posing it as the third term between two primary terms' (Metcalfe and Game 2008: 18). In discussing the ideas of the child psychologist Donald Winnicott, they suggest, like him, that this reliance on Euclid fails to communicate the different type of space that is made in moments of 'creativity'. Euclid's geometry is based on a loss of embodied experience, a plunging of three-dimensionality and temporality into two dimensions. The phenomenological attitude to this is to see 'the geometer' as one who 'will not think of exploring, besides geometrical shapes, geometrical thinking' (Husserl in Paterson 2007: 61). But this opposition of embodied experience, being-in-the-body-in-the-world to an abstracted mathematical model, does not quite articulate the formlessness of just being. It is a state of 'un-integration' that does not differentiate between states of outer space and inner personal space but combines the two into what Winnicott calls 'potential space' (Metcalfe and Game 2008: 18).

The potential space opens from a single focus through the wider vision and the differing perceptions of others. The sense of this space is informed from differing viewpoints which converge or diverge into multiple spaces. 'The sense of social community and of shared (or, indeed, disparate) interests pervades the vision of the field of possible action. The field is always already populated, the sense of self is partly mediated through the eyes of others, and the world is profoundly "dialogic" in that sense' (Bakhtin 1981: 13; Hastrup 2004 : 235).

I am keen to experience notions of speed and risk. Some of the work that I have been making over the last year or so has been partly motivated by trying to embrace chance and to allow the freedom and vitality of those first sketch phases of an idea to come right through to the final piece, building structure through line, the construction of a textile, it is three-dimensional (albeit compressed), not a surface.

As we worked together an objective emerged from conversations. This was to consolidate an understanding and initiate a strategy for the project by questioning and comparing working methods. Shared motifs and concerns began to emerge as a list of words that provided a physical description of volume, space and movements through and onto surface and surrounding contexts (Figure 3.1). The words served to identify positioning, interruptions, boundaries and states. They formed a declaration of starting points, places

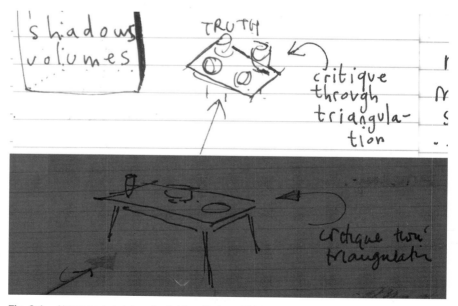

Fig. 3.1.   Notes and sketches for *Pairings* Project, 2009. Gates, Webb. Photograph: David Gates

where making could be examined and which could provide a portable tool kit carried away to geographically different locations. They were

Behind
Text as piercing
Holes
Surface
Volume
Planes
Penetrating
Shadow
Light
Interior
Exterior
Back
Front
Perspective

David likes corners . . . Jane is making words intangible and Alice is looking for line.

Am interested that although embroidery might be seen as a surface or layering technique, it cannot avoid having a back and front through its construction, and while not as constructed perhaps as some weaves, there is an undeniable three-dimensionality, to my eyes and hands.

The accidental or secondary on the reverse, leaving clues to the building of the front.

'Potential space' does mean a conflation of differences between the body and space, the inner and outer, but a constant state of tension in difference. In his article 'A Typology of Thresholds', Georges Teyssot discusses the etymology of the word 'between'. He notes that '[t]he English "between" . . . contains the word "twain", thus conferring the idea of the "two". The "between" is a mark of the spacing inherent to difference, one that is both "separateness and toward-ness"' (Teyssot 2005: 105). Like the Shakespearean role of the audience as 'third point', the between position holds the potential space perpetually open. Thus 'potential space' 'is holding space because it can hold possibilities, without seeking to resolve the space through definition' (Metcalfe and Game 2008: 19).

I have to start where I am and I think my response is to use stitch in response to you. David is essentially into three dimensions on hard material, and Jane is the metaphor and implicit reference. I am going to respond to and interpret your imagery and to carry your voices within my material.

I don't know what I am going to make yet, but I like being in that place for the moment.

Unfortunately, at this point Jane left due to the unexpected death of her father. She explained that she could not continue with the project, but David and Alice would not let her leave permanently. They held her place open and accepted that her participation was suspended, but her presence was still evident and essential.

DAVID'S AND ALICE'S STUDIOS

During this time, Alice and David worked together and visited each other's workshops, bringing form to the words that had been discussed. They created a thematic framework that gave them licence to explore ideas rather than demonstrating skills or testing tools. As a collection of words they required attention to meaning and analysis as to how they could be interpreted and transformed into material and visual form. In those words were the descriptive ingredients for the recipe for physical processes which would inform a cycle of making, thought and word. The thread became a navigational tool to negotiate a third dimension around and into the wood. The thread separated from its fabric ground was used to tie and bind, to disappear into holes and to emerge in knots and lines around rigid struts and boards smelling of cedar.

This open-ended experience was an improvisation with the familiar and unfamiliar of each other's making where the material was investigated and passed on. The divesting of ownership of material into shared authorship was part of this experimentation. Alice and David imagined what Jane might have done with her words if she had been there. They became her interpreters.

The holding space created by Gates, Kettle and Webb can be understood in relation to improvisation as discussed by Elvin Jones, John Coltrane's drummer. 'Coltrane did a lot of experimenting . . . even though it gave an impression of freedom, it was basically a well thought out and highly disciplined piece of work' (Cox and Warner 2008: 250). Improvisation is not completely free but is an action that moves around agreed structures and understandings between members, also emerging from and through established practices and traditions. The practice undertaken by Gates and Kettle echoed this same pattern, based on structured knowledge of skill acquired over time but circulating within the contained area of the shared holding space. The workshops of Gates and Kettle were inherently suited as physical manifestations of a holding space being, as Hastrup describes theatre 'a new poetics of space, a poetics that makes us experience the possible rather than the already manifest' (Hastrup 2004: 226). The workshop is always full of latent potential.

I would like some copies of pages from the little landscape drawing sketchbook to be in the display case. Gifting me that book on day one actually changed/brought in something new to what I do.

Both Alice and David enjoyed the way their collaboration provided an alternative to what can sometimes be a stifling self-reflexivity when working alone in the workshop. They noticed differences in the rhythm of the practice at different locations. They realized that a workshop is usually a very privileged space, a personal territory. Though both felt respect for their location, there was also a delight in being able to explore someone else's workshop and the alternative ephemera, the tools, the materials, the drawings, the miscellaneous twines and ties of another practice. The intimacy of the workshop locations were completely different from the spaces that Alice, Jane and David had previously met in, as these had always been neutral and transitional. The workshops were both familiar and unfamiliar—a homely space comfortable to all makers but one that becomes strangely other when predicated upon other materials and processes.

> The red shot through lines toward the top. Have a look. A third of the way down over on the right-hand side, an inch from the edge. Is it there? Is this the hole for your golden thread coming back? Can we do something with it? I like it. Going through, back and front and beyond the surface. You will be asked to place a wooden line in three-dimensional space.
>
> Yes it is there, I can see it. I would like my golden thread to go beyond the surface. The new surface speaks with a voice of its own and yet with familiar undertones.

The shift from a transitional space to situated studio locations 'owned' by Gates and Kettle was an important part of the developmental process. Workshops are inherently suited as physical metaphors of a holding space, being laboratories promising material transformation and drama. In his discussion of space as capacity, Alberto Corsín Jiménez (2003) notes that 'the world is not a known place that exists prior to our engagements with it . . . on the contrary the world happens with us' and through our practices (Jiménez 2003: 141). This antiessentialist perspective describes the world as one in which social life is central to the fabrication of our knowledge of the world (Burr 2003). Sense is made of the world through the interactive nature of collaborative working and the ongoing reformulations of culture at a local level. Indeed, Gates connects talk as social action and collaborative craft practice in his argument for 'making-in-interaction' (Gates 2013). For the workshop to emerge as a heightened space of becoming, beyond the usual state of how we live our lives, it has to be rejected as a personal, known territory that already existed, prior to activity. In other words, it has to be opened up to time and in so doing to 'choices and possibilities . . . paths [and] . . . histories' (Jiménez 2003: 142). Both Gates and Kettle dispossessed their usual spaces, tools and skills and allowed them to become again in what Jiménez sees as the 'double constituency of space' that he calls 'capacity' (Jiménez 2003: 142). Gates and Kettle understood this as making work, not as separate makers collaboratively but through divesting their separateness and by working within the between, 'potential' space.

> I think we really need to work out what stays in and becomes more and different, and what we shall take out? I quite like the idea of everything going together as one installation or composite 'form'.

WORK MADE, CONVERSATION CONTINUED

The bringing together of work to make public had always been part of the *Pairings* project. The exhibition was rehung many times to allow for developments in work and to keep the conversations between makers open (Figure 3.2). For David, Alice and Jane the act of unwrapping, and curating relational groups

Fig. 3.2. Triangulation Theory Workshop, 2010. Gates, Kettle, Webb. Photograph: David Gates

of work made was central to its construction. This was also Jane's first opportunity to rejoin the group, and the unwrapping worked better than any verbal explanation. But this activity was as important for Alice and David as the
reopening helped to quickly relocate everyone. We were in a momentum of
energy that felt like the making process itself, it seemed of the moment, not
reflecting on what had happened. Orchestrating the component parts meant
nothing dominated—it was like a (still ongoing) narrative. Alice asked Jane to
write on a large piece of stitched wood that Alice herself considered to be a
sketchbook. Struggling to think how to write, Jane chose to write with the construction, describing what the building of the pieces suggested to her as the
tableaux emerged.

> I am very happy that we closed the first loop . . . as a threesome. Somehow com-
> ing back round. It still feels like the beginning though, I have so much to learn
> from you two!

The 'fixing' of these objects in this neutral space equated to the workshop
making but without the individual associations of practice and tools. The process of connecting with objects and with one another, and of negotiating relationships between works, echoed those of the workshop dialogues. We began
to select things and put them in an order, objects placed side by side. But in
a crucial second curating, the stitched and notated wood sketchbook became
the ground for the rest of the objects, and we began to build, layering and
stacking. The work became a treasure of small interventions and three dimensions, a complex micro-macrocosm, a new space (Figure 3.3).

> Perhaps it is easier for you two to get together as you are already there, I trust you
> both. I think . . . the Munich pieces should probably come out . . . but I was so
> struck by how well they looked on the embroidered and written board that I would
> like something there if possible.

*The threeing did not adhere to the model proposed by Paul Ryan, that of the
roles of initiator, respondent and mediator (Paul Ryan, www.earthscore.com).
Rather the triangulation of Gates, Kettle and Webb can be better seen through
the metaphor of theatre as the roles of actors and audience were adopted organically between the three. This audience role was not as one might expect,
a passive one, rather it was following Hastrup's model of historic theatre, audience as active member, responsive to the events on stage. This fluid transition
between roles happened unconsciously and at irregular times and is perhaps
how the three worked to create a between space, which as Donald Winnicott
has noted, is crucial in holding open the potential space central to spaces of
creativity (Winnicott referred to in Metcalfe and Game 2008: 18).*

*Holding is a flexible metaphor. It allows for things to be held together but also
to be held apart, allowing shifting positions and the opening up of sight lines.*

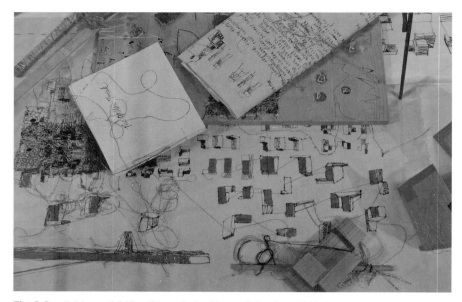

Fig. 3.3.   *Pairings* exhibition, Triangulation Theory Collection, 2010. Gates, Kettle, Webb. Materials: Thread, linen, wood, cotton, cloth. Photograph: David Gates

One can hold onto individual views to offer them into the space because as Metcalfe and Game suggest, this is a 'holding space because it can hold possibilities' (Metcalfe and Game 2008: 32). There is a literal manifestation of holding too, of tools and materials. We are reminded that as with many metaphorical constructs there is a grounding or reflection in physical experience. That for all our construction of a void—a space, there was and is the very real construction through making. And through this there is a sense of holding (onto) one another as knowledge, experience and identities entangle. With this fluidity must come a willingness to participate in new configurations and an ongoing negotiation along a continuum of chaos and order as we come together and move apart.

The list of words that Gates, Kettle and Webb identified as their manifesto of making describes the holding space. The words speak of spatial arrangement but lack overt structure, instead they invoke a geometry of the imagination. The words do not prescribe the material or manner of making, breaking with the material-bound literature on craft, they offer a method and framework to work within.

CONCLUSION

The objects that were created as a result of our collaboration were all aspects of ourselves but were slightly altered or unfinished, leaving room for the others.

David's work asked Alice to work with form and space, whilst he considered malleability and surface. Both provided a subject and a ground for Jane to write. The final combination of elements created a tableaux which was added to by a ghostly figure representing the sense of narrative and presences and absences that had gone into making the work. All three of us found it problematic to rationally explain how the processes and connections came about. This can be seen clearly in the work exhibited in the *Pairings* tour. An amalgamation, elements are partly fused but with ragged edges—overlapping here and with gaps there. The results have elements speaking to and across each other. We might claim that the work is dialogic, polyglossic, each material utterance responding to, supporting, or prompting another. Each stitch, strut or word causing each other, defying a linear concept of experience and space. Because of this intimacy, each one of us was changed by the other, perhaps for good.

For all these references to materials and making, it is notable that our most potent tool at many moments in the project was, and is, a list of words. The portability that the words afforded, provided something tangible and shared that could be carried across geography, as thing and as idea. The words reflected back and provided us with markers whilst simultaneously allowing us to look forward, prompting thought and action. Something of the interaction taken from the shared space of meeting to the space of shared potential, the workshop.

Let's make a CAKE while we chat . . . I agree, to do something as a different thing to the academic presentation. Words, Chinese whispers, consequences . . . our project is still open . . . our talk should remain so too . . . But I WILL NOT reinterpret our experiences through the medium of contemporary dance. . .

NOTES

1. *Pairings* exhibition, June 2009 Special Collections Gallery, Kenneth Graham Library, Manchester Metropolitan University, followed by tour 2009–2012. Thirty-two artists/makers were brought together in collaborative practice, curated by Alex McErlain, Stephanie Boydell and Alice Kettle and supported by MIRIAD, Manchester School of Art (Gröppel-Wegener 2009).
2. David Gates is currently working on a PhD thesis.

REFERENCES

Bakhtin, M. (1981), *The Dialogic Imagination: Four Essays*, Austin: University of Texas Press.

Burr, V. (2003), *Social Constructionism*, 2nd edn, Hove: Routledge.

Cox, C., and Warner, D. (eds) (2008), *Audio Culture Readings in Modern Music*, London: Continuum.

Gates, D. (2013), 'History in the Making; the Use of Talk in Inter-disciplinary Collaborative Craft Practice', in M. Partington and L. Sandino (eds), *Oral History in the Visual Arts*, London: Bloomsbury.

Grimshaw, A., Owen, E., and Ravetz, A. (2010), 'Making Do: The Materials of Art and Anthropology', in A. Schneider and C. Wright (eds), *Between Art and Anthropology: Contemporary Ethnographic Practice*, Oxford: Berg, 147–62.

Gröppel-Wegener, A. (2009) *Pairings*, Blurb.com.

Hastrup, K. (2004), 'All the World's a Stage: The Imaginative Texture of Social Spaces', *Space and Culture*, 7/2: 223–36.

Jiménez, A. C. (2003), 'Space as a Capacity', *Journal of the Royal Anthropological Institute*, 9/1 (March): 137–53.

Metcalfe, G., and Game, A. (2008), 'Potential Space and Love', *Emotion, Space and Society*, 1 (October): 18–21.

Paterson, M. (2007), *The Senses of Touch: Haptics Affects and Technologies*, Oxford: Berg.

Ryan, P. (n.d.), 'Earthscore,' <www.earthscore.org> accessed 25 April 2011.

Teyssot, G. (2005), 'A Typology of Thresholds', *Home Cultures*, 2/1: 89–116.

–4–

The Creation of a Collective Voice

*Brass Art: Chara Lewis, Kristin Mojsiewicz
and Anneké Pettican*

INTRODUCTION

The collaborative practice of Brass Art is hybrid, performative and playful in nature. Artist, collaborator and academic Charles Green describes the production of collaborative work as 'an act of individual disappearance, born ... from the desire to neutralize the self in order to clear out a useful new working space' (Green 2004: 74). We see our collaborative practice as an indivisible whole that amounts to more than the summation of its parts, allowing space for the loosening of individual identities and the creation of a collective voice.

In this chapter, we will focus on several aspects of our collaborative practice—including the double, the phantasm, the hybrid and the revenant.[1] We will examine different manifestations of our creative methods as well as collaborations with outside agencies, industry and other creative practitioners.

Since our collaboration began in 1999, we have slowly appeared (and disappeared, only to reappear again) as the subject of our practice—the figures of three artists repeatedly inscribing themselves in landscapes. We have examined the nature of the double—what it means to engage with an alter ego, in playful ways, and how this is manifest in our work. We have further replicated our bodies—using digital technologies, handcrafted materials and three-dimensional facsimiles printed from three-dimensional body-scan data—to become six, nine or more. This has enabled us to inhabit miniature worlds: to loom large as video or light projections or to become vaguely opaque shadow forms in a digital zone. In previous explorations/incarnations, we have represented ourselves as digital desktop sprites, solid black-clad trespassers, acrobatic filigree silhouettes and hot-air balloon pilots.

The genesis for self-replication and doubling derives from our desire to explore spaces from which we are excluded. We imagine a shift in scale, form, volume or material as a means to facilitate this freedom. The choice of location affects the transformation we undertake; each requires an alter ego that plays off the material qualities of the selected location, made manifest through a different kind of materiality—from inky watercolours and porcelain-like three-dimensional prints, to Web-like digital data. Our approach to making allows for both the literally handmade: 'captured' hand shadows, the hand-painted or hand-drawn image, the handmade curve of neon glass tubing, medium format photography, as well as the potential to interrogate digital possibilities: photography, video, three-dimensional modelling, three-dimensional scanning and printing and Kinect scanning.[2]

THE UNCANNY DOUBLE AND THE COLLECTION REANIMATED

Our response to invitations to view collections has been significant for the production of our collaborative work. In any collection there are implicit issues around visibility, status, gender, colonialism, power and value—our status as artists has its own implications; we have freedom to explore and respond unconstrained by ideas of museum protocol, archival or taxonomical propriety. We are neither part of the collection nor guardians of it but slip between roles and artefacts. The most interesting aspect for us—beyond the usual excitement at juxtapositions of objects and collapsing time frames, values and categories—is the invisibility of objects and specimens not on display; the 'in between' status of a collection in storage. The stored works are unseen and invisible to the public gaze, in some cases even uncatalogued and invisible within the archived collection itself. In these cases it seems there is a dual collection—one visible, one not—and that in this doubling there is an implicit negation; for every visible object there is an 'invisible' counterpart.

An early curatorial and collaborative project at Bury Museum and Art Gallery—*Paradise Revisited*[3] (1999–2000)—began with an invitation to reanimate two distinct collections with different audiences and culminated in a diverse body of work, including the photographic series *All That Is Dead Quivers* (2001). These large-scale images present an uncanny reanimation of long-neglected taxidermy specimens, along with our own reflected (doubled) and fragmented figures in the store. By turns, the specimens and our reflections appear both living and dead. This uncertainty is central to Jentsch's and Freud's definition of the uncanny[4]—fear of the inanimate becoming animate. Marina Warner observes, 'The theme [of the double] is intertwined with technologies of reproduction, first optical, then, increasingly biological. Representation itself acts as a form of doubling: representation exists in magical relation to the apprehensible world, it can exercise the power to make something come alive *apparently*' (Warner 2004: 165).

In *Sojourn* (2002) we employed a bronchioscope[5] to probe a miniature architectural artefact. As it moved from exterior to interior, another camera recorded the scene for what became a dual screen video installation. Inside, the accumulated dust became rubble in a seismic shift of scale, activating the interior space. Temporarily populated by miniature hand-made models of ourselves, filmed and magnified in situ, a strange disjuncture occurred between the views seen by the two distinct cameras.

The exploration of liminal space in *Sojourn*, informs recent work *Still Life No. 1* (2011; Figure 4.1) commissioned by the Whitworth Art Gallery. We explored and responded to the collections, including zoology (palaeontology and arthropods) and mineralogy at the Manchester University Museum. It is significant that we eschewed important cultural artefacts and ethnographic collections, and have, in the main, been drawn to specimens that once lived and breathed, now held in suspended animation. Our engagement with these specimens acknowledges the possibilities for transformation and disguise and references other Brass Art works.[6]

The reanimation of animals—whole or partial (e.g., antlers, horns, feathers, skins)—has been part of human ritual for more than 30,000 years.[7] Rendered either as line drawings or ritual 'performance' the reanimated animal can be seen to represent a state 'outside of time'. The arrested decay of the museum specimens, whether hunted or happened-upon, all exist in temporal limbo within the collection.

Fig. 4.1.   *Still Life No. 1*, 2011. Brass Art. *Dark Matters: Shadow Technology Art*, The Whitworth Art Gallery. 3D printed objects in resin, mixed media, motorised light. Photograph: Brass Art

For *Still Life No. 1* we wanted to evoke the enormous time span covered by the museum collection as a whole, and the cyclical nature of cosmological events. The mineralogy samples represent 'slow', geological time, and we selected them as individual sculptural forms, rather than as hidden within a geological landscape. The imagery of the comet, of which we make use, is a recognized motif for the idea of cyclical return, and a historical marker for reoccurrence. Lisa Le Feuvre and Tom Morton in their essay suggest, '[The comet] draws together the past, present and perhaps even the future too' (Le Feuvre and Morton 2010: 9).

Our constructed-landscape installation produced an expansive shadow-play toying with different timescales: the slow movement of a light travelling round a table top is cut across by the speed of a shadow accelerating and enlarging as it passes closest to the light, and slowing down and diminishing as it moves farther away again. We replicated each of our figures three times, at different scales, so that we are represented multiple times in the landscape, from different perspectives, engaged in different actions. The importance of this 'tripling' effect is evident in the shadow-play itself—the shadows skip past one another and out of the field of vision—the morphing of one form into another continues to change as other elements (rock, landscape, animal, antler) come into play.

The impression is that of an unstable vision; the cyclical nature of the installation and its presentation requires multiple viewings to connect objects and artefacts with their shadows. To accept the repetition of reappearing figures, seemingly co-existing with their doubles within the same time span, is to question what it is to be in the world and to understand it. Art historian Louise Milne posits that, rather than a linear experience of time, our perception is that 'the present moment and the collective past are embedded in each other, and in the perceiving self, in a simultaneous space-time frame' (Milne 2008).

The artefacts and figures revealed as objects in *Still Life No. 1* are momentarily lost in the darkness only to reappear cast as enormous, and suddenly, unfamiliar shadows. There is a sense of the sublime and wonderment in the limitlessness of this realm, its continuous shifts and its transformations. Viewers may return and, becoming part of this shadow world, review what they think they have seen. What has occurred may reoccur.

WONDER AND NONEXISTENCE

The phenomenology of wonder, 'the experience of astonishment before the world' (Kingwell 2000: 85), is an aspect of our encounter with the museum collection. It is evoked by the overwhelming quantity of specimens in the collections, the surprising juxtapositions and revelations at the turn of a handle or the opening of a drawer. Taking the collection as a whole, including miscellaneous oddities, we drew parallels with the popular Wunderkämmern of the Renaissance; their diverse displays of incredible creatures and object curiosities collapsing conventional, scientific time frames and genres. The objects we discovered for ourselves encompassed the handmade and the mass-produced: the unique, bespoke collector's object and the collectable souvenir. Their material qualities were little changed over time or else were degraded into a carapace of dust. For *Still Life No. 1* we selected museum objects to put through the same transformative scanning and printing process used to create our own doppelgängers. Their resulting translucency affects a denial of their original material presence only to appear solid once again in shadow form. There is no difference in the appearance of the original and the copy cast as shadows.

Our eclectic wandering within various collections in different museums (some rigorously collected, catalogued and monitored, others less so) has informed an approach to drawing which, as a tool, has evolved to become a key method in our practice, linking several ongoing projects, and acting as creative catalyst for new ideas and research trajectories.

Our first shadow drawings formed a series titled *Proteiform* (2006). The protean nature—to change shape and form, to become unrecognizable at will—is balanced by the need to recognize us physically as individuals in the work. It is through our gestures, posture and profiles that the notion of collaborating individuals is defined. This kind of drawing for us is a direct and active form of collaborative play—a way of effecting transformations that bring our individuality, gender and humanity into question. In *Proteiform*, miniature cut-outs of our shadows encounter grotesque forms made by crude hand shadows. The hand shadows, no matter how benign in origin, loom large and demonic over our tiny figures, representing the manifestation of a collective will.[8]

In 2010 we substituted the entomology storeroom in Manchester University Museum for our studio to work, in situ, alongside curator Dimitri Logunov and his collection. Zoological convention specifies that, if a specimen has not been classified within the existing phylum or species in the collection with a date and provenance, then it is effectively nonexistent and unseen: invisible within the museum. This double nature appealed to us—the possibility of being essentially 'out of place'—present and unseen at the same time. Heidi Gilpin, citing surrealist writer Louis Aragon,[9] writes, 'The act of disappearance is the most enabling, fascinating, difficult, and unavoidable performance we can enact or witness. Disappearance, like displacement, proliferates its own presence within absence, its own birth within death. The act of disappearance can be witnessed only in the moment of its passing, at the threshold between presence and absence, between birth and death' (Gilpin 1996: 113).

In the museum storeroom, our physical presence and proximity to specimens, artefacts and objects increased our sense of wonder, and the conscious desire to translate this experience in a visual form. Using a single light source, paper and pencil, we sought to literally 'pin down' the hybrid 'creatures' formed by the shadows, cast by artist and artefact. The images produced as *The Unnamed* during these intense periods in the museum stores, possess humorous, grotesque qualities but may be a much darker proposition. It was our intention to confront anxieties about the processes of preservation, suffocation, dissection and disappearance: of the proximity of certain specimens and their specific qualities.

The series of images shows the particular intimacy of working with the collection in this way—and our 'working intimacy'—to push and cajole, to pin and hold. It is clear we are not afraid of challenging one another, and the sometimes brutal acts or events suggested are balanced by delicate rendering in pencil and watercolour. In a small, dark corner of the store, the physical contortions required to hold poses and capture the shadows, mirrored the surroundings—pinning the subject in the glare of a spotlight. The drawings are 'framed' as tight crops—limbs disappear, faces are lost; the artist and specimen become one shadow form, a grotesque manipulation that continues outside of the frame. This expanded view of our handcrafted shadow play is also explored in *The Myth of Origins* (2008–) series in which we capture the artists' bodies more fully, revealing the *mise-en-abyme*, a play within a play.

Fig. 4.2.   *Moments of Death and Revival,* 2008. Brass Art: *Skyscraping at Yorkshire Sculpture Park*. 3D printed objects in acrylic polymer, dimensions variable, height from 19cm to 25cm, garden railway, torch, plinth. Photograph: Brass Art

DISAPPEARANCE AND THE COLLECTIVE VOID

What draws us to the shadow is that, in performing, the shadow is both distinctively us, something we recognize (*heimlich*) and at the same time unfamiliar (*unheimlich*). This sense of being both familiar and unfamiliar is heightened with props and disguises, enabling others to inhabit our shadow worlds, standing alongside and between us. Thus, the realm of the imagination, in its desire to see these fictive encounters between our selves and 'others' emerge and unfold, is awakened, and through our play, images and ideas emerge. Louise Milne states that, 'in Brass Art's phantasmagorias, animated shadows have the quality of spatial singularities; they open another dimension inside the photographic world, a dream-like register' (Milne 2008) (Figure 4.2).

By developing the importance of site in our drawing performances, we wanted to convey the specific qualities of both a physical space and the transient performance taking place within the heart of that space. The means of recording this would expand our engagement with liminal space, and offer a different perspective on our 'doublings' or alter egos—the masking and unmasking of which would be captured simultaneously. This has resulted in the new series of works *Shadow Worlds | Writers' Rooms* (2010–).

We drew parallels between our imaginary realm and the realm evoked by other female artists[10] and approached the domestic space of the Brontë family parsonage as an expanded theatrical tableau, employing the skills of photographer Simon Pantling and programmer Spencer Roberts to capture the scene as a whole. The shadows of the artists, photographer, props, furniture and curator were captured as part of the scenario, surveyed by a Kinect scanner, as directed by Roberts.[11] As anticipated, the Kinect system could be adapted to produce its own shadow play: the shadows are formed when an object obstructs the laser, and the resulting occlusion appears as black shadow but is in fact a lack of data—something the eye cannot perceive. Comparing the two forms of light-based technology, the photographed shadows seem solid and tactile while the Kinect scans confound any sense of solid bodies: people seem to move through spaces where there are walls or objects in unexpected spatial transformations, viewed in full 360-degree rotation. There is a temporal mutability inherent in the Kinect footage that contrasts with the still moment of the same scene captured by the camera. It is an area full of possibilities and, as yet, uncharted parameters.

CONCLUSION

Retrospectively, one of the most interesting aspects for us has been the 'loss of self' in the watercolour images, photography and even three-dimensional scans. A genuine misrecognition of which of us was the subject in drawn or scanned poses has led to a misprision regarding our self-re-presentation. Warner posits, 'Doubling offers another disturbing and yet familiar set of personae in ways of telling the self; permutations of inner and outer selves catalyse uncanny plots about identity' (Warner 2004: 163).

The focus of our practice—embodied experience, the body in space, doubling—demands recognition as three artists working as one; however, the production of a collective voice entails a necessary negation of the self to some extent, and this blurring of forms extends our narrative. The actual process of collaborating is often concealed, yet is at the forefront of our practice.

We three do not look alike but recognize that we have begun to resemble one another in sometimes unexpected ways. Unsurprisingly, we have all picked up some of the other's gestures and traits, which prompted a conscious decision to see whether we could accurately mimic one another and share expression. This was particularly successful in the three-dimensional scanning booth, where we could quickly achieve a sculptural, 'photographic' likeness—a true doppelgänger.

In psychological terms, this materialization of our doubles would be a cause for concern—not only their presence and potential to harm the self but also the death of the double is always linked to the (symbolic) death of the self, and our disappearances are enacted over and over. Perhaps it is this accumulation of miniature versions of ourselves that is the most uncanny aspect of our practice; an ever-growing corpus of revenants, phantasms and doppelgängers, suspended in animation.

We do not describe ourselves, or our work, within the context of craft but see the work we make with three-dimensional scanning and printing as an expanded sculptural practice. We make clear decisions about the 'well made' quality of the work and, despite the automated process of three-dimensional printing, carefully select the specific kind of printing process that suits the form required and the way in which it will be seen. It is possible for the three-dimensional prints to appear porcelain-like in quality, luminous when backlit, or clear as cast glass.[12] Our sculptural practice combines the handmade with the use of new technologies and collaborations with technologists and industry leaders in three-dimensional body scanning, modelling, printing and animation, X-ray tomography and four-dimensional biomedical capture.[13]

The ways in which the scan data are treated rely on 'a skilled hand'; the virtual stitching and repairing of 'holes' in the data is a laborious and difficult process and must retain detail required for a 'true' photographic likeness. It is possible to describe our three-dimensional print work as the production of autogenic[14] objects if the term is understood poetically to suggest that the three-dimensional prints are 'of us', on a fundamental, material level. The three-dimensional print process enables mass production of our three-dimensional forms, but working contrary to this, many of our forms are extremely fragile and require skilled technical supervision to 'release' them from their support material. It is probable that each time one of our forms is printed it differs in subtle ways from the previous.

We are acutely aware that our kind of collaborative practice raises suspicions of authorial compromise—we are neither combative nor competitive with one another. Working together began as an organic process led by mutual interests and an open approach to the possibility of collaboration. It is unwise, however, to mistake a lack of antagonism for a lack of rigour—we debate every creative decision and every word. In a close, working relationship such as ours, we do not reveal or ascribe roles to individuals but have a necessary shorthand in practical matters and communications.

Contemporary collaborative practices are commonly read as strategic methods of production and points of consumption for the contemporary audience, born out of necessity. To contextualize our practice against other models is difficult—to paraphrase Irit Rogoff, a valid point is made about groups of like-minded artists being historically 'recuperated in the literature by the cult of individual genius' (Green 2001: xv), but our collaborative practice is our main creative practice as artists, which cannot be teased apart. Our identity as a fully integrated practice of individuals is better served by Homi K. Bhabha's suggestion that this way of working comprises 'an interrogation of the discursive and disciplinary place from which questions of identity are strategically and institutionally posed' (Rogoff 1990: 39).

We have yet to meet other collaborations of three women artists that function like ours. However, our collaboration is not the artwork itself, but the fact that we function as a collaborative whole informs the production of work and has an impact on its subsequent reception. We have encountered a desire to untangle our roles and research contributions which we resist. When we present at conferences, talks or symposia, we are usually physically present as three co-authors, and we speak individually with one collective 'voice'. In any working dynamic, people's views or ideas shift over time and negates predictable patterns of collective behaviour. As with our gestures and expressions, we have moved closer to one another's way of talking, writing and even thinking, whilst stubbornly (and vitally) retaining our own ways of making sense of things and having contrary opinions.

Over the course of a long collaboration, we have created a body of work that expresses by our collective, composite voice that cannot be unpicked. This is perhaps most evident in our drawing practice—a space to test out ideas that are fragile, playful, ridiculous, partial and interlinked, entangled in our extended interests. It has become a particular way of 'performing' the collaborative process. It is a space where we can freely comment on the nature and assumptions of collaboration, make creative mistakes, work with the most elemental technologies and create doubles at will.

NOTES

1. We use these terms poetically to convey notions of repetition, return and reanimation.
2. Kinect is a sensor technology developed by Microsoft.
3. Paradise Revisited is composed of work produced by and curated by Brass Art. Invited artists were Eggebert & Gould, Louise Milne, Jane Benson, Kathrine Sowerby, Sarah Carne, Lisa Louise, Martell Linsdell and Jane Sebire. <http://www.brassart.org.uk/worksmenu.php?showProj=1 8&page=1&tm=curatorial> accessed 13 March 2013.
4. Freud (2003); Jentsch ([1906] 1996).
5. Bronchioscope filming sponsored by Pentax Medical UK.
6. *All that Is Dead Quivers* (2001) and *Moments of Death and Revival* (2008).
7. The Chauvet-Pont-D'Arc caves in Southern France are amongst the best-known and preserved records of Paleolithic cave painting. In 2010, Werner Herzog was granted access to the caves with a three-dimensional camera to record the forms on the walls of the cave complex dating back more than 30,000 years. See the French government Web site The Cave of Chauvet-Pont-d'Arc for more information: <http://www.culture.gouv.fr/ fr/arcnat/chauvet/en/index.html> accessed 22 February 2012.
8. We recollect a myth attributed to the origins of painting and recounted by Pliny the Elder. He tells of a shepherdess who traced her lover's shadow onto the wall with her crook the night before he left for battle.
9. Aragon (1963), cited by Gilpin (1996: 106–28).
10. Writers Charlotte Perkins Gillman; Charlotte, Emily and Anne Brontë; artist Francesca Woodman et al.
11. Custom built software created by Spencer Roberts and Microsoft's Kinect sensor and on-range camera technology. The system provides full-body three-dimensional motion capture, designed to fit domestic gaming spaces and work under any ambient light conditions.
12. This encompasses acrylic polymer and nylon prime part.
13. Companies: 3D Systems, EOS, Formero, Huntsman, Henry Mosley X-Ray Imaging Facility, Invision, Ogle Models & Prototypes, Wicks and Wilson, XYZ Innovation.

    Collaborating Institutions: Liverpool Museums Conservation, London College of Fashion, Manchester Metropolitan University, University of Glasgow, University of Huddersfield, University of Manchester Museum.

    Technical supervision: Chris Charlesworth, Simon Dunning, Oliver Garrod, Bogdan Matuszewski, Wei Quan and Ertu Unver.

Freelance professionals: Ricardo Creemers, Jennifer Colquhoun, Reuben Fleming, Alison Mealey, Jay Payne, Daniel Roberts, Spencer Roberts and Adam Shepherd.

Supported by: Association of Art Historians, Arts Council England, Edinburgh College of Art, Friends of Yorkshire Sculpture Park, Manchester Metropolitan University, Meadow Arts, University of Huddersfield.
14. Autogenic describes a self-generating process, that is, material for a skin, a muscle or a tissue graft.

REFERENCES

Freud, S. (2003), *The Uncanny*, London: Penguin.

Gilpin, H. (1996), 'Lifelessness in Movement, or How Do the Dead Move?' in S. L. Foster (ed.), *Corporealities*, London: Routledge, 106–28.

Green, C. (2001), *Collaboration in Art, from Conceptualism to Modernism*, Minneapolis: University of Minnesota Press.

Green, C. (2004), 'Doubled: Five Collaborations', *Cabinet*, 14: 71.

Jentsch, E. ([1906] 1996), 'On the Psychology of the Uncanny', *Angelaki*, 2/1: 7–21.

Kingwell, M. (2000), 'Husserl's Sense of Wonder', in *The Philosophical Forum*, 31/1: 85.

Le Feuvre, L., and Morton, T. (2010), 'In the Days of the Comet', in *The British Art Show 7*, London: Hayward Publishing.

Milne, L. (2008), 'The Broom of the System: On the Quarrel between Art and Narrative', in *Unreliable Witness*, Glasgow: Tramway.

Rogoff, I. (1990), 'Production Lines', in S. Sollins and N. Castelli Sundell (eds), *Team Spirit* [exhibition catalogue], New York: Independent Curators Incorporated.

Warner, M. (2004), *Fantastic Metamorphoses and Other Worlds,* Oxford: Oxford University Press.

List of Works, in Order of Reference in the Text

All That Is Dead Quivers (2001), series: C-type prints, mounted on aluminium, 125cm × 125cm.

Sojourn (2002), two-screen video projection, dimensions variable, colour: 3 min. 20 / black & white: 6 min. 40, looped, with sound. Bronchioscope sponsorship: Pentax Medical UK.

Still Life No. 1 (2011), installation: 2 m table with revolving arm and light. 9 SLA figures and antlers. Cellophane, paper and props. 3D material sponsorship: Hunstman. 3D print sponsorship: Ogle Models and Prototypes Ltd. Commissioned by Whitworth Art Gallery for *Dark Matters* at Whitworth Art Gallery, Manchester, UK.

Proteiform (2006), series: small watercolour drawings on paper.

The Unnamed (2010), series: medium watercolour drawings on paper. Unframed dimensions 50cm × 40cm.

Myth of Origins (2008–), series: large watercolour drawings on paper. 220cm × 140cm approx.

Shadow Worlds | Writers' Rooms (2011–), series in progress: large-scale photographs–Brass Art & Simon Pantling. Kinect video shadowplay–Brass Art & Spencer Roberts. Brontë Parsonage, Haworth, UK.

Moments of Death and Revival (2008), installation: 3D printed objects in acrylic polymer, dimensions: 19 cm to 25 cm high. Version 1: 9 figures, 3 morph figures, 2 skeletons, train, track, lights, plinths. Commissioned by Yorkshire Sculpture Park for Skyscraping at Yorkshire Sculpture Park, Bretton Hall, UK. 3D material and print sponsorship: 3D Systems.

PART II

THE GENERATIVE POWER OF CRAFT

Introduction

Helen Felcey, Alice Kettle and Amanda Ravetz

Material is a key property within the craft constellation, and materials figure prominently in the following chapters. Through the 'merging and clashing [of] materials' (Belford) and the cross-fertilization of science, technology and craft, the generative power of craft is revealed. The result can be innovative technological and aesthetic change driven through practical necessity, experimentation with the limitations of established practice or acknowledgement of the potential of craft ideals. The resulting extension of boundaries can be categorized in simple terms as scales of production (Binns), construction (Solomon), function and communication (Cleverly) and a desire to go deeper into the nature of the material ingredient (Belford). It is a stance which recognizes the importance of the crafts' relationship to technology and a desire to acknowledge crafts' efficacy as ethical, environmentally responsible and central to current socio-economic debates.

The writers see the crafts offering a relationship to materials through 'the trace de la main'. For Belford this has the potential of 'opening the seemingly hard world of science to a wider audience by using "softer" textile-making processes [. . .] to deliver a beautiful but rigorous scientific message for "ways to change the world".'

In generating new material and new material thinking, each contributor examines a combination of known and unknown, diverse technical, commercial and cultural territories, and of divergent and convergent knowledge, offering possibilities to contest established material processes and expand purpose. This comes from a direct desire to 'facilitate new forms of engagement' (Cleverly and Shear) or as the result of more open-ended experimentation. It can enable 'mindshifts' across 'seemingly utterly different environments' (Binns).

The undercurrent of science and art relationships run throughout this section with a level of professional synthesis—textiles and chemistry and business (Belford); ceramics and earth sciences and manufacturing (Binns); craft and computing science (Cleverly); fashion materials and surgery/medicine (Solomon). Outcomes include unique products for manufacture and new processes for industries with possibilities and sensibilities that are ethical, innovative, highly crafted, aspirational and sometimes idealistic.

For Jones and Gallison (1998), art and science are not as divorced as we have come to imagine. A poignant reminder of the enforced separation between them is Belford's memory of being made to chose between apparently opposing disciplines of chemistry and art and her eventual fusing of the two in collaborative projects with Morrow and Storey. It can be seen through these chapters that collaboration through craft can sometimes be a means to rejoin that which has historically been broken.

In Belford's work, craft is a translator, even a trickster, enabling material metamorphosis or alchemy, which goes beyond dressing and seductive beauty—although its tendency to transfix is also powerful and useful: 'the crafted, sensory and emotive process of material exchange could be used to draw in the public in a significantly powerful way' (Belford).

Cleverly and Shear write of 'sensitive fabrication' and craft's role in 'augmenting the sense of place'. Their poetic description of the digital interface (glossing Weiser and Seely Brown 1996) evokes a new vision of an existing world: 'The periphery connects us effortlessly to a myriad of familiar details. This connection with the world we call "locatedness."' The interactive craftworks of Cleverly and Shear are described as both 'augmented' and 'located'—there is an ability to extend temporalities, to be expansive into a virtual world, yet recognize and remain connected to the material present.

In Solomon's chapter, we recognize a two-way benefit from sharing craft, in 'creating an even better mend, thereby enhancing aesthetics in addition to functionality'. Here, crafting can be seen to run like a seam, joining two parallel territories of material knowledge. There emerges a situated knowledge which is generated through experiential learning whilst bringing together separate practices with distinct embedded cultures.[1] The assumptions of each are shifted through the seam. A new cloth is made.

The chapters in this section in some way act on what Binns (glossing Edlekoort) talks of as 'a future where industry embraces the sensitivities of craft production. A future in which a closer working relationship between the two fields ensures sustainable quality and design style'. There are clear shifts 'from developing craft-based artefacts to products applicable to industrial scales of production' (Binns) which recognize the importance of tactile materials. In Belford's case 'Tactility Factory brings to market new ways of delivering concrete skins to the built environment' with the expressed desire to retain qualities that are sensory and emotive. The hand-crafted is an explicit means for Cleverly and Shear and Solomon to generate interaction and knowledge exchange. The process of augmentation, of enhancing product and experience, is cited by Cleverly and Shear but is present in all these chapters. They enter expansive territory—in terms of manufacture, human interaction and human sciences—whilst simultaneously harnessing knowledge that is situated.

Eco-responsibility and the development of new sustainable practices is part of this expansive practice. In Belford's case this is in the form of a dress acting as a metaphor for serious issues in relation to air pollution. For Binns eco-responsible practice uses waste from other processes to innovate new high-performance, aesthetically sensuous building materials. In terms of impact and scope, the possibilities are increased through this interaction with technology, enabling craft to 'think big', moving between local and global. It is not so much craft and manufacture coming together that is remarkable here—there are many historical precedents—but that craft is able to offer a mode of situated knowledge which brings the objectified, rarified cultures of each practice into a shared focus of new analysis and examination with new sets of negotiated principles.

Craft is one element to examine, to provoke and to question within a 'stage by stage crafting of new materials through multiple processes and strategic work' (Belford). The assumption in all cases is that craft is not separate or distinct but part of an integrated process of applying technological industrial and academic skills. It is one element amidst a complex network of cultural exchange, technological advancement and aesthetic concern. It seems that the qualities, the substance of craft, can have an important role to play in the process of integration—seeping across boundaries—crossing different worlds. This integration and fusion of the handcrafted with the upscaled hybrid approach is perhaps the 'avant garde of the future', described by Greenhalgh 'not based on individuals it seems but individualized companies' (Greenhalgh 2002: 3).

There are also difficulties. As Solomon points out, the seaming of territories, real or imagined, is not easily negotiated and matters of expertise collide with those of taste. In the case of plastic surgery, there may be a 'difference in opinion of aesthetic outcomes—the visual expectations of a patient not always being met by surgical endeavour. Could the project help to align these factors? Or is this purely a symptom of differing taste?' The mismatch of approaches, of intentions and objectives is constantly negotiated. The crossing of scientific objective analysis and the fluid, fanciful and subjective, requires new languages and modes of communication. The extremes of the handmade and the industrially made, the commercially orientated and the personal endeavour, the medical necessity and the surgery of beauty expose the battle lines. The language of 'craft' must navigate through and within these polarized positions whilst keeping sight of both the specificity of material, of visceral bodies and the potency of assemblage—cooperation between human and nonhuman agents. The message we are left with is that in the presence of new tools and technologies the responsibility of the crafts—and craft— to address today's environmental issues or to be sustainable within its own practice is emphatically collaborative.

NOTES

1. Donna Haraway contrasts situated knowledge with the rhetorics of complete objectivity that seem to promise the 'infinite exchangeability' of data; using the metaphor of embodied vision, she outlines 'partial, locatable, critical knowledges situating the possibility of webs of connections called solidarity in politics and shared conversations in epistemology' (1995: 185). Situated knowledges demand specificity and difference and these in turn require that we learn to see faithfully from another position and point of view.

REFERENCES

Greenhalgh, P. (2002), *The Persistence of Craft*, London: A&C Black.
Haraway, D. (1995), 'Situated Knowledges: The Science Question in Feminism and the Privilege of Partial Perspective', in A. Feenberg and A. Hannay (eds), *Technology and the Politics of Knowledge*, Bloomington: Indiana University Press, 175–94.
Weiser, M., and Brown, J. S. (1996), *The Coming Age of Calm Technology. Beyond Calculation: The Next Fifty Years*, New York: Copernicus.

Catalytic Clothing and Tactility Factory: Crafted Collaborative Connections

Trish Belford

INTRODUCTION

This first-person account discusses two collaborative projects where textile knowledge engages, informs and develops new ideas with science, fashion and architecture. Catalytic Clothing is a collaboration with Helen Storey, internationally known for her fashion activism. The project centred on a concrete and textile dress, a metaphor for serious issues in relation to air pollution. Tactility Factory is a partnership between me and architect Ruth Morrow, a great ambassador for textiles who challenges the perception that textiles are simply the subservient dressing for architecture. The core aim in this collaboration is to 'mainstream tactility in the built environment'. In both projects my contribution was to interact in these domains using my textile technology, craft, industrial and academic skills. My collaborative partners are respected colleagues and experts in their own fields with a clear understanding of what textiles could bring to their own practices, whilst I recognize the potential to expand textile knowledge.

My fascination with chemistry in relation to textiles underlies my collaborative career. During my penultimate year at school, pondering the subjects that would determine the rest of my life, I began to realize that arts and sciences are considered opposing disciplines. When my naïve request to study art and chemistry was pronounced impossible, I had to choose between them and picked art and ultimately textiles. But at the beginning of my textile career, I found myself uncomfortable in the role of the solo textile designer who initiates a process from a blank page. I tried studio work but found that with my hands clean, there was no alchemy involved in the process of designing prints for 'anywhere' with an unknown result. This shaped my determination when setting up my own business, Belford Prints, in 1986, to learn about the chemistry of dyes and to find ways to stay in touch with how a paper design comes alive on cloth. My commitment depended on understanding processes and the ability to make space for my secret pleasure in play as a means to bring about a tactile alteration to a known substrate. 'We are so made that nothing but using brain and hand together, in some *way* or other, enables us to grasp facts,' wrote Minnie McLeish (1920: 277). For me, the union of hand, dyes and the screen became a way to skip the dreaded blank sheet of paper and unknown client. Working with high-end fashion designers (Helen Storey, Vivienne Westwood and Jasper Conran), I developed a strong ability to interpret their requirements, working up technique samples and offering ideas on cloth that they would not necessarily have had the knowledge to initiate. This apparently casual form of collaboration was reliant on good technical translation. In the pre-digital era designs were developed using a wealth of processes: discharge, devoré, flocking. A way to achieve an exciting print was to be creative in translation, making real mastery of the processes crucial. For this reason the final textile was not a copy of an original document but evoked the designer's desired look, offering a richer experience when printed on cloth. If the original design looked better on paper, then the end result had failed.

The value of the knowledge gained during this business phase was to be later utilized and reinvented for Catalytic Clothing and Tactility Factory. The process of devoré, or 'burn out', which during the early 1990s was commissioned from Belford Prints by Jasper Conran, English Eccentrics and Helen Storey has been of particular importance. In its simplest form it arises from an understanding of fibres, their construction and subsequent destruction via an acid burn-out process. Using this knowledge and experimentation, I have claimed a new role for the devoré process beyond the cheap clothing copies now produced in China. My move to research has resurrected the thinking behind this process to create the base for concrete adhesion in the Catalytic Clothing concrete dress and velvety concrete, the most tactile of the Tactility Factory concrete surfaces. Prior knowledge of the process, with an altered approach to thinking, provoked by collaborative discussion, has been the grounding for these two diverse but successful projects.

One of my early clients at Belford Prints was fashion designer Helen Storey, whose prolific career as an international fashion designer from 1983 to 1995 saw her twice nominated for British Designer of the Year (1990/1991). During our work together in industry, we built up a relationship of respect and trust, which continues, albeit in a different mode from the catwalk. Now we use textile processes as a method of translation for Storey's radical arts and science-based work. In 1997, the Helen Storey Foundation (HSF) was created with Caroline Coates in response to projects that required brand-new ways of working and thinking. The HSF seeks to inspire new ideas by instigating cross-collaborative art, science and technology projects. Storey embarked on a collaboration that made a profound new contact between the worlds of art and science, a 'mindshift' that has been the driving force behind all the foundation's subsequent projects.[1] Storey is currently professor of fashion and science at the London College of Fashion, an activist searching for 'ways to change the world' with a real sense of meaning beyond the catwalk. The vehicle for this comes about through her collaboration with scientist Professor Tony Ryan. Ryan never laughed at Storey's suggestions, instead using them to think differently, providing real solutions through science.

Architecture has also played a significant role in my current research practice. The work of my collaborator and business partner architect Ruth Morrow is invariably project based with multiple outputs, also underpinned by an activist and collaborative instinct. We are co-directors in Tactility Factory Ltd,[2] operating as a spin-out company from the University of Ulster. Tactility Factory challenges and brings to market new ways of delivering concrete skins to the built environment. By embedding textiles within the surface, aesthetic qualities are supported by increased technical enhancement of beneficial acoustic and thermal benefits. This collaboration has been constant since 2005, building on and drawing from other elements derived from very diverse technical and cultural territories. In conversation with Morrow, she has often verified tacit thoughts I perhaps had not considered to be relevant, such as how much architecture may look like and even appropriate textile technologies but rarely with the feel of textiles. At Tactility Factory we have become committed to the textile designer's ability to take 'hard-core', chemical and mechanical processes and use them to transform and combine yarns into an artefact that evokes a strong physical and emotional response.

Successful collaboration requires working with different disciplines and thinking processes but above all for me, feeling comfortable with what may seem like 'just making' and giving this substance beyond the aesthetic. Multidisciplinary conversations have reinforced my belief that craft processes have a role to play in science and in architecture. I would never have considered that the process of devoré printing would one day spark a trigger for a scientist in his lab, underscoring the relevance of the maker who informs other processes and just as significantly empowering confidence in my own role as a researcher, beyond being able to make a beautiful scarf.

TEXTILES AND SCIENCE

Catalytic Clothing[3] sets out to deliver solutions to air purification using textiles as a catalytic surface to purify air and employ existing technology in a new way. It is the brainchild of artist/designer Helen Storey and chemist Tony Ryan who have worked in recent years on highly successful art/science collaborations.

The three of us first collaborated on The Wonderland project which was set up to address problems of waste, beginning with a provocative question posed by Storey to scientist Ryan: 'Can a plastic bottle have an intelligent relationship with its contents?' Storey, recognizing my particular skills, tasked me to make a beautiful polymer material in the form of disappearing dresses. The rationale was that the crafted, sensory and emotive process of material exchange could be used to draw in the public in a significantly powerful way. Opening the seemingly hard world of science to a wider audience by using 'softer' textile-making processes, we were able to deliver a beautiful but rigorous scientific message for 'ways to change the world'.

At the outset of The Wonderland project, all collaborators did a show and tell of their discipline. This memorable five minutes in the science labs in Sheffield University in 2005 reinforced my belief that the instinct to create the new is universal across different disciplines. During my brief introduction to the scientists, I spoke glibly about the process of devoré, where one fibre remains and one is removed via a chemical printing method. I was nervous of my bucket chemistry approach in front of such an esteemed chemist but to my surprise our conversation sparked new thoughts for Ryan in relation to his lab which he later reflected upon in 'The Wonderland' report.

Our research on tissue engineering has adapted some of the technology used in the production of textiles for haute couture to fabricate scaffolds for the culture of cells in replacement organs. Devoré is a process for making delicately patterned fabrics by weaving and printing a dense cloth with a variety of materials and then removing some by dissolution in acid. When making nanofibres by electrospinning, we faced difficulties in controlling the pore size and fibre diameter independently. If the pores were big enough for the cells to come through, the fibres were the wrong size for them to attach to, and the scaffold did not work. We used devoré to control the pore size by spinning two different fibres. 'We wanted one at a certain diameter and a sacrificial fibre that set the pore size and could be subsequently dissolved away.'[4]

This revelation from Ryan generated my confidence to go forward with the belief that textile material processes have a deeper value beyond the common perception that they are only 'the dressing to a body or surface'.

From the success of Wonderland, I was invited back to contribute to the Catalytic Clothing project, demonstrating the potential of catalysts that purify air when added to textiles via the domestic laundering process. As a co-investigator in an Engineering and Physical Sciences Research Council (EPSRC)[5] feasibility study, I was required to develop the beauty of the material components to aid delivery of the serious message to an audience that might be turned off by charts, figures and preaching.

The aim was to provoke debate utilizing textiles, fashion, film, bespoke and social media, introducing the concept that clothing/textiles could purify the air—ultimately, to improve public health but also to engender public debate

Fig. 5.1. Helen Storey and Trish Belford adding final touches to *Herself*, 2010. Location: Tactility Factory Belfast workshop. Materials: Concrete & velvet. Photograph: Trish Belford

and interest. The way to achieve this was to make a concrete and textile dress—that aptly came to be called *Herself* (Figure 5.1)—pushing the boundaries of what would be possible in terms of bringing materials with polarized characteristics together and showing them in a beautiful and provocative form. Existing technology, used in sunscreens and glass cleaning, was diverted towards the development of a textile that could potentially deliver a solution to air pollution. By subverting existing textile processes and normal technical procedures, the research for beauty with purpose was the underlying concept.

To begin, a series of playful but consciously serious experiments were carried out in practical development sessions using a wide range of challenging procedures, all trying to identify methods of 'joining' a soft tactile fabric to concrete in ways that maintained fluidity. When I embark on these trials, no matter what the desired outcome is, importance is placed on play. I close my ears to cries of 'that will never work'. So far, the process of crafting techniques has never failed to deliver, even if it is an undefined spark at the beginning of the process. However, to initiate some form of strategy before the play/research session commenced, I self-imposed a series of questions:

1. How will the photocatalytic carrier be deposited on the fabric?
2. It is nanoscale, so how will I know the best method for depositing?
3. Can the concrete recipe be printed?
4. Can I sandwich concrete and textiles in a lattice format?
5. Will the dress be wearable?
6. Will it last outside during the science show-and-tell sessions?

By working through strategic practical experiments blending known textiles processes—devoré, printing, bonding, indigo dipping, spraying, embellishment and cutting—I eventually arrived at a matrix of separate working samples. These then had to be made to work as one to create a dress able to withstand the extremes of demonstrating the catalytic effect. Like building a pyramid of cards, each process was linked in a crafted manner, fulfilling the brief of creating a beautiful, thought-provoking dress which would travel to science events, delivering the message of air pollution in an accessible way, provoking public debate.

This research is ongoing with worldwide attention and is currently at the serious phase of making it happen in reality. The projects with Storey and Ryan are perhaps vulnerable to cynicism, demanding and suggesting as they do intelligent change through brave collaboration and experiment: using fashion as the Trojan horse worked as a string and provocative metaphor for our disappearing world. But the inclusion of textiles and with them the crafting of connected processes helped deliver this message in a tangible and beautiful way, aiding the serious science warnings we are used to, allowing the public to enquire into and be a part of the debate and not simply being told they are destroying the planet.

TEXTILES AND CONCRETE

Tactility Factory, my collaboration with architect Ruth Morrow, embraces textile and craft knowledge to make hard surfaces soft with the notion of creating a tactile warm environment. If it is a familiar feeling to stroke a soft scarf for comfort, then why not evoke this sensual familiarity within interior space, enhancing the user experience? Tactility Factory began its life as 'girli concrete', our initial off-the-cuff name that stuck. To develop a serious following in the extra-textile field, we felt it necessary to alter the name, thus raising a whole debate around gender and association I had not considered when ensconced in the field of textiles. By combining beautiful, crafted tactile processes into the skin of the hard concrete, we acoustically and thermally enhance a ubiquitous global material, thereby engaging on a more serious level with architects, who, when they first encounter the product, regard it as 'art' with no serious design intention but who, on further investigation, see there are serious underlying benefits beyond the aesthetic.

To try and address the issues around embedding delicate textiles in a hard alkaline environment, putting aside the challenging issues of crossing disciplines, the only way to initiate thoughts and conversation was to evolve ideas and techniques through the mechanisms of play and dissemination, while at the same time trying to answer an overarching research question: can a collaboration between an architect and textile designer result in making hard surfaces soft? This highly conceptual question has resulted in many unique outcomes evidenced in international patents, numerous citations, international interest, exhibitions and awards. The core aim of the project was to mainstream tactility in the built environment. The objectives by which this aim was met were to apply textile technology, technique and thinking to the manufacture of concrete surfaces; to place architectural and design thinking at the heart of the fabrication processes; and to build creative, technical collaborations that lead to innovation.

As a textile designer, I wished to take on bigger challenges and work with new materials, while Morrow recognized what craft and technology textile practitioners tend to forget when involved in the depths of making. As a strategic thinker, Morrow saw in these textiles technologies and processes a much bigger picture and one that could deliver a new product to the precast construction industry. This echoes Irish engineer Peter Rice's call to reinstate 'the trace de la main', as a way to 'make real the presence of the material in use in the building, so that people warm to them, want to touch them, feel a sense of the material itself and of the people who made and designed it' (Rice 1994: 76). The initial experiments were in part the controlled madness of embedding textiles in concrete, playing with the mix to create a flow through the voids, wanting the surface to feel it was one and, in the case of stitching, as if the concrete had been carefully worked under the sewing machine. We were not isolating the textiles from the concrete and adding one to the other. The methodology applied was similar to Wonderland and Catalytic Clothing: stage-by-stage crafting of new materials through multiple processes and strategic work to understand how to refine and develop the textiles to survive and look beautiful. After many sessions of sifting through images, staging exhibitions and generating critique, we gradually whittled the surfaces down to three must-develop techniques. Although each technique had the same applied thinking process, the outcomes were varied and the routes different, but each was underpinned by a blending of process, discipline and collaboration. This joining up of textile skills in practice with those of an architect were provocative and rewarding. However, I had not considered the challenges of bringing together two culturally diverse industries of textiles and construction and had to find a new language to demonstrate a serious desire to scale up textiles into the built environment. In this case the science behind the beauty gave weight to our product. With this depth of research and knowledge, we can confidently argue that Tactility Factory produces functional and aesthetic concrete skins, using textiles to add to the profile and not just mimicking structural performance.

Consideration has also had to be given to the resultant hybrid products; do they fall within the category of design, art or craft? We remain within the territory of design as opposed to art but are increasingly aware of the value that craft brings to the process. The craft person often speaks to a limited audience and knowledge occurs within the act of making; design is more often associated with the thinker. Working collaboratively with Morrow across textile processes and architecture makes it possible to join these models, whereas this would not have happened by working alone in textiles without provocation and discussion.

The textiles are specifically designed to include voids, making surfaces whereby the patterning is produced as much by the concrete as the textiles, bringing a handcrafted, antique feel, despite being created using multiple textile processes. This fossilization of textiles is most noticeably achieved in the following three patented techniques:

1. Linen concrete: Linen as a fabric has a rich heritage in Ireland, and part of its textile processing is an alkaline pretreatment. Extensive testing was carried out on the yarns, proving that linen could survive in concrete. Laser cutting meant predetermined patterns could be cut and bonded onto a semipermeable backing, holding the linen in place and allowing the selected flow of the concrete to unite the textile and concrete into one surface. In this surface, the qualities of each separate material are gently forced together, giving rise to a new surface. The processes do not fight one another but instead use one another to create a unique and tactile designed surface.

2. Stitched concrete: To make the surface look as if it had been stitched under the machine, this process was developed in line with the dissolvable polymer work carried out in the Wonderland project,[6] shifting the processes to adapt to the environment of concrete. Threads in a range of colours and weights can be used to create endless variations in pattern

and design. This development has unintentionally led Tactility Factory into marketing and branding opportunities, as the designs can be tailored to respond to the application of logos.

3. Velvet concrete: This began its life as an attempt to flock onto concrete prompted by a comment from scientist Ryan (in relation to Catalytic Clothing) 'that to add to a concrete surface in this way would increase surface area by a factor of 500'. The flock process was not initially successful, but the solution lay again in revisiting my knowledge from fashion printing days. After many months of sourcing a specific fabric construction, experimenting with print recipes and concrete mixes, we finally succeeded in making velvet-like concrete and concrete-like velvet. Prior industrial and technical knowledge of textile processes made development of a fabric purpose built for the concrete initially complex but ultimately successful and solved though a collaborative understanding of the end use. The velvet concrete embraces all the qualities we were looking for: tactility, warmth, acoustically enhancing hard, cold surfaces (Figure 5.2).

In its early stages, Tactility Factory was driven by a singular collaboration between a textile designer and an architect. This remains at the core of its development, but it has also progressed to include collaborations with precast

Fig. 5.2. Printing the velvet for concrete wall panel, 2011. Location: University of Ulster Research Centre. Materials: velvet mix suitable for devoré and concrete. Photograph: Trish Belford

specialists, mould makers, digital textile designers, weavers, embroiderers, graphic designers, marketing consultants, business advisors and patent attorneys. Whilst many of those who contribute to the project do not come from identifiable 'creative' professions, they all contribute through their expertise and efforts to the application of creative ideas. Within Tactility Factory we recognize and give credence to the personal motivations of all involved. Some are motivated by the wish to experiment with familiar technologies, others by holding true to a work process. Finding the balance between personal motivations and the direction of the company starts with an understanding of the strengths of each person. For example it is understood that the textile designer brings a wealth of knowledge and an established track record in the textile design industry.

She or he offers:

1. Profound technical skills, a natural curiosity and confidence to experiment within new and unfamiliar technologies.
2. An acute sensibility in creating rich tactile surfaces.
3. A fastidiousness about the fabrication of the aesthetic; trialling, testing and ultimately crafting and controlling each technical move to ensure quality outcomes.
4. An ability to lead trend-sensitive markets.

By comparison, the architect/academic brings:

1. A strategic clarity to complex process.
2. A conviction in linking the conceptual, theoretical intention to the visceral lived experience.
3. Skills in communicating across languages and cultures i.e. from visual to verbal, from conceptual to operational, from artistic to engineered (Morrow 2010).

CONCLUSION

I am primarily interested in craft processes and how materials connect, the same pattern speaking a different language, textiles and craft provoking and teasing new surfaces. The wealth of the collaborative experience and success is not solely as a result of merging and clashing materials but also due to open conversation combined with implicit trust and respect. Collaborating with Storey and Morrow has given me the opportunity to expand the applications of textile processes and at the same time develop ideas I would not have considered during my career in industry. Catalytic Clothing and Tactility Factory are a testament to the fact that thinking with other disciplines and in turn being challenged by science and architecture can have positive outcomes, far beyond the requirement to deliver textiles to a fast-moving and demanding industry that often has no time for reflection and debate. The importance of craft and its place in multidiscipline thinking cannot be underestimated. Working through these projects has underlined the fact that the processes of textiles have led to tactility, emotional and cultural expectations being profoundly challenged and challenging. Perhaps in the initial stages of my career when I became a textile designer and engaged more confidentially with the soft perception of making, I did not give much thought to the wider view. A new language and understanding had to be developed which for me has meant making explicit the importance of play, crafting and using knowledge of processes to bring about new tactile solutions to everyday issues. Although this has inevitably been challenging, it has led textiles, craft and the act of making into a wider and more influential field.

NOTES

1. H. Storey, MBE professor of fashion and science, London College of Fashion; Helen Storey Foundation, <http://www.helenstoreyfoundation.org/> accessed 18 March 2013.
2. Tactility Factory, <http://www.tactilityfactory.com> accessed 18 March 2013.
3. Catalytic Clothing, <http://www.catalytic-clothing.org/> accessed 18 March 2013.
4. Tony Ryan, personal communication.
5. Engineering and Physical Sciences Research Council, <http://www.epsrc. ac.uk> accessed 18 March 2013.
6. 'Wonderland', Helen Storey Foundation, <http://www.helenstoreyfoundation. org/pro7.htm> accessed 18 March 2013.

REFERENCES

McLeish, M. (1920), 'Colour and Form', *The Cabinet Maker and Complete House Furnisher*, 8 May: 277.

Morrow, R. (2010), 'A Hybrid Practice: Between Design and Craft', paper presented at Design and Craft conference, Brussels, September.

Rice, P. (1994), *An Engineer Imagines*, Zurich: Artemis.

—6—

The Aesthetic of Waste: Exploring the Creative Potential of Recycled Ceramic Waste

David Binns

INTRODUCTION

Bernard Leach, in his seminal essay 'Towards a Standard' (1940), severely criticized (ceramic) manufacturers for designing without consideration for materials and processes, insensitive to form or beauty. He did however acknowledge the potential for collaboration with craft makers, believing their commitment to such values in their own work could be positively applied to the betterment of industrially produced ware.

Li Edelkoort (2003: 69) echoes Leach's earlier optimism, writing, 'Borders are now blurring between disciplines: craft is using industry, industry is transforming design, design is approaching art. Suddenly, the traditional feud of the industrial versus the artisan, and craft versus art, becomes irrelevant'.

Edelkoort goes on to envisage a future where industry embraces the sensitivities of craft production. A future in which a closer working relationship between the two fields ensures sustainable quality and design style.

This chapter outlines an evolving project that bears out Edelkoort's and Leach's optimism that positive collaboration between craft and industry may facilitate the development of products beyond the resources and ambition of traditional studio craft practice, making possible the creation of products that have enduring quality and style. The project that started life as an offshoot of my ceramic practice has at the time of writing evolved through collaboration with scientific and industrial partners to a point where an industrial manufacturing plant is being established.

The research for this project has been undertaken at the University of Central Lancashire, in Preston (UK), where I currently lecture in ceramics and three-dimensional design. In parallel with my lecturing, I also run my own ceramics studio in North Wales, dividing my time between teaching and research at the university and making my ceramic artwork.[1] Since the late 1990s my craft practice has been informed by a more formalized and systematic approach to research, increasingly involving collaboration with fellow researchers, scientists and more recently, industrial manufacturers. Parallel to this has been a change in emphasis from developing craft-based artefacts to products more applicable to industrial scales of production.

The project involves the development of a unique material made almost entirely from recycled ceramic, glass and mineral waste that offers a sustainable alternative to traditional ceramic and stone tiling and surface cladding products. In parallel with the material being developed commercially, knowledge gained through this collaborative process continues to inform and enhance my own craft practice.

The primary question driving this research project has been how the combination of recycled waste glass with mineral waste materials in a casting process can be used to develop a 'value added' material of unique aesthetic quality? Subquestions include whether the material can offer architects, designers, artists and craft-makers new creative applications or opportunities; whether value can be added to recycled waste materials through the application of design; how the production process might be applied to industrial/commercial manufacturing; and what impact manufacture of the material might have on waste material stock and the environment?

BACKGROUND TO THE RESEARCH

My interest in collaboration and embracing an interdisciplinary approach was shaped early in my career, whilst still studying for a degree in three-dimensional design at (the then) Manchester Polytechnic. I had embarked on my studies intending to become a cabinetmaker, drawn to this discipline through my love of both the natural beauty of wood and the precision required when working this material. Clay at that time seemed too malleable and unstructured to offer any great interest, serving more as a therapeutic diversion to the technical rigours of cabinetmaking. It was only through collaborating with fellow students on kiln-building projects, that I eventually got drawn into ceramics. I learnt to recognize the value of working with others from a variety of disciplines, sharing ideas and solving problems together. It is interesting however to see how the experience of working in wood has come to inform my ceramic practice. Both the geometric aesthetic vocabulary of wood and technical processes more commonly associated with woodworking, such as cutting and polishing, have been adopted within my ceramics.

After graduating in 1982, I first worked with the respected ceramic maker David Roberts, before establishing my own ceramics studio, whilst simultaneously embarking on a teaching career. Since the late 1990s my craft practice has been concerned with making sculptural forms in clay that relied on the clay body alone to provide the focus of visual interest. I was (and remain) interested in the idea that what is seen on the surface, passes through the core of the material; having long favoured materials in an unadorned state and valuing the principle of 'truth to materials'.

The process I developed involved adding coarse, granular material to plastic clay to enhance the aesthetic properties of the fired clay form (Binns 2006). The intention was to enrich the clay's visual and textural properties, developing a body that required no further adornment or application of glaze. The work was conceived and produced alone within a traditional craft studio environment—developing over time a personal vocabulary of form and surface.

DEVELOPING COLLABORATION

To expose the visual richness of the matrix of clay and aggregate inclusions I was adding to my work, I found it necessary to grind and polish the fired clay surface, in much the same way a stonemason polishes stone to reveal its natural beauty. As my material was extremely hard following firing, it was necessary to investigate an efficient method of grinding back the top surface layer—a process rarely used within ceramic practice. This led to another experience of collaboration within my craft practice. Aware that glass artists often employ a grinding and polishing process, I consulted with a glassmaker colleague at my university. She explained the various techniques used by glass artists and suggested a power tool commonly used within the granite and glass industries. The process involves working through a series of removable diamond pads, from very coarse to fine polish. Guided by my colleague's knowledge, we undertook an extensive series of tests using different types of grinding medium and systems, before settling on a procedure that seemed most applicable to my work. The grinding process is also important in refining forms to the exact geometry I desired—giving crisp architecturally inspired shapes that do not conflict with the visually rich surfaces. As grinding and polishing has become such a fundamental element of my craft practice, I now realize how important this early collaboration was in shaping all my studio practice and the recent moves towards developing a commercial, architectural product.

Continually searching for ways of increasing the visual drama of the fired clay surface led me to consider the possibility of introducing small amounts of crushed glass—a material that is closely allied to ceramic materials in its chemical makeup. I gradually increased the proportions of glass, eventually reaching a point where plastic clay was almost eliminated from the process. I found that the finely crushed glass when mixed with ceramic aggregates and fused together formed a hard, durable material, which had an aesthetic appearance that was unlike either conventional glass or ceramic. The process involves blending together the various constituent parts of the mixture, packing it in a mould and firing it in a kiln—a process closely allied to traditional kiln cast glass. During the fusing process, the material becomes molten before solidifying on cooling. On removal from the kiln, the solid mass of material is broken out of the casting mould and then cut, ground and polished to define the form and reveal the fused matrix of glass and aggregate material.

The first tests using entirely glass and ceramic aggregate materials were undertaken at the end of a residency at the International Ceramics Studio in Kecskemet, Hungary. I began with a hunch that finely crushed glass when mixed with crushed ceramic aggregate, heated to a point of melting, might possibly give an interesting hard material on cooling and solidification. The investigation had very humble origins, starting with a series of simple moulds from made plaster of Paris, cast over small plastic storage containers purchased at the local market. Tacit knowledge of ceramic materials and firing suggested parameters for predicting the most appropriate blend of materials and fusing temperatures. My starting point was a 50/50 blend of crushed glass and finely ceramic aggregate—prefired and crushed pottery. Later tests involved gradually increasing the ratio of glass to ceramic to increase the glassy qualities of the material. Knowing that most common forms of glass become fluid between 700 degrees and 1,000 degrees Celsius, I undertook initial firings within this range. The test samples appeared promising, showing that it was possible to produce a hard material with interesting visual properties, quite different from either conventional glass or ceramic material. On returning to my own studio, I continued developing the process, integrating the material into my repertoire of work. The new work was similar in form to previous clay work but with a wider range of surface qualities. The process provides a surface that has greater 'visual depth' than conventional fired clay, due to the translucent properties of the glassy component of the material.

Moulds, an integral part of the process, offered another important opportunity for collaboration. Plaster moulds were used initially, similar to those traditionally used in glass casting. They were however found to disintegrate at the firing temperatures required, creating problems within the casting process. At this time I was supervising the doctoral project of Alasdair Bremner (2008) at the University of Central Lancashire. Bremner's PhD research involved exploring the aesthetic and creative potential of refractory concrete.[2] Recognizing that the refractory concrete might have potential as a mould-making material, Bremner created a series of test moulds, which were found to withstand the higher casting temperatures and could be reused, unlike the sacrificial plaster moulds. Our initial sharing of ideas led to collaboration on a number of projects, including developing a body of work for the Brick Project (2007), an international design project organized by the European Ceramic Work Centre (EKWC) in the Netherlands. We collaborated on two prototype architectural products for the project—a wave-shaped facing brick and six large cladding panels. The schemes combined our joint skills. Bremner brought to the project his knowledge of the refractory concrete material and associated methods of mould-making. I brought knowledge of the glass/ceramic material, including the firing schedule. We developed the designs through discussion and an evolving shared aesthetic. The work produced for this project featured in a number of exhibitions.[3]

The finishing of these projects, which required resources not available within either my own studio or the university, led to my first encounter with industry. As a large-scale diamond saw was required to dimension the cast bricks, I contacted a local granite worktop company. A machine operative in the granite company, with no previous knowledge of our project, but high levels of skill in his field, was able to offer far more efficient and accurate solutions to the machining of the cast forms, solutions that we did not envisage, having no previous experience of industrial stone-finishing processes. The collaboration proved a valuable insight into utilizing knowledge and skills outside the domain of the craft environment, bringing a recognition that seeking out specialist expertise can increase accuracy and efficiency. Furthermore, this first experience of collaborating with an industrial partner unexpectedly opened up many new opportunities. I started recognizing that linking up with an industrial partner would allow me to extend my creative ambition beyond what is possible within a craft studio environment.

Further collaboration between Bremner and me led to a number of other projects, including production of a pair of large sculptural forms commissioned by a garden designer. The making of the sculptural forms combined my vocabulary of form with Bremner's expanding knowledge of refractory concrete.

RESEARCH GRANT

As I continued exploring the cast glass and ceramic material within my own practice, a growing awareness of eco-responsible practice led me to start introducing waste glass and ceramic material, as an alternative to virgin raw materials. Using locally or regionally sourced recycled waste would alleviate the consumption of nonreplenishable raw materials, whilst simultaneously reducing the excessive embodied energy associated with transporting raw materials huge distances around the globe.

Recognizing the potential for developing a more extensive research project around the process, Bremner and I prepared an application for research funding from the Arts & Humanities Research Council (AHRC) 2008. The bid was successful, providing us with both time and resources to develop a more structured investigation into the development of a range of materials made from recycled ceramic, glass and mineral waste. The primary aims of the project were firstly to identify and investigate potential recycled, mineral-based

Fig. 6.1.   Waste bone china tableware. Furlong Mills Ltd, Burslem, Stoke on Trent, UK, 2010. Photograph: David Binns

waste materials and then explore how they might be combined within a kiln-casting process. A second phase of the research involved examining potential applications for the material, including the creative possibilities for architects, designers, artists and craft makers. Once the commercial potential had been identified, the final phase involved exploring how the process of making could be adapted for industrial-scale manufacturing.

The investigation, fuelled by a growing awareness of materials and the waste industry, led us to explore utilizing a wide range of waste industrial material: recycled container glass, waste from the tableware and sanitary-ware industries, steel smelting, coal-fired power stations and ash from incinerated domestic waste (Figure 6.1). As testing progressed, we found the new material not only had unique aesthetic qualities but also appeared to be highly durable, with functional properties, suggesting, in particular, applications within an architectural context.

WORKING ACROSS BOUNDARIES

Crucial to the success of the research has been collaboration with Dr Richard McCabe, a material scientist from the University of Central Lancashire's Centre for Materials Science. The collaboration with McCabe provided material analysis, allowing a deeper understanding of the chemical and physical characteristics of both the unprocessed recyclate and the finished prototypes. Feedback from this scientific investigation helped shape the emerging research, informing the best possible combinations of materials and optimum temperatures and firing cycles.

The ceramic studio and the material science laboratory are seemingly utterly different environments, each with very different working practices and lexis. To develop a meaningful and fruitful dialogue between two environments of such polarity, it was important to spend time working in both laboratory and workshop. As such, Bremner and I were inducted into using the electron microscope, whilst McCabe involved himself with making moulds and preparing batches of materials for casting within our craft studio. Becoming familiar with these contrasting environments allowed everyone concerned to become confident in contributing to every aspect of the evolving research. It was interesting to discover that in many ways these two apparently alien disciplines have many parallels, with 'craft knowledge' fundamental to both. The idea of craft within a science environment may at first seem alien, but when working with McCabe, I saw many similarities in approach. Firstly, I noticed McCabe's tacit understanding when fluently handling the 'tools of his trade', albeit microscopes, rather than kilns or saws. Secondly was his joy in solving problems creatively, through the use of materials and equipment, finding beauty in effective solutions, albeit formula, rather than artefact. Without this collaboration, it would have neither been possible to develop the knowledge of the recycled raw materials nor verify the functional properties of the new material.

Having an informed understanding of the studio-based process and properties of the new material has led McCabe to consider other potential applications that will require further investigation—applications that focus more on the chemical and physical properties of the material and less on the aesthetic qualities. It will be interesting to involve ourselves in this research, where the activity may swing towards craft that supports the science, rather than science that supports the craft.

DEVELOPING COLLABORATIVE ENTERPRISE

Whilst the waste raw materials were obtained from a variety of sources, a recycling company—Recycling Lives,[4] local to the university—served as the main supplier of our crushed waste glass. Whilst the core business of Recycling Lives is essentially the collection and processing of waste, it is important to them to find economic and viable use for their processed waste, rather than simply rendering it safe for landfill—applications that add value to an otherwise low-value material. As such, they became increasingly interested in our evolving research and involved in supporting our project. Rather than simply providing us with materials crushed to a standard size, through increasing cooperation, they developed methods of crushing and grading the glass to suit our requirements and sourcing specific waste streams we required.

As it started to become clear that our material had commercial possibilities, involving the consumption of large volumes of raw material, it has been important to ensure we have a sustainable and lasting source of raw materials. Recycling Lives have been able to assure us of long-term supplies of crushed glass. Recognizing the mutual benefit of collaborating more closely, Recycling Lives and the research team started discussing potential routes towards manufacturing. We have the knowledge and skills to make the material, albeit only on a scale limited to a small craft studio. Whilst Recycling Lives have none of the technical knowledge, they have the resources to collect and process to our specification many of the waste raw materials we require. Furthermore, the company has large-scale industrial premises, a workforce and business infrastructure. Once a production facility is fully operational, the manufacturing unit has the potential to create employment for a number of semi- and highly skilled operatives. My role in the project would then interestingly further broaden to include training and skill development.

At the time of writing, a large kiln had just been procured, together with other ancillary equipment necessary to set up a fully operational pilot manufacturing unit. The unit will enable the material to be manufactured on a larger scale and give us the opportunity to explore many new ideas than would ever have been possible using our existing craft-based resources alone. It is our intention to start producing a limited number of product ranges which we will then start marketing to architects and designers. Initial products will include a 'slip' facing brick, normally made from imported stone. Other likely products include ranges of roughcast and polished wall tiles, eventually moving on to larger format cladding tiles and counter surfaces (Figures 6.2 and 6.3).

One of the primary aims of the unit however is to retain a strong craft ethos, creating ranges of products that have design and aesthetic qualities that would be lost if the intention was simply increasing output through industrial production. One example of how a culture of craft will be retained relates to craft historically being 'place orientated', utilizing locally available raw materials, and/or engendering a sense of place through visual appearance. A unique attribute of the material is its ability to link materiality with place; allowing the development of short batch production or bespoke products that will be sited in the same locality in which the waste raw materials were originally sourced. Damaged stone masonry or brick could be crushed and introduced into the process, providing both a direct visual and conceptual link between material and place.

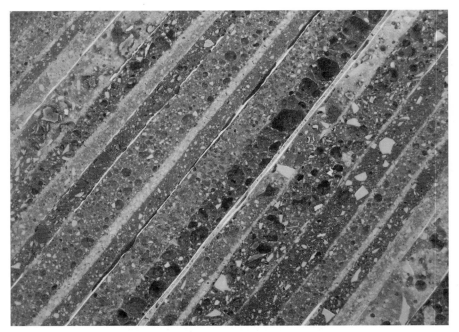

Fig. 6.2. Cast tile. Fused waste trimmings—kiln cast waste glass and recycled ceramic aggregates. Ground and polished post firing. 30 × 30 × 3cm. 2010. Photograph: David Binns

Fig. 6.3. Prototype cast tiles. Kiln glass waste and recycled ceramic aggregates. Ground and polished post firing. 30 × 30 × 3cm. 2010. Photograph: David Binns

CONCLUSION

As the project moves towards fruition and a fully operational manufacturing plant, it is important to reflect on the original intentions of the project. Through collaboration between ourselves and other external partners, Bremner and myself have successfully developed a cast material made from up to 100 per cent recycled waste, that has a unique range of aesthetic properties, unlike either fired clay or glass. We have made a number of prototype products, including tiles, cladding sheets, table-tops, bowl forms and sculptural artefacts, in a range of different colours and textures. Being made primarily from low value waste, these products clearly add value to the original waste raw materials, many of which being otherwise destined for landfill. Between them, the range of prototype products we have developed, demonstrate the creative potential of the material for artists, designers and craft makers. Launching a range of prototype samples at the 100% Design international trade fair,[5] we were inundated with interest from architects and designers, reassuring us that we have developed a product that is both aesthetically unique and has significant sustainable credentials. Whilst at the time of writing, the manufacturing plant is not fully established or operational, the process has been adapted within the craft studio, in readiness for industrial production. Unless the intention was to eventually make huge volumes of the material, requiring fully automated processing facilities, the current intended scales of manufacturing will still rely heavily on hand (craft) skills and an intimate knowledge of the materials. Increased production volumes are now feasible because of investment in a large kiln, space and increased crushing capacity both provided by our industrial collaborative partner, Recycling Lives.

Regarding impact on the environment and waste material stock, only time will tell, once the manufacturing plant is fully operational. These do remain important concerns and therefore will be closely monitored. Any beneficial impacts on the environment would be due to significantly decreasing landfill of certain waste materials and reducing consumption of nonreplenishable, virgin raw materials.

The material would never have reached fruition without collaboration underpinning every stage of development, from two people sharing ideas and solving problems within the craft studio, embracing scientific methodologies, to commercial collaboration, with an established industrial partner. If it is successful, then we will feel that the optimism Leach and Edelkoort had for fruitful collaboration between craft practice and industry has been realized; a product and idea that was born within the context of craft practice, maturing as an idea through collaboration with an industrial partner.

NOTES

1. I exhibit my work both in the United Kingdom and overseas and am a member of the International Academy of Ceramics and UK Crafts Council Index of Selected Makers, and a fellow of The Craft Potters Association.
2. 'Refractory concrete' is the term used for a wide range of materials with similar chemical and physical properties. In simple terms, it is a heat-resistant concrete made with high-alumina or calcium-aluminate cement and a refractory aggregate. To date, refractory concretes have been used almost exclusively as a furnace-lining material in the high-temperature steel and chemical industries. The aim of Bremner's PhD research was to investigate the creative potential of this material, developing 'aesthetic' properties that might be used by artists and craft makers.
3. These exhibitions included Rotterdam 2007 European City of Architecture, 2009 Dutch Design Week in Eidhoven, and two exhibitions examining innovations in ceramic materials and design curated by internationally regarded designer Marek Cecula: *Object Factory—The Art of Industrial Ceramics* I and II. These exhibitions were shown at the Gardiner Museum in Toronto, Canada, in 2008 and the Museum of Art & Design in New York 2009. <http://col lections.madmuseum.org/code/emuseum.asp?emu_action=advsearch&ra wsearch=exhibitionid/,/is/,/472/,/true/,/false&profi le=exhibitions> accessed 10 March 2012.
4. Recycling Lives is a Queen's Award–winning waste management and reprocessing company, based in Preston, United Kingdom. Supporting their recycling core business, the company also runs a programme of social rehabilitation, providing education and life-skills training. The Recycling Lives charity acts as a safety net for vulnerable and marginalized people, helping them back into full-time work.
5. 100% Design is a major international design fair. The annual event situated at Earls Court exhibition centre in London, acts as a showcase for many of the best design-led products, attracting an international audience of architects, interior designers and design buyers.

REFERENCES

Binns, D. (2006), 'Additions to Clay Bodies: A Research Project', *Ceramics Technical*, 23: 57–62.

Binns, D. (2007), 'AHRC Research Grant: The Aesthetic of Waste—an Investigation of the Creative and Commercial Potential of Kiln Cast Re-cycled Mineral Waste', <http://www.ahrc.ac.uk/Funded-Research/Pages/The-Aesthetic-of-Waste--an-investigation-of-the-creative--commercial-potential-of-kiln-cast-re-cycl.aspx> accessed 15 March 2013.

Bremner, A. (2008), 'An Investigation into the Potential Creative Applications of Refractory Concrete', PhD thesis, University of Central Lancashire, Preston, UK.

Brick Project (2007), *European Ceramic Work Centre (EKWC)*, <http://www.designartnews.com/pagina/1brick.html> accessed 5 March 2012.

Edelkoort, L. (2003), 'CRAFTS: On Scale, Pace and Sustainability', *Prince Claus Fund Journal*, 10a: 60–69.

Leach, B. (1940), 'Towards a Standard', in *A Potters Book,* London: Faber & Faber.

Object Factory (2009), *Museum of Art & Design, New York,* <http://collections.madmuseum.org/code/emuseum.asp?emu_action=advsearch&rawsearch=exhibitionid/,/is/,/472/,/true/,/false&profile=exhibitions> accessed 10 March 2012.

7

Designing Collaboration:
Evoking Dr Johnson through Craft
and Interdisciplinarity

Jason Cleverly and Tim Shear

INTRODUCTION

In recent years there has been a growing interest in creating interdisciplinary collaboration between makers, scientists, curators and academics, and we have witnessed the development of a number of unique, site-specific initiatives in museums and art galleries.

In this chapter, we discuss the background and ambitions that have informed the creation and installation of an interactive craftwork designed to engender new forms of visitor engagement. In particular we discuss the design development and implementation of the *Interactive Table and Escritoire* exhibited at Dr Johnson's House, London. This work was the result of an invitation to submit a proposal for the *House of Words* exhibition held at Dr Johnson's House during the summer of 2009 to celebrate the 300th anniversary of Dr Johnson's birthday.[1]

Dr Johnson is largely remembered for his dictionary, which was compiled and written at 17 Gough Square in the City of London. The house was built in 1700 and is one of the few residential houses of its type still surviving, containing panelled rooms, period furniture and paintings (Figure 7.1). Published in 1755, Johnson's dictionary is the most influential in the history of the English language. Its development involved the gathering together of etymological information from a range of sources, a task made possible through the assistance of a number of clerks, or amanuenses, who worked standing up at a large table. The dictionary was completed in about nine years and in the original contained 42,773 words, with the innovation of definitions and illustrative quotations. The *House of Words* exhibition[2] involved a number of contributing artists, each selecting a different part of the house to respond to (Peters and West 2009).

The project proposal was initiated by Jason Cleverly, a maker with a track record of working on interactives and interpretives for museums and art

Fig. 7.1. Dr Johnson's House, 17 Gough Square, London, 2009. Photograph: Jason Cleverly

galleries.[3] Cleverly chose the top floor, or garret, the actual room in which Johnson worked. Proposing to use a digital system and needing to work within the constraints of Web servers, virtual machines and high-resolution print, the work quickly became interdisciplinary as Cleverly drew on the support of Tim Shear, a research technologist with an interest in pervasive and physical computing and a professional background in computer simulation design and network technologies.

Our aim in this chapter is to contribute to an ongoing investigation and understanding of design sensitivities through documenting the life cycle of a collaborative design project. We are interested in how the use of new technology can facilitate new forms of engagement, encourage informal learning and enhance collaboration both in the intended audience and in ourselves as makers, through the construction of novel interfaces. We will consider how, as collaborators, we shaped the project from design to museum to Web. What for example was the impact of our partnership on the content generated? We also hope to illuminate the design processes as the sum of its collaborators, which included maker, technologist, commercial partner, museum curator/ moderator, social/computer scientists and museum visitors.

The installation we developed was a playful recreation of Johnson's furniture which included a table, an escritoire, a book and an inkwell, with the whole being augmented by technology (Figure 7.2). The digital pen-and-paper system used in developing this project offers an appealing and suitable combination of traditional media (pen and paper) and digital and Internet-based technology. The pen reads tiny watermarked dots printed on paper, which

Fig. 7.2. *Interactive Table and Escritoire*, 2009. Jason Cleverly and Tim Shear. Photograph: Jason Cleverly

enables the capture of drawings and writing via a USB dock or inkwell. The pen has associated software, enabling the translation of handwriting into text-based data, which is transmitted to a database available to view via the Internet. The watermarked augmented paper is customized to create a pro forma, allowing different tasks to be performed when certain active areas are written on (Figure 7.3). The visitor is encouraged to add words of his or her own devising or to write idiosyncratic definitions of existing words to add to a collaborative online dictionary. The furniture in the garret room was fabricated using digital routing and laser etching; this digital tooling was intended not only to echo the use of the digital pen and paper but also to resonate with the current concerns within the crafts around new manufacturing processes.

Cleverly was determined to examine the dictionary compilation process and how the creation of a work of such importance and lasting impact by Johnson contrasts and compares with a number of current preoccupations. Contemporary search engines and databases, notably Wikipedia and particularly perhaps its sister project Wiktionary, rely on contributions from the online community to shape and edit the contents. A key idea was the notion that language is evolving and expanding continuously and relies on an ever-increasing series of subjective definitions emerging from popular culture, slang and emerging technology.

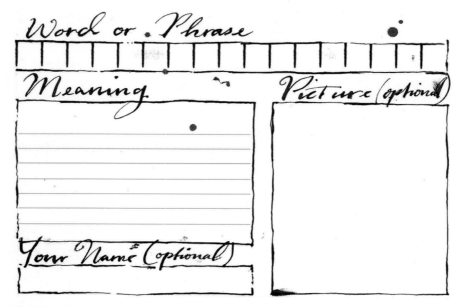

Fig. 7.3. Pro forma, 2009. Jason Cleverly and Tim Shear. Photograph: Jason Cleverly and Tim Shear

In summary our aims and objectives were to enhance visitor experience and to engender participation by creating a new craftwork that wove digital media technologies into a tangible object. We also sought to augment the sense of place palpable at Dr Johnson's House—to interpret and evoke the significance of Dr Johnson's endeavour and legacy.

THE DICTIONARY AND THE WIKTIONARY

It is reputed that the garret at 17 Gough Square had a high table around which Johnson's assistants worked. Johnson's biographer James Boswell recounts in his famous *Life* that Johnson had 'an upper room fitted up like a counting house for the purpose, in which he gave the copyists their several tasks' (Boswell 1791). The image of a paper-strewn table surrounded by Johnson and his staff sharing, working on and collating data, seemed like an eighteenth-century search engine or indeed an analogue Wiki to Cleverly, and it was this which became the inspiration for his design.

Regarded as the pioneer of the Wiki, Ward Cunningham introduced the Wiki-WikiWeb in 1995. Ward's keynote for WikiSym 2006 offered the 'Design Principles of Wiki' (Cunningham 2006). In reviewing these Wiki design principles, four in particular can be seen as a significant to the design, configuration and ambition of the *Interactive Table and Escritoire*:

1. Organic principle (co-evolution)—the structure of the site is expected to grow and evolve with the community that uses it.
2. Mundane principle (undistracted)—a small number of conventions provide all necessary formatting.
3. Universal principle—the mechanisms of editing and organizing are the same as those of writing so that any writer is automatically an editor and organizer.
4. Observable principle—activity within the site can be watched and reviewed by any other visitor (Cunningham 2006).

Although our participants had a relatively limited contribution to the design and structure of the installation, their interactive contribution was neverthe-less the key ingredient for the success of the work. The use of digital/tan-gible assemblies allowing multiple authorship has been examined previously through projects such as Automake, which enables artefacts like jewellery to be designed remotely, resulting in a shared practice using online design tools that 'challenge definitions of authorship, concepts of provenance, char-acterizations of practice and models of consumption' (Marshall and Bunnell 2009). These kinds of projects require simple structures, conventions and procedures that allow for a shared influence.

THE CALM INTERFACE

In order that the museum visitor might engage with the *Interactive Table and Escritoire* in an intuitive, familiar manner we wanted to employ the notion of the Calm Interface (Weiser and Seely Brown 1996) in the design, something closely allied to ubiquity of a Wiki. We also aimed to be sensitive to the unique environment of the museum by augmenting the sense of place, or located-ness, and evoking to some modest degree the scale of Dr Johnson's original project in 1755, a studio or workshop where words are carefully considered, assembled and crafted together to form a larger whole.

In *The Coming Age of Calm Technology*, Weiser and Seely Brown (1996) outline the 'locatedness' we aimed to achieve in our work on the Dr Johnson project by embedding open source Web 2.0 technologies into the piece. In 'designing for the periphery', the design problem is not merely one of camou-flage but of rendering the complexity of the hardware and software as a subtle augmentation of the mise-en-scène; the compositional process is particularly aided by a forceful site specificity. 'The periphery connects us effortlessly to a myriad of familiar details. This connection with the world we call "located-ness"' (Weiser and Seely Brown 1996).

Through this sensitive fabrication of workshop/garret, and the provision of appropriate tools for the task, we hoped that the visitor would feel at once the experience of being in an eighteenth-century workspace, and yet be part of a Web 2.0 project collaborating with past and future visitors on a larger shared endeavour.

EXTENDING THE VISIT

Discussing the potential of digital bookmarking, the use of PDAs,[4] kiosks and Web sites by visitors during their movement around museums to record and save data of personal interest or relevance, Silvia Filippini-Fantoni and Johnathan Bowen (2007) suggest the obvious attractions and increasing prevalence for museums and collections of an extension of the museum experience beyond the visit. 'The ability to save an important part of the content encountered during the museum visit and access it at home or in another context allows the visitor the possibility of focusing more on discovery and the aesthetic experience while in the museum and to leave the more traditional didactic aspects for later' (Filippini-Fantoni and Bowen 2007).

Encouraging the visitor to act out and contribute to the Johnsonian task, and to enable the subsequent remote review of their own contribution, and that of others via the Internet, allowed the physical space to extend beyond the environs of the garret room and to create digital iterations of the dictionary and therefore extend the visit. This transposition tool permits visitors to collaborate in the making of a holistic structure through and by an augmented craftwork.

DESIGN SENSITIVITIES

Relying on a historical portrait or mise en scène which informed and defined the aesthetic approach, Cleverly began collaborating within an interdisciplinary environment to work out the rules for new media (Web and tangibles) he was now designing for. Creating an ecology based on the Johnsonian artefacts, the design process also drew upon reproductions of Johnson's own handwriting laser etched into the birch-ply table. Once the concept of conflating historical and contemporary writing tools was devised, a digital palette was developed informed by other cues from the ecology of artefacts, which cascaded through the table, escritoire, book, digital paper, USB inkwell, embedded screen graphics and fonts.

Luigina Ciolfi's PhD thesis on 'Situating "Place" in Interactive Design' explains that 'sensitivities suggest relevant issues and inspire creative design, rather than imposing rigid rules on the design. Sensitivities do not impose pre-determined solutions, but rather define spaces for discussion on how the design of interaction could deal with the issues that they express' (Ciolfi 2004: 144). Our process of creating this located craftwork evolved to identify our key sensitivities at the design stage and to incorporate them to our development processes in building and deploying the piece.

During the design stage, our key sensitivities were

1. To be sympathetic to the environment of Dr Johnson's House, resulting in the development of an *ecology of artefacts* used by Cleverly to embed the piece into the garret.
2. To focus on the augmented paper interface in the museum and not to devalue that experience by allowing entries remotely.
3. To not obscure reliance on the digital, despite technology being embedded in the user's periphery.
4. To embed the procedures of participation (protocols) in the augmented paper pro forma (also a significant collaborative moment in the project).
5. To be mindful of the technical constraints of the digital pen and paper system and the necessity to build in the ability to moderate visitor input, in case of indecent words or drawings.

DESIGN AND CONSTRUCTION

The scheme of table and book, conceived at an early stage in the design development, was in some ways a rather straightforward choice of composition given the location. However, the concept was formulated to accommodate embedded content and a calm interface as discussed above and could be arranged sympathetically and easily within the given space, whilst affording a variety of extended configurations as the collaborative, shared design emerged.

Research revealed a curious lack of information on the exact items of furniture used by Johnson. Images of Johnson at work (which mostly come from a later period) are celebratory and their accuracy is not easy to confirm. However, assumptions could be made about approximate style and function. The design was largely informed by examinations of a small amount of furniture extant in the Johnson house alongside images of contemporary items both photographic and illustrative. A wealth of Georgian prints and drawings informed the composition. Satirical portraits by William Hogarth, and Thomas Chippendale's *The Gentleman Cabinet-makers Director*[5] (Chippendale [1754]

2000), revealed an aesthetically pleasing use of crosshatching and stylized perspective. In the case of the Chippendale directory, this exaggerated perspective is a deliberate projection used to show clients a range of views in a single image.

The design, informed by two-dimensional images, was to be regarded as a kind of stage set, as if drawings had been cut out and reassembled, an indication of the original table and an escritoire. The construction of the work included the deliberate use of CAD/CAM: the structure of the furniture was made with a CNC Router, and the trompe-l'œil surface details using laser etching. The employment of digital processes is to be seen as a counterpoint to the digital/analogue pen and paper.

Working from Cleverly's original brief, Shear searched for an Anoto server-based solution; Anoto server products can be coded to process the captured form data. It soon became clear that no preexisting product would work for the concept, but XMS Penvision's Formidable server could be configured to our requirements. Shear then preceded to negotiate with XMS Penvision and its UK suppliers eventually bringing in a commercial company, Celtic Internet, as the digital pen and paper consultants to sponsor the project.

Utilizing Celtic Internet's product knowledge, Shear carried out a risk assessment for the technology that was to power the piece which resulted in a very bespoke use of the Formidable server. The most risky issue was the unknown but reportedly basic Internet connection in the garret. Without a constant stable connection, the piece simply would not run. In order to control the risk we decided to build the Formidable server, the digital pen drivers, the Drupal-powered ersatz Wiki, the bespoke Web services and Adobe Flash client used to power the display all into the escritoire, enabling the piece to run with or without Internet.

As previously stated, one of our core design sensitivities was the museum's requirement to moderate visitor input before publishing entries to the web. The server embedded in the escritoire processed entries to the dictionary within seconds to a Johnsonian style screen, independent from the publicly viewable Web site. The online site[6] was only updated once the museum curator had approved the entries via a separate content management screen, and synchronized the local dictionary with the online version; this obviously did require an Internet connection, and for the exhibition we patched in a power line Ethernet connection to the garret room in the house.

Perhaps the element of the work requiring most collaboration in design, and the most critical for visitor engagement was the pro forma. Shear was able to make different areas of the paper active in collecting visitor entries, whilst Cleverly was concerned with the visual quality of the form, drawing on images of Johnson's correction notes for the second edition, which featured characteristic smudges and drips. Collaboratively, they worked on visitor intelligibility, with methodologies, including tests on un-briefed work colleagues, friends and children.

The design had to account for the creation and spelling of new words and the conflict with software spelling correction systems. Iterations of the form were subject to further testing on subjects, and the final design included written instructions as part of the page layout. Working together on the form Cleverly and Shear developed perhaps the most significant collaborative element of the work.

Shear used graphics, fonts and logic from the pro forma to develop the software that ran the digital display in the escritoire, in keeping with the Johnsonian aesthetic of the piece. Outside the garret, the Web site, although using the same graphics and colours as the form, was published with an almost default Web 2.0 interface, corresponding to design sensitivities in order not to obstruct the Web 2.0 aspects of the work.

THE CAREER OF THE INSTALLATION THROUGH ITS COLLABORATORS

Clearly, the exhibition curators and the designer/maker hold both the influence and power during the planning and commissioning stage. Cleverly had worked on the proposal for some time prior to starting the collaborative journey in 2009. In order to illuminate the collaboration, we need to distinguish between influence and power. Throughout the collaboration process, power to sanction deliverables resided with the designer/maker, whereas decisions about the exhibition resided with the curators and the museum.

The whole project was seeded with the idea of a physical crafted structure that gradually took on a hybrid structure, with the tangible form influencing the digital form and vice versa until a compromise was reached.

From a craft perspective, the more organic part of the collaboration happened before we were locked into the procedures of participation. Those pre-collaborative months for Cleverly and the initial few weeks collaborating with Shear were not a programmer/client requirements analysis phase but two designers working in each other's areas, with Shear having to think like a maker and Cleverly, conversely, having to think like a programmer.

Of particular interest is how the level of influence shifted through the initial design, design and development, exhibition setup, public exhibition and evaluation stages. With each new collaborator, at least one threshold moment occurred making their level of influence clear. The main threshold moment for us was the design of the pro forma for the digital paper. This was the first point at which all the major collaborators' influence became clear. Working across disciplines can become challenging unless participants immerse themselves in that discipline or collaborate closely with someone from that discipline; small details can quickly become major challenges. What provisionally appeared as a simple task of designing the pro forma, rapidly turned into a problematic process accommodating the previously described key design sensitivities. Our solution required close collaboration with the digital pen and paper supplier and commercial partner. To make the pro forma work to requirement, to enable users to make up new words and to allow the captured data to flow through the servers to the embedded screen and onto the Web site, Celtic Internet undertook the high-resolution colour print run of the digital paper. The simple pro forma generated an 80 gigabyte print file, with sample prints taking ten minutes per page on nonindustry laser printers. A Drupal-powered content management system was built into the design allowing the museum staff simple access to moderate entries; those entries were then served to the screen in near real time (in reality there was a fifteen-second processing delay). As an Internet connection was not guaranteed, the local database used by the piece was uploaded to the public Web site, pending approval by the moderator.

PARADIGM TRANSITION OF INFLUENCE

The exhibition setup was the paradigm transition of influence for the collaborators; the role of the museum/moderator now clearly emerged. A shift in influence occurred when Cleverly, after conceiving and setting up the physical structure of the piece, took a more minor role, leaving Shear to work with the moderator to ensure the stability of the installation during the exhibition. Celtic Internet and the exhibition curators having completed delivery, respectively, became less involved.

During the three-month public exhibition stage, both the moderator and most important the visitors became very influential, effectively leaving the previously highly influential collaborators on the sidelines, including both Cleverly and Shear. A key design sensitivity now emerged forcefully: the removal of material considered vulgar or indecent by the moderator. This bowdlerization process informed the legacy of the work as viewable on the Web-based archive.

RESULTS: THE COLLECTIVE OUTPUT FROM INSTALLATION AND OBSERVATIONS

A video-ethnographic study of the installation (Patel et al. 2011) primarily focuses on the methods of word construction employed by visitors. From video evidence it would appear that visitor collaboration in constructing words was fragmented and distributed (nonlinear) as opposed to site specific, and in most cases did not rely on real-time co-participation. Many visitors used the paper-based book to review previous entries, rather than the limited, rolling eight to twelve entries on the embedded screen. After consulting the book or screen, some visitors would then make an entry; hence, we describe this as 'fragmented and distributed visitor collaboration'.

It was always appreciated that visitor numbers would not be high, as traditionally, the museum does not have a large flow of visitors. The final count was 742 entries from the exhibition uploaded to the Web site, all of which were approved by the moderator. With hindsight, we should have requested that any unapproved entries also be retained to give us a true idea of all the entries. But the moderator was quite open-minded. In regard to actual visitor numbers, the exhibition curator stated, 'I can report that the Trustees of Dr Johnson's House have been thrilled to discover how much their visitor numbers increased over the period of the show. In comparison to the same months in 2008 there was a 28% increase in June 2009, a 30% increase in July and a whopping 75% increase in August' (Peters 2009).

The *Interactive Table and Escritoire* was one of seven works at the *House of Words* exhibition, and there was also much contingent publicity around the Johnson tercentenary, so this boost in footfall cannot be attributed directly to this one work alone.

CONCLUSIONS

To reiterate, the primary motivation for this chapter was to identify and highlight cases of design sensitivity, whilst examining the impact on content as a result of the input the collaborators had on the project. Earlier we identified key design sensitivities around the project which amounted to the need to balance artistic vision, curatorial duty (moderation) and technical constraints. In connection with this, we highlighted the functionality of the digital paper which in turn informed the layout and design of the book used by the *Interactive Table and Escritoire*. This threshold moment not only inspired close examination of the installation's career but also underlined this moment as the point at which we coded the procedures of participation.

The procedures of participation are the result of collaboration, and although fixed at a point in the design and development, the collaborators' level of influence rose and fell through the career of the installation, resulting in the massive shift of influence towards the museum during the exhibition.

Our results, some not anticipated, can all be traced back to trade-offs made when designing the procedures of participation. These shaped the design, development, use and moderation of the installation. We acknowledge an ignored opportunity to develop a more collaborative Web 2.0 site, or true Wiki, choosing instead to reinforce the value of the tangible interface, preserving exclusivity and enhancing new forms of participation in the museum.

We retained the ambition not to obscure the digital nature of the piece, whilst showing sensitivity to the museum's visitors thus affording a calm interface within which to participate in an online work.

For Cleverly, the project is a continuation of a practice examining the design and development of situated interactive interpretive assemblies in museums and art galleries. However, the introduction of the digital-augmented content provided through collaboration with Shear enhances this practice, allowing the work to become more meaningful for the visitor through the playful reflexivity of the designed task and the conditioning narrative this affords.

Shear's engagement with the project also forms a continuation of practice, allowing experimentation and deployment of new media, the considered alignment and management of bespoke and off the shelf software. The creation of a novel visitor interface forms a satisfying and unique balance between digital and analogue, with further possibilities for collaboration of this kind.

Collaborative design is all pervasive, for example in film production or car design; these modes of production rely on teams of specialists engaged in Fordian divisions of labour. But what might be considered more unique within collaborative design is the manifestation of small-scale curious and engaging design projects, museum interpretives with site-specific constraints aimed at informal learning, that continue to afford possibilities for the wider use of calm interfaces and embedded technology.

As the pairing engaged with such a project we consider that an individual designer would have approached our design problem differently. Working as a team we formatted a deliberate balance to the tangible to concentrate on an evocation of Dr Johnson's working and domestic environment. Our deployment of a calm interface was a nuanced alternative to a more mainstream Wiki experience, which could be considered more Craft 2.0 than Web 2.0.

The visitor flow in the garret on the fourth floor of Dr Johnson's House, when combined with the procedures of participation, created what we describe as fragmented and distributed visitor collaboration. We think this fragmented and distributed visitor collaboration is the new form of engagement aimed for, allowing museum visitors to collectively or individually participate with a digitally augmented museum exhibit, or augmented craft. In this case this involved a work that is at once analogue and digital, allowing for an elegant structure situated concurrently at a single, highly specific location and at any subsequent location or time.

NOTES

1. The *House of Words* exhibition (2009), Dr Johnson's House Gough Sq., London, curators Tessa Peters and Janice West.

2. See Peters and West (2009).
3. Other work by Cleverly includes *Deus Oculi*, an interactive piece designed to engender participation and collaboration, devised in conjunction with colleagues from King's College London, discussed and evaluated in Crafting Participation (Heath et al. 2002).
4. Personal digital assistant (electronic handheld information device).
5. Thomas Chippendale became the first cabinetmaker to publish a book of his designs titled *The Gentleman and Cabinet Maker's Director*. Three editions were published, the first in 1754, followed by a virtual reprint in 1755, and finally a revised and enlarged edition in 1762.
6. See <http://drjohnsonsgarret.net/words/how>—original version created by visitors to the *House of Words* exhibition 2 June–29 August 2009.

REFERENCES

Boswell, J. ([1791] 1992), *The Life of Samuel Johnson*, London: Everyman Library.

Chippendale, T. ([1754] 2000), *The Gentleman and Cabinet Maker's Director*, New York: Dover Publications.

Ciolfi, L. (2004), 'Situating "Place" in Interaction Design. Enhancing the User Experience in Interactive Environments', PhD thesis, University of Limerick, <http://richie.idc.ul.ie/luigina/LCThesis.pdf> accessed 16 August 2012.

Cunningham, H. (2006), 'Design Principles of Wiki: How Can So Little Do So Much?', Keynote, WikiSym: International Symposium on Wikis, <http://c2.com/doc/wikisym/WikiSym2006.pdf> accessed 16 August 2012.

Filippini-Fantoni, S., and Bowen, J. (2007), 'Bookmarking in Museums: Extending the Museum Experience beyond the Visit?', in *Museums and the Web 2007, Proceedings*, Toronto: Archives and Museums Informatics, <http://www.museumsandtheweb.com/mw2007/papers/filippini-fantoni/filippini-fantoni.html> accessed 16 August 2012.

Heath, C., Luff, P., vom Lehn, D., Hindmarsh, J., and Cleverly, J. (2002), 'Crafting Participation: Designing Ecologies, Configuring Experience', *Journal of Visual Communication*, 1/1: 9–34.

Marshall, J., and Bunnell, B. (2009), 'Developments in Post Industrial Manufacturing Systems and the Implications for Craft and Sustainability', *Making Futures*, 1, <http://makingfutures.plymouthart.ac.uk/journalvol1/papers.php> accessed 16 August 2012.

Patel, M., Luff, P., Heath, C., Cleverly, J., and vom Lhen, D. (2011), 'Curious Words and Public Definitions—Engaging Visitors in the Collaborative Creation of a Museum Exhibit', paper presented at Digital Engagement '11, 15–17 November, Newcastle, UK, <http://de2011.computing.dundee.ac.uk/?page_id=197> accessed 16 August 2012.

Peters, T., and West, J. (eds) (2009), *The House of Words*, London: Dr Johnson's House Trust Ltd and Luminous Books.

Peters, T. (2009), email, 3 October.

Weiser, M., and Brown, J.S. (1996), *The Coming Age of Calm Technology. Beyond Calculation: The Next Fifty Years*, New York: Copernicus.

sKINship: An Exchange of Material Understanding between Plastic Surgery and Pattern Cutting

Rhian Solomon

INTRODUCTION

This chapter draws together the seemingly disparate practices of plastic surgery and pattern cutting for fashion.[1] Through research that I have conducted into collaborations within this setting, it has become apparent that many striking similarities exist between these professions, particularly with reference to making techniques and material considerations.

Both are concerned with the crafting of the body—the reconstruction or enhancement of oneself through the tailoring of cloth—and both require high standards of dexterity, attention to detail and similar considerations when selecting material fit for purpose in creating a desired silhouette. But despite these and other direct links between these 'craftsmen',[2] specialists within this area seldom work in collaboration with one another.

Through the research program I have founded, entitled sKINship,[3] I am keen to understand how subject-specific knowledge of materials and making can transcend disciplines to add value to practitioners within each of these respective fields. The key focus of this chapter is to communicate the potential for cross-disciplinary working across art and science specialisms, in particular plastic surgery and pattern-cutting professions. How for example can the techniques by which the skin is cut and manipulated during plastic surgery be applied to informing new designs of garment cut and shape? And how can the techniques by which garments are designed, planned, cut and constructed inform surgical practice?

BACKGROUND

There has long been preoccupation with the boundaries that exist between skin and cloth. Striking visual representations of this relationship can be traced to the late Renaissance period and Andreas Versalius's graphic ana-tomical documentations in his text *Fabrica—De Humani de Corporis* (Connor 2004: 14–15). Here flayed ecorches[4] appear animated, peeling one's own skin as if removing clothing from the body.

In contemporary cultures artists have continued to share this curiosity in exploring and presenting notions of identity through metaphorical repre-sentations of the body and dress. The work of French artist Orlan (Hauser 2008: 83–89) for example brutally depicts this correlation through the continual reinvention of self and identity in performative plastic surgery transformations.

Innovations in textiles technologies have been developed in recent years by studying the materiality of skin. Works such as that of Oron Catt's *Victim-less Leather* (Senior 2008: 76–82), promoting the culturing of skin cells within a laboratory environment to grow bespoke seamless garments from one's own skin and the creation at the University of Manchester of a machine that can print living skin cells onto a substrate to be harvested for skin grafts (Camber 2005), have evolved our thinking around the potential outputs cre-ated in extending this line of enquiry.

In the context of fashion, themes of plastic surgery and changes in body shape have begun to be explored by contemporary designers, including Marios Schwab (Gregory 2011) and Shelley Fox (2008). In these settings, the science of surgery and anatomy have informed the concepts of the garments and the cuts and aesthetic outcomes of designs. Fox's creations for her Fat Map collection 2008 for example explore how patterns of clothing change as garments are altered for different-sized bodies. This was achieved using MRI scanners to monitor changes in the internal and external body fat of six vol-unteers under a controlled exercise and dietary regime.

The work of Paddy Hartley is also pertinent in transferring knowledge across these disciplines to combine surgical technique with the crafting of fashion objects. Inspired by his earlier research in uncovering the identities of injured servicemen from the First and Second World Wars, Hartley now applies tech-niques of facial reconstruction (taken from pioneering plastic surgeon Harold Gillies)[5] to create decorative face masks to be worn by style icons such as Lady Gaga. Here the craft of surgery has been translated directly into cloth, resulting in 'second skin' facial adornments. In this setting, it is the surgical cut followed by the manipulation of the cloth that has informed the overall de-sign and outcome of these bespoke products.

It is important at this stage to acknowledge the role that material has to play in the construction techniques in both surgical and pattern-cutting practices, as the former inherently informs the latter. We begin by document-ing material qualities. How does the make up of skin and cloth impact on 'procedures'?

COMMONALITIES—MATERIALS AND MATERIALITY

Grain—Physical Qualities

As the grain of cloth must be considered during garment design and construction—to achieve a variation in drape, a good fit and desirable aesthetic—so too must the grain of skin be considered during surgical procedures.

In textile practice, the grain of the majority of fabrics is relatively consistent and is dictated by its method of production, whether this be woven, knitted, crocheted or knotted. The way in which this cloth is then cut in accordance to the garment pattern and selvedge edge[6] (straight grain,[7] cross grain,[8] on the bias[9]) will dictate how the fabric will drape, ultimately informing the overall style and aesthetic of the garment. The direction in which the grain travels across a cloth may vary between pattern pieces, and potentially cloth may be cut on a number of grains. This direction may also vary dependent on where they feature on the body.

Skin similarly mimics this grain in the multidirectional layout of collagen fibres across its surface. The ways in which these fibres align themselves creates lines of cleavage that are characteristic of their respective limb. Named after the anatomist whom discovered them, they are known by surgeons as Langer's lines.

Langer's observations have allowed plastic surgeons to understand the variation in directional grain of the skin. This has informed surgical practice in guiding the direction in which an elective incision must be made during a procedure. Generally a surgical cut will be carried out following their direction, as incisions made parallel to these linear pathways heal better and produce less scarring. Incisions that run counter tend to gape and tear more so (Langer 1978: 3–8).

SURFACE—AESTHETIC QUALITIES

In addition to considering the direction in which the grain of skin is traveling, skin quality must also be addressed by the surgeons, with regards to its age, thickness and its coloration. Hair also is another factor to contend with, ensuring that the direction of growth is maintained once sections of skin have been transposed. There is much variation in each of the qualities mentioned above, across the body surface, and from patient to patient. Great care must therefore be taken to match skin qualities particularly when grafting or transposing skin.

Variations in skin quality by no means rival the variation of cloth that is available to the pattern cutter and fashion designer, though similar considerations must be adhered to in this context. The consistency of a printed or woven surface pattern for example may need to be continued and matched across the garment, despite multiple cuts and pattern components. Also the pile[10] or sheen of a cloth in offering different colour variations and aesthetic qualities can dictate the direction in which light falls upon the garment. Close consideration must be made of these elements during cutting and construction processes to dictate how they feature upon a garment. To maximize or minimize such characteristics tends to be the decision of the pattern cutter and designer together and is fundamental in informing the style of the garment.

It is important to note the role that taste and style have to play in relation to the designing of fashion. When developing garments it is common for the 'voice' of the designer to be expressed through the design of dress. This may be achieved through the selection of cloth and colour and the combinations in which it is cut and featured on the body.

Personalization of materials promotes much variation within this field, with garments reflecting a designer or a brand. Both may be subtly or extremely dependent on which specialism the designer is creating for. Couture fashion perhaps could be viewed as an accentuation of the human body, with tailoring a more formal and less obvious enhancement of oneself.

By outlining the qualities of the corresponding materials of each trade, we begin to see how their inherent properties inform the assemblage and manipulation of 'cloth' within the professions. We must now look to the techniques and processes utilized by each to plan and construct, delving further into their correlations.

COMMONALITIES—TECHNIQUE

Planning

In their preparatory stages, both plastic surgery and pattern-cutting for fashion require bespoke planning to proceed with their product or outcome. In couture trades, particularly, several fittings will be made upon a client or live model and a toile[11] or several will be constructed to obtain the perfect fit (Fischer 2009: 58–9), the alterations being carefully marked onto the fabric.

In reconstructive surgery, procedures also can consist of several consultations and perhaps even several operating stages, dependent on the complexity of the operation.

Generally, a plastic surgeon will plan for a procedure by marking out the areas of incision using a pen. The lines marked onto the body provide a useful guide for the operation as the tension of the skin alters once initial incisions have been made. Variations upon technique are specific to each plastic surgeon. The design of a procedure will also be informed by shared knowledge from within their respective field, inspired by pioneering works conducted by colleagues. These may be modified by the individual surgeon to suit their patients physique or requirements.

As a fashion designer can become recognized for a trademark style of dress, plastic surgeons may too become known for a style or specialist procedure. The design and/or craftsmanship of their work can also be recognized, commended, shared and potentially adopted both nationally and internationally by other practicing surgeons. With reference to pattern cutters utilizing toiles to plan garment construction, surgeons throughout history have similarly used simplistic models as a means of planning procedures.

The following stages of this chapter will now look to examples to highlight how knowledge of making and craft techniques has begun to be shared across disciplines.

GEOMETRY—THE OPENING AND CLOSING OF ANGLES

A technical consideration that is followed in each of these professions is the use of geometry, in particular the opening and closing of angles as a means of throwing fullness or achieving body-contoured outcomes (Fischer 2009: 30–31). In fashion, this takes the form of darts,[12] pivots, pleats and gathers and in surgery, the manipulation of flaps of skin through the approximation of operative wound edges—creating or abolishing standing and lying cones[13] (Limberg 1984: 13).

In a surgical context, fullness can be both desirable and undesirable in its placement or application, in the former setting, in the reconstruction of a nose, in the latter, in reducing gathers of excess skin that form upon the body surface. This can be controlled by carefully planning the size of the angles of incisions prior to the surgical procedure or through the excision of excess tissue which will permit the conical gatherings (standing cones) to lie flat (Papel et al. 2009: 30).

Fashion mimics these aesthetic and constructive considerations in creating structured areas of a garment that can alter and enhance the silhouette of the body, offering shape and volume through such techniques and cosmetically in managing or accommodating undesirable defects, such as an anomaly in posture or weight, by creating a balanced physique through the tailoring of dress. Could the introduction of padding, interlining, corsetry and quilting be considered the prosthetic implants of the fashion world?

TEXTILES FOR PLANNING—HAROLD GILLIES

The pioneering work of surgeon Harold Gillies (1882–1960) prominently references skin as cloth in his documentation and planning of reconstructive procedures. Here cloth patterns were used to calculate the surface area of skin required to repair the damaged faces of First World War soldiers (Hartley 2005).

MODELS FOR PLANNING—ALEXANDER LIMBERG

Towards the middle of the twentieth century, Russian surgeon A.A. Limberg focused much of his work upon the design of pedicle skin flaps, again using fabric and paper models as a means of calculating and planning procedures on the surface of the face and body (Limberg 1984). Unlike many of his predecessors, Limberg studied the body surface geometrically (as opposed to topographically) and was innovative in developing complex mathematical indexes to plan procedures. These strategies would then be simplified and placed into practice through the use of moving origami models constructed from linen, rubber, tin, plywood and paper. They would communicate how the skin would respond during surgical operations once it had been incised, transposed and stitched. As expected, some materials were more representative of skin characteristics than others; however, during this period, paper was the material of choice solely due to its abundance and cheapness in training surgeons. Paper however only yielded crude exaggerations of procedures to be performed.

GARMENTS FOR PLANNING—R.J. WISE

A reference that poetically draws these two specialisms together, which has been catalytic in the conception of the sKINship project, is the work of surgeon R.J. Wise. Here the patterns of undergarments were used to directly inform both the planning and undertaking of surgical technique. The Wise 'skin' pattern, developed in the 1950s, is a system used to plan breast reduction surgery (reduction mammoplasty). Its inspiration was drawn from the units of a brassier pattern and the corresponding size index associated with breast size (32A, B, C). Consisting of three key components that were used to mark out and manipulate the breast, this technique revolutionised this method of breast surgery and continues to be practiced in medicine today (Wise 1956). We begin to see a direct correlation between the processes of pattern cutting and plastic surgery and how one can begin to inform the other.

FASHION SURGERY

To test the value of applying surgical technique to fashion-based disciplines, the sKINship research project has sought to obtain practice-based evidence in understanding how surgical cutting and construction techniques can be applied to the cut and construction of garments today. How can new modes of cutting cloth for fashion (using surgical technique) inform new styles and shapes of garments? This has involved a direct collaboration between me and innovative pattern cutter Paul Rider. A handful of simplistic surgical procedures from A. A. Limberg (Limberg 1984) were scaled up, cut into cloth, manipulated to mimic the movement of skin during a surgical procedure and then freely draped upon a dress stand, aiming to develop interesting neck-lines and garment styles.

Findings from these exercises suggest that there would be great potential in promoting more focused collaborations between practitioners from each field, perhaps based more specifically upon the region of the body that practitioners may specialize in. Potential future collaborations will look to pair a surgeon specializing in breast surgery with a cutter for body contour[14] garments, a hand surgeon with a glove maker, a milliner with a craniofacial surgeon. This will be developed as the next stages of the sKINship program.

CONCLUSION

To date, the sKINship project has recognized and developed an openness to collaboration amongst professionals from both plastic surgery and pattern-cutting specialisms. More specifically, findings from a national survey conducted by the project in 2010 have shown that plastic surgeons are more open to collaboration than pattern cutters, with a higher percentage of these practitioners already looking broadly to fashion and textile-based knowledge to inform their discipline. This chapter has also illustrated a prevalence in existing applications of the language of pattern cutting to plastic surgery techniques, the transfer of this knowledge is more direct in its application than knowledge exchange in the opposing direction.

It is evident through the research that it is the *planning* of surgical procedures that has been informed by the use of garment patterns and the *design* of clothing and their pattern components that has been developed by surgical cutting and construction technique. This collaborative process has also served to inform the education and communication of subject-specific knowledge within and across disciplines, at the same time attempting to remove hierarchical professional barriers.

The language of making has transcended the technical terminologies sometimes associated with these professions. It has also provided an access point to the project and to these specialisms for a wider audience, challenging our perceptions of the relationship between skin and cloth, the body and dress, craft and science. Could this new knowledge perhaps, in the future, inform patient care in developing techniques of communication between surgeon and patient?

It is important to consider collaboration in the context of quality of 'making'—a 'good mend'. During this project, I have become aware of just how inter-related function and form are in these professions. In both settings, one must comply with anatomy—regardless of whether that means respecting blood supply, structure, surface and form. But what about the aesthetic considerations? Could craft techniques be used to inform further the quality of making skills in plastic surgery—to create an even better mend, to enhance aesthetics in addition to functionality? A key challenge that occurs frequently in plastic surgery is the difference in opinion of aesthetic outcomes, the visual expectations of a patient not always being met by surgical endeavour. Could the project help to align these factors? Or is this purely a symptom of differing taste?

Fundamental factors that have contributed to the success of this program to date have resulted from 'good' collaboration. The ability of professionals to be open, to share knowledge, to take risks, and to trust in other practitioners has been paramount. Although the abundance of research conducted on this topic suggests a strong correlation between the craft of pattern cutting and plastic surgery, there still remains a large amount of territory to explore. This line of enquiry will continue in more depth in the following stages of the sKINship project.

NOTES

1. For the purpose of this study, the terminology 'pattern cutting within fashion' or 'fashion professions' refers to the use of patterns in the following disciplines—menswear, womenswear, bespoke tailoring, millinery and cordwaining—which utilize a variation of patterns across their practices.
2. An artisan who practices a handicraft or trade.
3. sKINship—a professional forum and research program that seeks to promote cross-disciplinary collaborations between art and science, <www.skinship.co.uk> accessed 18 March 2013.
4. The term 'ecorche' means flayed and refers to anatomical figures depicted in drawings and sculpture showing muscle without skin.
5. Harold Gillies is a key pioneer of modern plastic surgery as we know it today. His practice in repairing the damaged faces of injured service members during the First World War inspired the recognition of plastic surgery as a specialist medical profession in its own right.
6. Selvedge edge is the edge of a fabric that will not fray or unravel, which is resultant of how a fabric is constructed.
7. Straight grain is made up of threads that run parallel to the selvedge edge. The grain line of pattern pieces to be cut with a straight grain will be arranged parallel to the selvedge.
8. Cross grain is made up of threads that run perpendicular to the selvedge edge. The grain line of pattern pieces to be cut cross ways will be arranged at a 90-degree angle to the selvedge.

9. Bias—The diagonal direction along the fabric which has stretch. The grain line of pattern pieces to be cut along the bias will be arranged at a 45-degree angle to the selvedge and cross grain.

10. In textiles, pile is the raised surface or nap of a fabric, which is made of upright loops or strands of yarn. Examples of pile textiles are carpets, corduroy and velvet. The word is derived from the Latin *pilus* (hair).

11. A toile is a version of a garment made by a fashion designer or dress-maker to test a pattern. They are usually made in cheap material, as multiple toiles may be made in the process of perfecting a design.

12. Darts are folds sewn into fabric to help provide a three-dimensional shape to a garment.

13. Standing and lying cones are gathers of skin that occur during surgical procedures when two edges of an operative wound are brought together or approximated. The closure of angles during operations results in what are commonly referred to by surgeons as 'dog ears', excess flaps of skin.

14. Body-contour pattern cutting refers to the cut and construct of underwear and swimwear garments, including corsetry, bras, knickers and swim-suits—designs that cling to the contour of the body.

REFERENCES

Camber, R. (2005), 'Tailor Made Skin from Ink Printer', *Manchester Evening News*, <http://menmedia.co.uk/manchestereveningnews/news/s/143230_tailormade_skin_from_ink_printer> accessed 23 March 2012.

Connor, S. (2004), *The Book of Skin*, London: Reaktion Books.

Fischer, A. (2009), *Basics—Fashion Design—Construction*, Lausanne: AVA Publishing SA.

Gregory, L. (2011), 'Marios Schwab: Designer, Artist, Genius', *Palatinate* (31 January), <http://www.palatinate.org.uk/?p=9869> accessed 23 March 2012.

Hartley, P. (2005), *Project Façade*, <http://www.projectfacade.com/index.php?/news/comments/gillies_pattern_making/> accessed 12 April 2012.

Hauser, J. (2008), *Sk-interfaces,* Liverpool: Liverpool University Press.

Langer, K. (1978), 'On the Anatomy and Physiology of the Skin: The Cleavability of the Cutis', *British Journal of Plastic Surgery*, 31/1: 3–8.

Limberg, A. A. (1963), *The Planning Plastic Operations on the Body Surface: Theory and Practice*, trans. A. Wolfe, Lexington, MA: D. C. Heath.

Papel, I. D., Frodel, J. L., Holt, G. R., Larrabee, W. F., Nachlas, N. E., and Park, S. S. (2009), *Facial, Plastic and Reconstructive Surgery*, 3rd edn, New York: Thieme Medical Publisher.

Senior, A. (2008), 'In the Face of the Victim: Confronting the Other in the Tissue Culture and Art Project Sk-interfaces', in J. Hauser (ed.), *Sk-interfaces*, Liverpool: Liverpool University Press.

Von Glasow, K. (2008), *Nobel Textiles, Shelley Fox and Peter Mansfield*, <http://www.cultureunplugged.com/play/5742/Nobel-Textiles--Shelley-Fox-and-Peter-Mansfield> accessed 17 March 2013.

Wise, R. J. (1956), 'Plastic and Reconstructive Surgery: A Preliminary Report of a Method of Planning the Mammaplasty', *Journal of the American Society of Plastic Surgeons*, 17: 367.

PART III

INSTITUTIONAL COLLABORATIONS

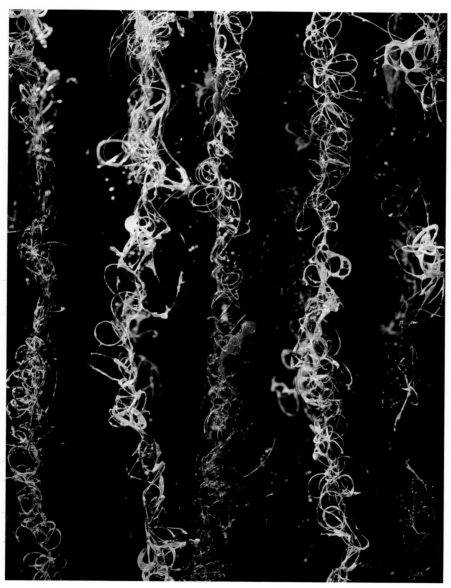

Plate 1 *Untitled* (detail). 2004. Machiko Agano and Anniken Amundsen. Commissioned for *Through the Surface*. Materials: Fishing Line, Paper Yarn, Paper Pulp. Photograph: Toshiharu Kawabe

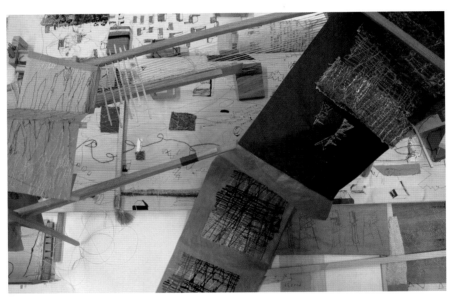

Plate 2 *Pairing*s exhibition, Triangulation Theory collection. 2010. Gates, Kettle, Webb. Materials: Wood, thread, linen, cotton cloth, paper, ink. Photograph: David Gates

Plate 3 *The Myth of Origins, Proteiform 3.* 2008. Brass Art. Watercolour 40.6 x 30.5 cm (unframed). Photograph: Brass Art

Plate 4 'Child's own tutor' alphabet fan, made in England, c. 1920. Courtesy The Mary Greg Collection of Handicrafts of Bygone Times, Manchester City Galleries. Accession number: 1922.453b. Photograph: Ben Blackhall

Plate 5 Ceramic flower bicycle, Ahmedabad, India, 2011. Photograph: Stephen Dixon

Plate 6 Sara leading, day 7; John listening, day 7. Rebuilding Mayfield. 2010. Photograph: Charles Roderick

Plate 7 *The Muster (Troops Drilling at Fort Jay)*. 14 May 2005. Allison Smith. A project of Public Art Fund. Photograph: Amy Elliott

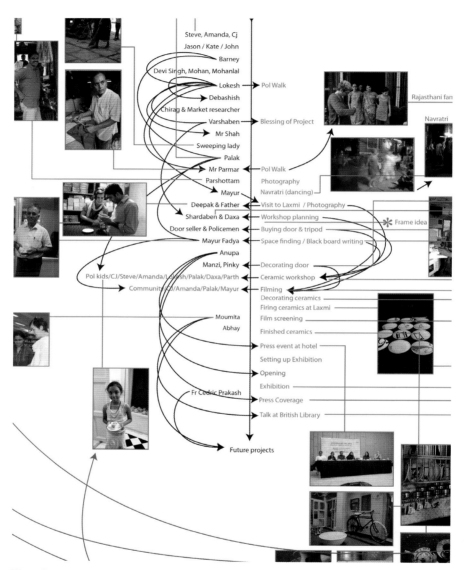

Plate 8 Diagram of connections between people, events, objects and place during The Pol Project (2010). Courtesy Cj O'Neill and Amanda Ravetz

Introduction

Helen Felcey, Alice Kettle and Amanda Ravetz

In this section we gain insight into collaborations across institutions where craft is taught, learnt and made visible either as a distinct entity or as a presence in related disciplines. The institutions are evoked by the authors as communities of practice and sites of debate and discourse, with possibilities for collaboration and friction. The proposition of this section is of craft at the interstices of institutions, to be found in the cracks in the walls, corridors and towers. The chapters negotiate existing frameworks and territories, reflecting on the shift from 'the crafts' to craft as a movement with imaginative potential and plateaux of engagement across horizontal plains and vertical geologies. Knott describes craft as a discomforting tool for collaboration; Hawkins and Wilson develop cross-disciplinary craft/art/science conversations; in Taylor and Payne's view, life skills are learnt through making; whilst Mitchell and Blakey's clashing of craft cultures is found to change institutional perceptions. The desire of all is to reclaim the power of skills and connected thinking where craft is not separated out as a distinctive field and thus to shake foundational attitudes.

Institutions are usually hierarchical structures and by dint of being established bring to mind something permanent, characterized by their physical manifestations and inhabited by members, artists, teachers, curators and all they do. The occupation of craft in these spaces is identified through the programmes of making, the paraphernalia of tools and of protocols. The rules of navigation and preservation are currently filled with the conflict of what to keep and how to look forward with a shared vision. In *On Craftsmanship*, Frayling describes an imagined future world of integrated practice constructed by students which is entrepreneurial and improvisatory and where products and services seem to be blending together (2011: 135).

These chapters all describe 'ground up' initiatives to change perceptions of craft and value whether directly or tangentially deliberate. Each highlights and explores new models and ways of working which subvert territories—often through simply trespassing, opening a door, sharing a tool, making visible the forgotten within collections, within institutions and within pedagogy.

The chapters describe craft utilized for provocation. Craft here is understood as an irritant, a different way in which to inhabit spaces and to think.

In Department 21 at the RCA students defiantly reconstruct studio spaces, subvert teaching programmes in a campaign for the 'liberation from departmental syllabuses and their tight, pedagogic structures' (Knott). Craft emerges as a liberating tool where it has not been explicitly intended. Both Mitchell and Blakey and Taylor and Payne describe 'making' as a tacit experience with all the challenges this carries of implicit knowledge—the personal, intuitive unspoken language. They describe informal learning spaces for the acquisition of skill and learning through example and by handling objects, which shifts educational and museum hierarchies and classroom layouts to apprenticeship studio models. This serves 'to encourage different thinking about intelligent craft production and how this can be translated into effective classroom pedagogy' (Taylor and Payne, this volume). Project Dialogue, described by Hawkins and Wilson, aims to create open spaces without specific intention or direction through a methodology of a space to play, to negotiate, to enquire and to craft. The authors regard this as 'space for reflection and collaboration in which students can experience a broader perspective on their studies'.

As we have seen in other sections, there is an underlying theme of loss with a nostalgia for the forgotten connections and methods that craft historically possessed. Taylor and Payne seek to rethink the relevance of lost skills to the current constituency of technologically engaged younger generations. They perform an archaeology of practical skill which can be pulled into the present with a new use for the future. Even Knott, wedded to craft as discomfort, sees traditionally acquired craft skills and tools employed as agents for change that reevaluate their function and purpose. Sitting alongside is the issue of preservation and conservation; Blakey and Mitchell highlight the paradoxical nature of material preservation and value posed through the Mary Greg Collection.

'Expertise' and the role of the expert, whilst assuming different complexions, is discussed by the contributors in terms of skill, competency, quality, refinement, the well made and perceptions of value. Rather than increasing mastery, Department 21 raises questions about what we both can and cannot do as individuals and collaborators with and without the sharing of skill; craft assumes a very different role here from its moral antecedent. The skill of the bricoleur (aligned to Department 21 by Knott) who adopts items for construction which happen to be available, acting in a resourceful and spontaneous manner, is subtly different from that of the 10,000 hours of the craftsperson implied in Taylor and Payne's The Making. However, the value of crafting skills evidenced in The Making and in Blakey and Mitchell's description of craft as fundamental to the understanding of the Mary Greg Collection also rests on achieving some form of 'informed spontaneity', not in the sense of working rapidly, but 'working knowledgeably and fluently' (Dormer 1994, quoted in Taylor and Payne) or as 'rummage [which] could be an intrinsically creative and serious act' (Blakey and Mitchell). We arrive at a form of expertise we might call 'informed spontaneity'—combined insight and intuition—arguably pure expertise. The process involves risk, the courage to embrace failure, to un-make and re-make, combined with the lightness of play. The 'contemplative space' described by Hawkins and Wilson, the 'free-space of Department 21, the 'off-radar' investigation of the Mary Greg Collection, are driven by significant national and human causes—and the instigators seek to effect positive change.

These chapters indicate that collaborations through craft are rich ground for exploring substantial research issues—and we are challenged to recognize the essential roles of 'craft' and 'collaboration' in this process. Collaboration reminds us that we do not operate independently and that craft can bring about cooperation and the fusing of disciplines. Interdependent cooperation is the professed aim of institutions, and in attempting to understand craft as intrinsic to this process, it is identified as sociable and able to navigate through and between territories of practice and modes of teaching. No wonder we grapple with the provinces of craft and seek to redefine its borders through collaboration with alternative theories and flexibility of frame and law. Could it be that it is in the context of institutions that the shifting definitions of craft we are currently seeing offer the best chance to move from 'the space of places to the space of flows' (Frayling 2011: 133)?

REFERENCES

Frayling, C. (2011), *On Craftsmanship*, London: Oberon Masters.

–9–

Department 21: The Craft of Discomfort

Stephen Knott

BEGINNINGS

It started with a portable desk and a box of oranges at a work-in-progress show at the Royal College of Art (RCA) in autumn 2009. It was from this platform that Department 21[1] first announced a plan to set up a radical, interdisciplinary workspace. Bianca Elzenbaumer and Fabio Franz—students from the communication, art and design department—were the chief protagonists, and along with their collaborators, carted the desk and oranges between the different sites of the RCA. They presented an invitation to students to join them in occupying a floor of the Stevens Building in January 2010 that was temporarily vacant after the relocation of the painting department (Figure 9.1).

In the first term of his post, the new rector of the RCA, Dr Paul Thompson, was willing to engage with the team of students led by Elzenbaumer and Franz, who valiantly persuaded the college authorities to give the project the green light. The students wanted something different: liberation from departmental syllabuses and their tight, pedagogic structures. As stated in the Department 21 book, published in June 2010: 'We wanted to create a challenging, inclusive, radical and productive environment which might steer the Royal College of Art towards new models of education' (Elzenbaumer, Franz and Hunter 2010: 1).

With funds secured from the college authorities,[2] students took over the space for six weeks and put together a wide-ranging programme involving roundtable discussions, workshops, film screenings, performances, lectures and social gatherings. After residency of the Stevens Building expired, Department 21 contributors continued to work together throughout the spring of 2010, most notably on a multi-authored collaborative publication, and the college acknowledged the momentum Department 21 had generated by handing over an internal courtyard space for the project during the RCA Graduate Show in June–July 2010. Fitted out with wooden decking, Department 21 ran a series of well-attended events during the show that demonstrated a broad enthusiasm for working across departments. The college responded to this widespread support for a communal, interdisciplinary space by granting the

Fig. 9.1. The vacated painting studios. January 2010. Stevens Building, Royal College of Art. Photograph: Stephen Knott. Courtesy Department 21

project a permanent workstation in the renovated Stevens Building from September 2010 to February 2012.[3]

I was in the second year of an AHRC-funded collaborative PhD[4] when I attended Department 21's first open roundtable discussion. Again, there were oranges, with blue '21' labels stuck on where the 'Del Monte' stickers should have been. The scent of citrus hung in the air as a panel of four speakers (including artist Richard Wentworth and architectural theorist Celine Condorelli) expressed their thoughts about interdisciplinarity with a vocal student audience.

At this early stage, two things were clear: the phonetic nightmare of using the word 'interdisciplinarity' in a roundtable reflected the many problems that people generally had with the term; and there was a conspicuous absence of any proposals about what sorts of activity would take place in the space and what the participants would actually do.

A COLLABORATION WITHOUT CRAFT?

Department 21 was never meant to be a collaboration through craft. The 'c' word was not mentioned in preliminary meetings nor discussed in any great detail throughout the project. Its stated aims were pedagogical: to provide an alternative space of independent learning free from departmental constraints, with a parasitical relationship to the college, dependent on its structures yet offering students some form of temporal and spatial reprieve (Elzenbaumer et al. 2010: 12–13). However, the emphasis on creating a neutral space within the college's structures unavoidably raised the question of what would be made to fill it and what skills would be exercised, learnt and exchanged in this process? It emerged that self-directed learning compelled participants to face up to the limitations and potential of their own skills in a collaborative environment.

Although hardly intended, Department 21 highlighted the unusual position (and problem) of craft within current paradigms of artistic education. Craft, in this context, is understood according to Glenn Adamson's criteria, not as a discrete set of disciplines but as 'a way of thinking through practices of all kinds' (Adamson 2007: 7). In this instance, craft encourages us to consider the position of material skill and production within models of art and design education, collaborative and otherwise.

A reading of Department 21 as a collaboration without craft would be consistent with the idea that post-studio art practice is divorced from actual making, an example of Nicolas Bourriaud's concept of 'relational aesthetics' par excellence. This describes a situation whereby production is subservient to the idea that art is experienced as an encounter, 'its theoretical horizon the realm of human interactions and its social context, rather than the assertion of an independent and *private* space' (Bourriaud 2002: 14). Bourriaud cites the artists Felix Gonzalez-Torres and Rirkrit Tiravanija as exemplifying this approach in which the gallery-goer is invited to participate in the work, taking away sweets from an unguarded pile in a collective elegy to a friend who died from AIDS-related illnesses, in the case of the former (*Portrait of Ross*, 1991) or in the latter, converting gallery spaces into kitchens and offering food to passers-by. If these artists, and many more besides,[5] seem to be prioritizing art as a social encounter or a performance in a discrete spatial-temporal moment, then Department 21 could be seen as doing the same for art and design education.

The number of events Department 21 hosted—from regular-themed dinner parties to film events, roundtable discussions and performances—suggests that the social experience of being there was more important than making anything. The budget for food and drink accounted for more than 50 per cent of expenditure (Elzenbaumer et al. 2010: 27–29), outweighing material costs and giving the sense that the project was an extension of the canteen or bar. Without obligation to exercise their skills,[6] each student, like each viewer-participant in an installation by Gonzalez-Torres or Tiravanija, made sense of Department 21 in his or her own way, and often this encouraged a model of collaboration through socializing in which craft was absent.

Critical to Bourriaud's notion of relational aesthetics, however, is the importance of subjective interaction with 'other territories it comes across as an evolving formation' (Bourriaud 2002: 91). In other words, interaction with otherness is both critical to the artist's engagement with a gallery audience and can be applied to the model of collaborative learning advocated by Department 21. The forms of social occasion were not 'other' enough for an audience of art and design students who knew how to behave in these settings.[7] But a far greater sense of the collision of 'other territories' became evident when participants were invited to bring their skills to the table to contribute to developing collaborative projects. Without the regimented structures familiar to programmes and project briefs occurring within each department, making and generating output in Department 21 followed an unusual trajectory, bringing to light particular manifestations increasingly prevalent within the art school environment. These include the importance of bricolage, recognizing the limitation of individual authorship and using craft as a strategy of discomfort, which I explore in more detail below.

BRICOLAGE

Craft in Department 21 was not characterized by the quasi-spiritual symbiosis of head and hand celebrated in Richard Sennett's philosophy of pragmatism (Sennett 2007). Neither were there courses in which students mastered a specific skill and subjected processes of learning to theoretical investigation in the style of Peter Dormer's calligraphy and sculpture tuition, as recalled in *The Art of the Maker* (Dormer 1994). Instead, craft in Department 21 was largely demonstrated when readily available tools and material were deployed in the spirit of Claude Levi-Strauss's bricoleur (Levi-Strauss 1975: 17). The bricoleur, in this context, realizes the limitations to individual skill and the inherent reliance on the hands of other labourers when making, yet continues to demonstrate individual skill within these constraints.

There were many moments during Department 21 in which collaborative objects were made, satisfying Roland Barthes's definition of interdisciplinarity, not as the gathering together of two or three sciences around a common theme but involving the creation of 'a new object that belongs to no-one' (Barthes 1986: 56). The Web site, the presence at the RCA graduate show and the publication effectively communicated the project's pedagogic and critical message and reflected the tremendous amount of work by Franz and Elzenbaumer in particular. However, collaboration was most palpable when it was materially manifest through objects, when students from different backgrounds exercised their skill sets to make objects that no one owned.

The mentality of the bricoleur was essential to Department 21 due to the limited budget: there was no possibility of buying furniture or materials. Participants made sure that all the excess material from the painting studio's deconstruction was kept and the large chipboard panels that previously compartmentalized the space into individual studios were particularly useful. These panels were made into tables for the workspace, a transformation of a 'separating element into a connecting element' according to Franz (2009), a neat encapsulation of the project's desire to break down departmental architectures that fostered isolation.

These scraps of wood, plastic, and 2 × 2 timber strips—all remnants of the room's former function—were deliberately organized into piles. This was part of Department 21's plan for the opening night entitled *Take a Seat* held on 12 January 2010, where instead of only mingling and drinking bottled beer, attendees were invited to contribute to the project by making chairs and benches (Figure 9.2). This was an example of the 'super handmade' nature of the collaborative project,[8] adding to the furniture that had already been built from the former studio walls. Department 21 needed seats and only through this mobilization of opening-party labour was the project able to get off the ground.[9] The electric drill was in constant demand on the night, and by the early hours, the scraps of wood had been turned into a haphazard array of chair designs, from simple wooden benches to chairs firmly entrenched in the Reitveld tradition.

These chairs were used throughout the six-week residency and then later became a prominent feature of Department 21's presence at the RCA graduate show. The chairs were piled up in a huge tower and put on sale to the public. I was in the space when a man had decided to buy the chair that I had made. I wondered why anyone would want to buy this scrappy, simply made chair, fabricated with various bits of wood and brass screws. I realized at this moment that this chair had never belonged to me: I had merely put together the different parts prepared into piles by the various participants of Department 21. My own authorship and (limited) craft skill were amalgamated into the collaborative venture as the chair's entire value, and meaning was predicated on the existence of Department 21. This loss of autonomous authorship within the collaborative project alerted me to a definition of craft that was radically nonindividualistic and not related to my own skill. Individual

Fig. 9.2. Department 21 chairs made during the opening of *Take a Seat in Department 21*. Stevens Building, Royal College of Art. January 2010. Photograph: Stephen Knott

expression was limited within this model of collaborative authorship, but it also provided a context in which alternative forms of production could flourish, as I mention in relation to 'collective silliness' below.

There were many other moments during Department 21's tenure of the Stevens Building where collaborative craft was manifest through bricolage. In the first workshop held in the space, goldsmithing, silversmithing, metalwork and jewellery students invited participants, drawn from the college's different departments, to form small groups and make something for a dinner party. There was hardly anything revolutionary about the contraption for dispensing wine, the trays for serving slices of pizza and crisps, and a poorly made dolly that was meant to carry food from one part of the table to the other. As a participant, I felt there was no arch-critique, no manifesto, just a bunch of students from an art college making inconsequential stuff. Moreover, making with what was to hand was easy within the art college environment, with the abundance of available tools and materials and the bottomless resources of a constantly replenished skip.[10] However, this collaborative labour reminded each contributor of his or her own skills and the resources of the environment around them. Scampering around the college was like an orienteering lesson, a portal into the different departmental spaces of the college that usually remain behind swipe card entry systems that regulate access.

This freedom from departmental structures allowed students to engage in 'collective silliness'. Collaboration meant output did not belong to any individual but a team, meaning that the competitive environment that usually surrounds any response to a brief or a challenge could be sacrificed in favour of play: the output could belong to no one and meet Barthes's criteria for the interdisciplinary object. The quickly made dinner-party accessories would not be added to any portfolio of works and offered participants in the workshop a bit of breathing space from trajectories of professionalization and single authorship that increasingly define postgraduate art and design education. Department 21's play had similarities to the work of Swedish craft collective We Work In A Fragile Material (WWIAFM), a group of practitioners who studied at Stockholm's College of Art and Design who periodically gather together to create collaborative work that departs from each member's specialism. Like making things for dinner parties, WWIAFM's projects are silly—ranging from playing paintball within a giant three-dimensional game, building a messy, papier-mâché structure in a South Kensington gallery and imitating Kylie Minogue's music video entitled *Slow* on an art studio floor (Adamson 2009: 61). Department 21 similarly offered the space to make things outside the rigour of departmental specialism, an increasingly popular form of diversion for artists seeking postdisciplinary solutions to overspecialization.

Craft in Department 21 also provided a way of understanding both the limitations to individual skill and the reliance in artistic production on the labour of others. Throughout the various guises of Department 21 workshops have played a key role—from creating animations[11] to open-source publishing. During my time in the Stevens Building I attended both a ceramics workshop and a session on how to make the most out of the blog publishing platform WordPress. On both occasions I was very aware of my own skill limitations: with clay I proved unable to make pinch pots without punching a hole in the bottom with an overenthusiastic thumb;[12] with the WordPress lesson, I quickly was unable to follow the complex HTML code that allows you to personalize the design. In both of these workshops, I engaged in a series of failed productions, yet it still constituted a form of learning: a form of reversed pedagogy through the realization of what you cannot do, helping to foster a greater appreciation of skill when you do encounter it.

CRAFT OF DISCOMFORT

This optimistic assessment of craft's valorizing role in Department 21—as awakening the spirit of the adaptive and responsive bricoleur, freeing practice under the umbrella of collaboration, and as way of understanding the limitations of individual skill and respecting the skill of others—does overlook one key tension. Collaborative labour within the context of the art school is largely comfortable, for despite the diversity of students from different departments, each with their own particular culture, most have a level of pre-education (art foundation courses for example) and picking up a spanner when you are used to scissors and thread is not much of a jump compared with the fear of tools a beginner faces when commencing his first do-it-yourself project. There is also widespread familiarity with relational aesthetics as mentioned above, so in a sense the project stayed on safe ground.

Craft could have been deployed more obviously as a strategy of discomfort. In the first roundtable discussion, an idea about interdisciplinarity emerged on this theme, based on encouraging awkward scenarios: Wentworth stressing the educational vitality of vulnerability and 'walking backwards' and Condorelli attracted by enforcing discomfort, stating, 'We can continue talking about the already known for the rest of our lives [. . .] and nothing expands' (Condorelli and Wentworth 2009). As argued above, the question as to what constitutes artistic skill was an unexpected issue that resulted from Department 21's activities, yet these aspects could have been further accentuated by enforcing an 'unknown' situation: intentionally asking participants to work with unfamiliar tools and materials. Denying participants access to the tools of their craft would have compelled the practitioner to more acutely consider the skills inherent to his or her discipline, encourage empathy for the abilities of other labourers and show the limitations of individual abilities, as well as encourage a more explicit exercise of the attributes of the bricoleur.

During the first weeks of Department 21, there *was* an initial sense of this tool de-territorialization: a discomfort through craft. Participants stood before a vacant floor with nothing but chipboard and timber leftovers. However, free to do whatever they wanted with the space and under no constraint from Department 21 organizers, students established their own workstations and brought in their tools. The absence of stipulations that was key to the openness and inclusiveness of Department 21 meant that the project became more of an extension or displacement of studio practice in a slightly refracted realm, rather than a terrain of unknowing. I brought in my laptop, and I was instantly comfortable.

Nevertheless, I pursued this idea of imposing a different tool order by handing out thirty paint-by-number kits to Department 21 participants with the instruction that they fill out the painting (of Times Square) with the tools enclosed. I initially wanted the project to be Department 21–focused, but many of the students could not commit to finishing the painting, so I started to give kits to other researchers, friends and family. Admittedly, giving a paint-by-number kit to an art student with its over-didactic grid, poor-quality paint and a stick-thin paintbrush that only allows limited control over the composition, was not the most exciting brief: you need an extraordinary degree of patience if strictly following instructions. However, this forced discomfort was designed to highlight how various people responded to a set of tools (Figures 9.3 and 9.4).

Fig. 9.3. Paint-by-number workshop. Department 21 at Show 2–Upper Gulbenkian Gallery Courtyard, Royal College of Art. June 2010. Photograph: Stephen Knott. Courtesy Department 21

Fig. 9.4. Discussion on the deck. Department 21 at Show 2–Upper Gulbenkian Gallery Courtyard, Royal College of Art. June 2010. Stephen Knott. Photograph: Fabio Franz

Six months after I had started to hand out the kits, and after a paint-by-number workshop during Department 21's presence at Show 2, participants started to return the paintings. Many were half complete, some kept to the lines, others decided to paint something completely different with the materials. Individual response was evident within the stipulations imposed by the paint-by-number grid: each participant expressed craftsmanship, risk, and the negotiation of uncertainly[13] within the confines of a mass-produced art kit. This imposition of limiting access to tools in a collaborative project reflects just one way in which craft has the potential to encourage situations of discomfort within art and design practice that helpfully reify existing skills, develop new ones and create genuinely collaborative objects.

CONCLUSION

Department 21 propounded an educational strategy of complementarity, a zone of free thinking that would help students reflect upon their work. In comparison to previous collectives, for example WWIAFM or the Art Workers' Coalition founded in New York in 1969 that attempted to 'underscore art's connection to labour' according Julia Bryan-Wilson (2009: 11), Department 21 held a much more ambiguous relationship to producing things. In many respects it was enough to develop a parasitical educational structure that provided breathing space for students overwhelmed by their intense courses: a terrain within the college of nonproduction that befitted current comfort with the idea of relational aesthetics and the importance of philosophical discussion. Thinking about learning was enough.

Yet the spectre of craft hung over the project, bringing the issue of materiality and skill to the fore. Polly Hunter, a Department 21 participant and editor of the publication, expressed her incredulity when she recalled the clay workshop: 'You don't come to the RCA to see a fashion student make a mess on a potter's wheel'.[14] Witnessing the failure of others would not appear to be an enlightening course of professional artistic education, but the tangible example of a lack of skill, failure and a willingness to participate accentuates the process-led nature of craft and what can be learnt from it: perhaps mess should have been encouraged more. Collaboration through craft in Department 21 seemed less about bringing one's skills to the mix and feeling good about it, and more about a feeling of trepidation when approaching new fields, encouraging an empathy between individuals with different skills and an awareness that production depends on everyone else as well as the individual. Through such tactics, and operating under the freedom that collaborative authorship provides, artists, designers and nonmakers alike might reap further benefits from collaborative craft practice.

NOTES

1. Department 21 was a radical, experimental educational project set up at the Royal College of Art in 2009 and led by Bianca Elzenbaumer and Fabio Franz. The idea was that students from all of the twenty existing departments at the RCA would come together to form a twenty-first department that was to be governed by independent learning, freedom from departmental syllabuses and the sharing of knowledge between disciplinary specialism.

2. Both the Rectorate and the Learning and Teaching Committee of the Royal College of Art contributed £1,000, amounting to a total budget of £2,000 (Elzenbaumer et al. 2010, front cover).

3. The most recent post on Department 21's Web site at time of writing is entitled 'Departed 21', 27 February 2012, <http://www.department21.net/?p=2284> accessed 10 July 2012.

4. During this time, I was the holder of the third AHRC-funded Royal College of Art/Victoria and Albert Museum studentship entitled 'Modern Craft: History, Theory, Practice'. I undertook my thesis about amateur craft practice in a cross-departmental context, with supervisors in both the history of design and the goldsmithing, silversmithing, metalwork and jewellery departments.

5. For example Jeremy Deller's work has a strong participatory element—such as his miners strike reenactment *The Battle of Orgreave* (2001) or *Valerie's Snack Bar* (2009) which invited gallery-goers of the recent Hayward Gallery show to sip tea in a recreation of the Bury Market original—as well as Clare Twomey who invites audiences to interact with the materiality of porcelain in *Trophy* (2006) and *Conscienceness/conscience* (2001–2004).

6. In the early stages of Department 21, organizers resolutely refused to stipulate any programme or force collaboration in any way (Franz 2009).

7. Hal Foster questioned whether hanging out and 'getting together sometimes' constitute an effective collaboration (Foster 2006: 194).

8. Department 21, 'Buildathon', <http://www.department21.net/?paged=11> accessed 10 July 2012.

9. Collaborative, bricolage-style chair making was also a feature of Luca Frei's collaborative project, *The So-called Utopia of the Centre Beaubourg—An Interpretation* (2007).

10. The Royal College of Art skip was praised as an 'ever-generative' source for Department 21. 'Ready to Go', Department 21 Web site, <http://www.department21.net/?p=1194> accessed 10 July 2012.

11. To see results from this workshop, see 'Monday Is Animation Workshop', Department 21 Web site, <http://www.department21.net/?p=630> accessed 10 July 2012.

12. For an account of the clay workshop, see 'Claytime' post from my blog (*rcabynumbers*) that recorded my experiences in the collaborative project:

<http://rcabynumbers.wordpress.com/category/21/> accessed 10 July 2012.

13. David Pye (2010) advances a definition of craft based on the notion of risk, with machines often imposing a sense of certainty that can reliably guarantee accuracy (Pye 2010).

14. Conversation with Polly Hunter, 16 December 2011.

REFERENCES

Adamson, G. (2007), *Thinking through Craft*, Oxford: Berg.

Adamson, G. (2009), 'Fragile's State of Mind', *Crafts*, 219 (July/August).

Adamson, G. (2010), *The Craft Reader*, Oxford: Berg.

Barthes, R. (1986), *The Rustle of Language*, trans. Richard Howard, Berkeley: University of California Press.

Bishop, C. (ed.) (2006), *Participation*, London: Whitechapel Ventures Ltd.

Bourriaud, N. (2002), *Relational Aesthetics*, trans. Simon Pleasance and Fronza Woods, Dijon: Les presses du reel.

Bryan-Wilson, J. (2009), *Art Workers: Radical Practice in Vietnam War Era*, Berkeley: University of California Press.

Dormer, P. (1994), *The Art of the Maker*, London: Thames & Hudson.

Elzenbaumer, B., Franz, F., and Hunter, P. (eds) (2010), *Department 21*, London: Calverts Co-operative.

Foster, H. (2006), 'Chat Rooms', in C. Bishop (ed.), *Participation*, London: Whitechapel Ventures.

Frei, L. (2007), *The So-Called Utopia of the Centre Beaubourg—An Interpretation*, London: Bookworks and CASCO.

Levi-Strauss, C. (1974), *The Savage Mind*, London: Weidenfeld and Nicolson.

Pye, D. (2010), 'The Nature and Art of Workmanship', in G. Adamson (ed.), *The Craft Reader*, Oxford: Berg, pp. 341–52.

Sennett, R. (2007), *The Craftsman*, London: Allen Lane.

Web Sites

Department 21, <http://www.department21.net> accessed 10 July 2012.

Franz, Fabio, Condorelli, Celine, and Wentworth, Richard (2009), *Initiatives in Institutions: The Power of Interdisciplinarity*, Department 21 roundtable discussion, 4 December, <http://www.department21.net/?p=83> accessed 10 July 2012.

Rcabynumbers, <http://rcabynumbers.wordpress.com/category/21/> accessed 10 July 2012.

We Work In A Fragile Material, <http://www.weworkinafragilematerial.com/> accessed 10 July 2012.

Skills in the Making

Simon Taylor and Rachel Payne

INTRODUCTION

In 2009, in response to a growing need, as we saw it, The Making, an arts education charity and crafts development agency based in Hampshire, United Kingdom, launched a new action research and education programme to bring craft and design directly into British schools.

Skills in the Making, supported by the Paul Hamlyn Foundation, is designed to improve the level of craft and design knowledge amongst schoolteachers. It is a three-year pilot professional development programme which enables art, design and craft teachers and trainees to meet some of the United Kingdom's leading makers, find out about their work and explore the value of learning through making. This knowledge, we hope, will in turn be passed on to pupils and help to improve the standards of craft and design education in British schools. Artists involved in the programme to date include highly respected figures such as metalwork artist Junko Mori, ceramist Kate Malone and Jerwood Prize winners Caroline Broadhead (jewellery/performance) and Phil Eglin (ceramics) (Figure 10.1).

The programme is being developed in an evolving collaboration with Oxford Brookes University, an important example of third-sector innovation delivering new solutions for education, teacher training and pedagogy. In this chapter, Simon Taylor describes the collaboration which is producing new models of best practice, using the intellectual assets of the artists, designers and makers involved. Rachel Payne describes how masterclasses in contemporary crafts practice for initial teacher trainees have explored new approaches to visual research. The trainees are using critical analysis and visual data collection methods to investigate the experience. These data are subsequently being analysed in relation to social constructivist learning theories to explore how active learning processes develop through making with an expert. This is a shared and collaborative model for learning through a sharing of craft methodologies and knowledge.

Skills in the Making also provides a timely and lively response to the latest surveys by British Government Inspectors, *Drawing Together: Art, Craft and*

Fig. 10.1. Drawing in three dimensions. 2009. Masterclass with Junko Mori and PGCE Art and Design trainees at Oxford Brookes University. Photograph: Simon Taylor. Courtesy The Making

Design in Schools (Ofsted 2009) and *Making a Mark: Art, Craft and Design Education* (Ofsted 2012), which found that craft and design were poorly taught or neglected in many UK schools: 'in more than half the schools visited, craft and design dimensions were underdeveloped, topics were unimaginative and there was a lack of response to pupils' cultural interests' (2009: 6). We believe this failure has a knock-on effect, resulting in fewer young people seeking careers in these subjects, the closure of specialist craft departments in higher education and, potentially, the decline in quality contemporary craft and design in the United Kingdom. The 2009 report noted that the underlying problem was often due to insufficiently trained teachers and called for continuing professional development for art teachers at all levels. Skills in the Making is designed to improve the offer to teachers with inspirational opportunities to further their knowledge through direct contact with leading artists, in an approach that goes further than the usual short-term residency model. New learning can be shared and disseminated in the school environment by the trainee teachers themselves. Organizations such as The Making can provide important connections between crafts-sector professionals and trainees, and this project will act as a catalyst for establishing the Ofsted report's aim of 'developing sustained partnerships between schools, the creative industries, galleries and artists in the locality' (2009: 7).

APPROACHES TO LEARNING, PEDAGOGY AND THE CRAFTS

> Ideas are not fixed and immutable elements of thought but are formed and reformed through experience . . . learning is . . . a process whereby concepts are derived from and continuously modified by experience. (Kolb 1984: 26)

Our philosophy has been one of using nondidactic techniques such as active dialogue, interpretation, observation and hands-on participation; learning is viewed as a self-reflexive process where knowledge is discovered, not simply imparted. We take a constructivist approach (Hein 1996), which means not viewing learners as empty bottles to be filled but as creative individuals who bring their own experiences, interests and skills to a session, whatever their age. 'Participation' then becomes a collaborative process between the artist/practitioner/workshop leader and the assembled group.

Learning is understood as a self-reflexive process of making meaning that it must 'go beyond merely doing things; the learner must come to reflect on that practical experience, to articulate something of what it means' (Salmon 1995: 22). The more traditional didactic transmission models of education are no longer appropriate in the context of experiential learning. A new 'constructivist' approach is required. George Hein explains this theory of learning, inspired by Dewey's 1938 publication *Experience and Education,* as follows: 'We have to recognize that there is no such thing as knowledge "out there" independent of the knower, but only knowledge we construct for ourselves as we learn (Dewey 1938). Learning is not understanding the "true" nature of things, nor is it (as Plato suggested) remembering dimly perceived perfect ideas, but rather a personal and social construction of meaning' (Hein 1996: 30).

However, it could be argued that for many learners, especially adults, making their own meaning is not enough, as resistance to new ideas often stems from their conflict with old beliefs, however crude or erroneous (Kolb 1984: 28). What could the roles of artists, teachers or gallery educators be in this situation? According to Kolb, 'one's job as an educator is not only to implant new ideas but also to dispose of or modify old ones' (Kolb 1984: 28). Kolb goes on to identify two mechanisms by which new ideas are adopted, a process of integration and one of substitution. Both mechanisms however are preferable to one of simple constructivism (Hein 1996) or personal meaning mapping (Adams, Falk and Dierking 2003), which can be problematic if these 'personal meanings' are never challenged.

In this context good teaching is seen to be the gradual rebuilding of inner confidence by providing the learner with empathy and a supportive 'interpersonal atmosphere'. The central role of the teacher is much more than a mere 'facilitator', and the experience for many in formal education is one of personalities (Salmon 1995: 24). This reflects the profoundly personal nature of the learning process which any 'practitioner of experiential methods cannot . . . disregard' (Salmon 1995: 24). It is clear that 'meaningful learning is integral with the personal identity of the learner' (Salmon 1995: 24).

Wenger develops this idea further, describing learning as social participation where individuals construct their identity through being active participants in social communities. This social learning leads to communities of practice, with individuals that have a shared domain of specialist interest, interact regularly and are, most important, practitioners (Wenger 1998). This social interaction and collaboration is also essential components of situated learning theory (Lave and Wenger 1991) whereby learning is embedded in authentic activity and context, rather than an abstract, classroom-based model. Guy Claxton and Bill Lucas, from the Centre for Real World Learning, based at the University of Winchester (United Kingdom), have also highlighted the importance of experiential learning, practical intelligence and embodied cognition within the undervalued field of practical vocational learning (Claxton, Lucas and Webster 2010). To be a good teacher within this field, an individual has to act as 'a role model, an explainer, a critical friend, and a coach of the "wider skills" that every learner needs' (Claxton et al. 2010: 14). Craft practitioners in particular can help learners to build habits of concentration and attention, smart practice and intelligent playfulness (or 'serious play'), controlled imagination and critical thinking (Claxton et al. 2010: 13). For Lucas and Claxton, the journey that individuals can make from amateur to expert suggests that 'learning proceeds through four stages from *unconscious incompetence* through *conscious incompetence* to *conscious competence* and finally on to *unconscious competence*' (Claxton et al. 2010: 7).

THE VALUE OF WORKING WITH CRAFT PRACTITIONERS AND MAKERS

For teachers the unique perceived benefit of Skills in The Making is that it provides contact with professionals; practicing artists, designers and makers are leaders in their respective fields and provide a 'way in' through their use of practical skill and process that is accessible to nonexperts. These individuals are not teachers but, importantly, self-employed freelancers, working in the real world, and what they can bring to the classroom is different but complementary to what is already there.

Makers can act as vocational role models with diverse backgrounds, bringing original approaches. For example Junko Mori trained as a welder in Japan before studying art in the United Kingdom. Junko's use of open-ended drawings (modular doodles of repeated patterns growing organically that develop themes of propagation and growth) and drawing in three dimensions with metal wire open up possibilities and encourage risk taking. Her approach is accessible at all levels and can be used to develop more experimental sketchbook work by creating an effective level of challenge. Drawings in three dimensions can be shared and worked on collaboratively, leading to discussion and students being more self-reflective in a way that is closer to the work of real-world artists. This questioning approach extends their literacy, fluency and visual language, is of particular value to students lacking confidence in their traditional drawing skills, and is in line with Ofsted's renewed emphasis on the importance of drawing in all its forms (Ofsted 2012).

Craft practitioners may also offer alternative career paths and have direct experience of routes into creative industries for example fashion, retail, one-off bespoke textile design. They have often built their career on skill, portfolio working and flexibility, creating opportunities for themselves by responding to clients, commissions, residencies, exhibitions and so on. Another important consideration is their ability to advise pupils on options or progression to further and higher education which can provide a substitute for often very poor career advice from schools (and parents), especially in arts subjects.

The partnership between The Making and Oxford Brookes University emphasizes the importance of engaging with contemporary craft practice by highlighting issue-based work that is nonfunctional. Textile artist Lucy Brown explores self-identity, gender and the body, through garments that have personal meaning. The recycling or deconstruction of old clothes that have social or cultural significance is a key part of Lucy's work and this translates very easily into an accessible classroom activity using old wooden picture frames as cheap weaving looms. There is great potential here for links with curriculum themes, including 'self-portraits' and 'cultural understanding' (Qualifications and Curriculum Authority [QCA] 2007).

Skills in The Making promotes cross-curricular applications working with contemporary crafts practitioners such as Rob Kesseler, a maker forging interdisciplinary partnerships. Kesseler, professor of ceramics at Central St Martin's College in London, has been collaborating with botanists at Kew Gardens to make pieces in glass, textiles and ceramics using visual imagery from nature: pollen and seeds which are then manipulated and coloured using Adobe Photoshop.

Through our work together we were able to explore the creative use of technology, including information and communications technology (ICT), in art using microscopes, digital cameras and sketchbooks (old and new technology). Art and Design trainees from Oxford Brookes University worked in partnership with staff from the School of Life Sciences at Oxford Brookes, and this innovative approach encouraged the joint use of equipment and the pooling of resources across departments, including science labs, microscopes, computers and cameras. 'I liked hearing about the development of the artist's interests—the lack of boundaries between things', commented one participant. This approach also links directly to the Qualifications and Curriculum Authority's recommendation in the New Secondary Curriculum for England that students should be 'thinking and acting like artists, craftspeople and designers, working creatively and intelligently' (QCA 2007: 23)

Contact with practitioners can provide much-needed cultural insight for teachers and knowledge of current events and exhibitions. Makers can provide links with high-profile cultural and commercial events such as London Fashion Week, the Clothes Show, Design Week and particularly in the crafts sector, Origin and Collect, the international fair for collectors of contemporary craft, now at the Saatchi Gallery. For example experienced textile artist Dawn Dupree uses contemporary urban imagery, which appeals to teachers and young people alike and encourages a free painterly approach to screen-printing using open screens, wax resists and mixing coloured dyes in situ.

LEARNING THROUGH EXPERIENCE AND CRAFT KNOWLEDGE

Contemporary craft uses experiential haptic learning, or learning through touch (Kolb 1984) that many educational psychologists believe is crucial to our cognitive development (Dewey 1934). However, rather than being seen simply as anti-intellectualism, Dewey's highlighting of the intelligent nature of artistic thought is more of a precursor to current ideas on the complex nature of human intelligence that value other abilities, not just linguistic or logical/mathematical. These issues are central to an understanding of art practice and many writers have been concerned with rebuilding the links between art and experience. In Dewey's words, 'to restore continuity between . . . forms of experience that are works of art and everyday events, doings, and sufferings that are universally recognized to constitute experience' (Dewey 1934:3).

Many educational psychologists believe touch is crucial to our cognitive development and contact with our environment from the earliest pre-reflexive stage of our childhood development (Piaget 1973) creates an awareness of qualities and experiences which influence our creative abilities. 'Well before we are able to assign words to those qualities . . . we experience them in their nameless state' (Eisner 1998: 17). This form of bodily learning reflects the phenomenological philosophy of Merleau-Ponty (1963) which has become the basis for contemporary interest in perception, embodiment and concrete human experience, of 'being-in-the-world'.

These theories further develop a concern for proprioception or haptics (McCullough 1996)—sensing our place in the world through our ability to tell the position and movement of our body. This form of spatial awareness relates to hands-on or craft skills, what Herbert Read called 'the will to form' (1931: 23), often referred to as 'tacit' (Polanyi 1967), or 'craft knowledge' (Dormer 1994: 11). Dormer explains that tacit knowledge or 'know-how' is a significant force in society but is slowly acquired. This craft knowledge is based largely on physical effort and practical expertise, is not easily described by language and is often difficult or even impossible to translate into theory. It is best learnt through experience and is easier to acquire with a skilled practitioner, teacher or trainer (Dormer 1994: 11).

'Tacit knowledge refers to a body of knowledge which we have gained through experience—both through the experience of our senses and through the experience of doing work of various kinds' (Dormer 1994: 14). This is not to claim that the development of craft skills or enactive learning, does not require intelligence. As Eisner says, 'a skill is not simply something we do physically, it is something that requires thought in the doing. Nothing can be done skillfully without thought' (Eisner 1998: 199). He goes on to explain that a highly skilled individual may give the appearance that 'skilled performance occurs without reflection', but we must never forget that 'even in the most rapid forms of information processing, cognition is at work' (Eisner 1998: 211). Without the engagement of the mind, action deteriorates into 'mere behaviour' (Eisner 1998: 212).

As a field, the crafts have suffered in the unwritten modernist hierarchy of art forms due to the fact that for many contemporary practitioners 'skills are regarded as technical constraints upon self-expression', especially in the West where 'a high value is placed on individuality and self-expression in the plastic arts' (Dormer 1994: 7). Craft knowledge, because it is essentially communal and collaborative (in the sense that individuals serve some sort of apprenticeship), conflicts with this notion of originality and it is generally assumed that craft is bound by rules that 'necessarily conflict with freedom of thought, imagination and expression'. Dormer also highlights the issue that many skilled craft practitioners 'are drawn irresistibly . . . into practicing skill as an end in itself' (Dormer 1994: 7–8). The goal of many practitioners is, however, to achieve some form of 'informed spontaneity', not in the sense of working very rapidly but 'working knowledgeably and fluently' (Dormer 1994: 85).

Working on a large scale, ceramicists such as Kate Malone utilize a spatial awareness coupled with expert understanding of ceramic materials and their capabilities. Interestingly, Kate's work is used as a case study in the National Curriculum and, inspired by natural forms, is a very accessible way to introduce pupils to working in three dimensions, as students can bring natural found objects in to the classroom as source materials and inspiration (QCA 2007).

Caroline Broadhead's work has developed from jewellery to body adornment, and she now makes sculptural clothing for installations, performances and collaborations with contemporary dancers. Working with Caroline encouraged the trainees in developing their tactile skills, spatial awareness and structural understanding. These skills only really come through material knowledge gained through hands-on making and 'tacit knowledge' (Dormer 1994), possible even when using low-cost materials such as paper and card. Most important, just as dance could be described as thinking through movement, craft can be described as thinking through making (Adamson 2007).

Dialogue with contemporary craft develops teachers' critical language and builds their confidence to engage with conceptual work. Artist-led sessions encouraged critical analysis, discussion and the exploration of meaning with trainees at the Institute of Education, within the University of London. Our programme encouraged a discussion-based model around the language of making, the importance of experimental and intuitive work (that is not outcome-led) and appreciating the handmade. This could be seen as a reaction to consumerism and manifests itself in movements such as Craftivism in the United States and Urban Knitting in the United Kingdom. As Richard Sennett states in his book *The Craftsman*, 'slow craft time also enables the work of reflection and imagination' (2009: 295).

The most effective approach was artist-facilitated discussion, followed by collaborative group work around a theme with open-ended outcomes. These included a mini group exhibition exploring mark making through a group drawing, by first creating the objects to 'make marks' using a limited 'palette' of found materials. This approach explores the three basic abilities that are 'the foundation of craftsmanship' according to Sennett: 'the ability to localize, to question, and to open up' (Sennett 2009: 297).

RESEARCH EVIDENCE, BY RACHEL PAYNE

In the current UK educational climate, the value of practical learning in secondary education is in danger of marginalization, in part by the championing of the English baccalaureate (Department for Education 2010). GCSE options are becoming narrower and opportunity to engage with the arts in fourteen to nineteen education reduced as a result of many schools' interpretation of political ideology (Adams 2011; Steers 2011). Two Craft Council publications (Eggleston 1998; Mason and Iwano 1998) analyse the relevance of pupils as craft makers and how people learn through making. Both reports indicate that teaching and learning through craft can support intelligent making, a process necessary in human development. In response, a key component of the PGCE

(Postgraduate Certificate in Education) course is to explore practical learning, engaging trainee teachers in a range of making activities which not only develop their subject and pedagogical knowledge but also develop their understanding of making as an intellectual activity. This is imperative if the trainees are to engage pupils in meaningful making and thinking during lessons to ensure pupils understand the purpose and value of making activity, especially in the current educational climate and Skill in The Making workshops contribute to this approach.

The research element of the project has been developed in partnership between Oxford Brookes University and The Making and is situated within socio-cultural theory. It attempts to explore how trainees' learning and professional practice develops when exposed to the practice of a craft expert within a PGCE learning community, working to the following research question: How does the trainees' professional practice develop as a result of working with an expert? Are they able to master or appropriate new learning to initiate effective craft-based learning in the classroom? How does social interaction and the cultural context affect how trainees learn about and through craft making, and what are the implications for this in relation to classroom practice? The aim of the research is to expose cognitive processes as they occur, identifying moments of active learning (Wertsch 2007); action in this context involves a deliberate relationship between technical skill and cognition (Crawford 2009). So, the purpose is to encourage different thinking about intelligent craft production and how this can be translated into effective classroom pedagogy.

Wertsch (1998) clarifies the purpose of socio-cultural analysis as the exploration of the correlation between human action and cultural, historical, social and/or institutional contexts. Human action is defined as the 'psychological moment of action' (Wertsch 1998: 23), an individual occurrence which cannot exist in distinction from the social dimension but as a moment in the whole process. This can be explored through 'mediated action' (Wertsch 1998: 24), or by focusing on the relationship between agent and cultural signs or tools. In this context, cultural tools refer to any artefact utilized by and for human activity, including all craft-based equipment and media to enable craft production. It is the creation and implementation of tools which alters the human environment and how humans engage with that environment; relationships with cultural tools alter human existence (Luria 1928 cited in Cole and Engeström 1993). The artefact or tool enables an activity to be performed through mediated means; indeed the cultural tool is two sided, involving both external and internal forms, including language. This relates to Vygotsky's theory of linguistic development in children where speech becomes the means by which socialization into a community and cultural forms of thought occur (Vygotsky 1978). Learners begin to apply to themselves the forms of behaviour applied to them by others, where language increases learners' abilities to perceive and understand, including concepts only partly or not yet perceived (Cole and Engeström 1993). So, learning 'not only occurs in context, it is driven by context' (Freedman 2003: 79). In this sense, action occurs in what Leont'ev (1978, 1981, cited in Cole and Engström 1993) called activity systems or learning communities. Here traditions are constructed and adapted according to ongoing mediation with cultural or making tools, and studying how mediation occurs facilitates understanding of not just 'what people know, but how they know' (Freedman 2003: 83).

Mediated action alters the process of knowing; transformation can lead to internalization of the learning process as mastery and/or appropriation (Wertsch 2007). Internalization begins when the learner demonstrates some understanding of the meaning, purpose and organization of tools during specific activity. Mastery represents the ability to move beyond replication towards independent means of engaging with making tools; this includes understanding the tool's properties, strengths and limitations when constructing craft artefacts. Appropriation suggests the ability to own the craft activity, to invest and respond meaningfully towards making where purpose becomes personalized. In this context, the role of expert craft practitioner is important in enabling the learner to grasp key characteristics of specialist tools and how to organize making activity with them. Without the expert practitioner, internalization would either not happen or indicate a slower, less consistent process of development.

In December 2010, fifteen PGCE art/design trainees took part in a workshop with a craft expert, one in a series of practical experiences aiming to develop formative understanding, skills and knowledge. The range and order of workshop activities provide opportunity for discussion and reflection, expert presentation about craft practice and group and independent craft production in relation to set themes. Learning develops through social interaction in specific environments through engagement with craft tools; what is communicated indicates how the trainees perceive. Communication is multimodal as trainees were asked to use cameras to capture still and moving images of the making processes; using these tools the trainees documented both explicit and implicit mediation (Wertsch 2007). These data have been used to explore the trainees' process of learning about craft; film footage was played back to the trainees after the workshop when they were asked as a group to consider: How has working with a craft based practitioner changed your professional practice? This was broken into three subquestions focusing on identifying key moments when learning changed direction, how collaboration contributed to learning and how key learning points from the workshop translate into classroom pedagogy.

The data analysis process involves identifying themes within the focus group transcript which indicate changes in learners' behaviour or quality of learning. Transformations are indicated by how learners choose to engage with practical craft activity according to their perceptions and personal histories, as well as how they engage with each other and the craft practitioner. In this sense, learning occurs when trainees gradually become aware of the meaning and function of craft tools and how to apply them in a different learning context.

The initial workshop activity involves the craft expert working alongside trainees; this process includes staged instruction of how to manipulate media through the construct of individual components to create a complete artefact. What is significant is the expert using visual and verbal instruction to assist the trainees in becoming fluent when using craft tools, revealing that the process of mastery starts socially through the interaction of expert and learner. Expert intervention implies tensions as well as benefits: the intervention attempts to alter the learner's approaches to making which limits personal interpretation; however, this approach enables the learner to develop an initial understanding of how to manipulate craft tools to create an artefact; it provides a starting point and demonstrates a method similar to the craft apprenticeship model.

The interview transcript reveals three trainee perceptions of the value of the initial making activity: how to introduce children to new media, how to teach a technical skill and how this supports later engagement with craft tools. At this stage learners have not been asked to produce independent artefacts and so visual evidence represents partial understanding of the making process. Initially, trainees can mimic the expert's actions but cannot demonstrate competence, which indicates that progression relates to an understanding that the tool is crucial in helping trainees organize making activity; the properties of the medium combined with the availability of specific equipment dictate how trainees engage with the practical activity and at what point learning occurs. Problem solving and adaptation are supported according to the trainees' history of craft making and their approaches to learning practical skill and techniques.

Another key moment of learning evident through data analysis is the importance of play and experimentation to foster risk taking. Eight trainees cite playing with new materials as key in developing mastery of craft tools and how the ability to engage in risk taking activity appears to link to confidence and freedom from the fear of failure. When analysing the social aspect of making it becomes clear that some trainees experience insecurities when making together, engaging in informal comparisons with their peers.

For example:

Sometimes I think that working collaboratively can have a negative effect (because) sometimes you're so pressured by what everyone else is doing that then affects your work. Sometimes, with me anyway, if I'm left on my own I'll just get on with my work—I'm fine—I'm not worried about anyone else. But when you're sat in a big social gathering you can be sat there thinking, Oh God, hers looks really good and mine's not so good. (Trainee Eight)

This indicates that internal skills are needed to overcome such tensions, implying emotional intelligence, such as resilience. In this sense, does the nature of craftwork exacerbate negative correlations, and does the experience of being included in a research project dictate additional pressure? However, not all trainees experience negative social comparisons, and some cite how important it is to make alongside others; five trainees refer to insecurities whilst four refer to the value of comparing different making methods to reveal diverse and/or new processes of engaging with craft tools. In addition, the experience of being challenged by external forces (such as media properties, set tasks and expert expectations) was viewed as important. Data reveal that certain trainees experience a moment of transformation owing to restrictions placed on them by the craft expert. Once trainees can demonstrate the ability to represent implicit processes (such as methods of construction chosen to represent personal interpretation of subject matter) externally and independently they begin to demonstrate internalization through using tools with awareness for a specific purpose. This becomes independent craft activity, not one created by mimicking the expert. Interestingly one trainee observed that whilst skill acquisition is vital, demonstrating that through highly accomplished outcomes is not important when considering the purpose of the activity.

Indeed it is crucial to reconsider the purpose of activity: researcher agency was not to produce expert craft practitioners but to encourage different thinking about craft making and foster opportunity to translate this into classroom pedagogy. Focus group responses indicate how trainees adapt diverse components of the workshop to embed into pedagogical planning; these vary depending on aspects which promoted interest, transformations or correlated with personal context. The depth of trainee understanding indicates that differing perception, experience and history are important in the mastery of craft processes. The following quotation indicates how one trainee forged a clear identity with specific pedagogical approaches:

> For me it was the importance of experimentation and play, and if it's a new material allowing pupils time to interact with it and take risks, and, you know, have a go rather than expecting them to produce something straight away. I thought that was vital. (Trainee Six)

This research indicates key findings which correlate to the properties of mediated action. For example mastery of craft processes begins socially through mimicry; tensions created through craft expert intervention are vital in developing an understanding of the tools' properties which dictate how craft activity is organized; the importance of risk taking and play in a secure environment; that social visual activity can promote insecurity as well as new investigations. Some findings haven't been analysed and warrant further investigation: the importance of emotional support from peers and the craft expert, the role the visual plays when problem solving, and the relevance of informal learning such as sharing and extending ideas through informal dialogue. Returning to the research question it is clear the trainees learnt and developed professional practice through craft expert facilitation of intelligent-making activity with specialist tools, evident through multiple moments of transformation. Most would have struggled to engage with the craft tools alone, or at least to develop the quality and variety of learning evident from this analysis, or relate this knowledge to the art classroom with as much insight. The research demonstrates mastery of craft activity has occurred but appropriation is more difficult to achieve or possibly measure. Is the gap between the two the time needed to practise, reflect, to work with colleagues, experiment and gain further experience and understanding in relation to how craft tools can inform pedagogy? Or is it about preferred making activities and personal histories of the art educator? One conclusion is that possibly the most effective art teachers are those who are able to appropriate making tools and embed this ownership within pedagogy and curriculum design authentically.

CONCLUSIONS

In terms of quality assurance for the work we do, during the course of this programme The Making and its host HE partners have been observed and received positive feedback from Ofsted and undergone quality assurance by the Centre for the use of Research and Evidence in Education (CUREE) on behalf of the former Training and Development Agency for Schools (TDA): 'The trainees gained a great deal at a very impressionable stage of their career. Your choice of maker and the focus of the workshop were skillfully combined . . . extremely positive and productive' (Ian Middleton, chief inspector for art and design, HMI, Ofsted).

In terms of our own evaluation methodology, we use a triangulation of techniques, questionnaires, observation and one-to-one interviews combined with longitudinal studies (one to two years) to find examples of increased confidence, evidence of transfer of skills into the classroom and the development of new schemes of work.

THE FUTURE

Further developments have been made in partnership with the University of London's Institute of Education, the Universities of Greenwich, Roehampton and Liverpool John Moores in order to provide an in-depth model for delivery that can be replicated by other initial teacher training courses throughout the country. This model is being developed with national and regional partners, including the National Society for Education in Art and Design to ensure the long-term viability and sustainability of the programme. Our aim is to deliver bespoke, affordable high-quality training that is subject-specific. The message needs to be loud and clear about the potential benefits both to schools in raising attainment, closing the achievement gap for boys (currently performing 20 per cent less well than girls at GCSE Art and Design A*–C grade), re-engaging disaffected pupils, and increasing self-confidence for individuals to engage reflexively with contemporary craft practice.

As we have highlighted, the wider context for this programme is massive change within initial teacher education provision by universities and there is a huge state of flux within the higher education sector. The UK Government's Department for Education has also announced a National Curriculum Review in England, and there are questions as to whether art and design, and design and technology will remain core subjects. As a result, any plans will have to be reviewed as soon as changes are announced.

However, despite all the uncertainty, our long-term aim is that the benefits of collaboration are made clear, and new communities of practice are being developed to meet the 'design challenges' for pedagogy and the crafts.

REFERENCES

Adams, J. (2011), 'Editorial: "The Degradation of the Arts in Education"', *International Journal of Art and Design Education*, 30/2: 156–60.

Adams, M., Falk, J., and Dierking, L (2003), 'Things Change: Museums, Learning and Research', in M. Xanthoudaki, L. Tickle, and V. Sekules (eds), *Researching Visual Arts Education in Museums and Galleries: An International Reader*, Dordrecht, Netherlands: Kluwer Academic.

Adamson, G. (2007), *Thinking through Craft*, Oxford: Berg

Claxton, G., Lucas, B., and Webster, R. (2010), *Bodies of Knowledge: How the Learning Sciences Could Transform Practical and Vocational Education*, London: University of Winchester and Edge Foundation.

Cole, M., and Engström, Y. (1993), 'A Cultural-Historical Approach to Distributed Cognition', in G. Salomon (ed.), *Distributed Cognitions: Psychological and Educational Considerations,* Cambridge: Cambridge University Press, 1–46.

Crawford, M. (2009), *The Case for Working with Your Hands: Or Why Office Work Is Bad for Us and Fixing Things Feels Good*, London: Penguin Books.

Department for Education (2010), *The Importance of Teaching: The Schools White Paper 2010*, London: TSO Information & Publishing Solutions, <https://www.education.gov.uk/publications/eOrderingDownload/CM-7980.pdf>.

Dewey, J. (1938), *Experience and Education*, New York: Kappa Delta Pi/ Collier Books.

Dormer, P. (1994), *The Art of the Maker: Skill and Its Meaning in Art, Craft and Design*, London: Thames & Hudson.

Eggleston, J. (ed.) (1998), *Learning through Making: A National Enquiry into the Value of Creative Practical Education in Britain*, London: Crafts Council.

Eisner, E. (1998), *The Enlightened Eye: Qualitative Inquiry and the Enhancement of Educational Practice*, Upper Saddle River, NJ: Merrill.

Freedman, K. (2003), *Teaching Visual Culture: Curriculum, Aesthetics and the Social Life of Art*, New York: Teachers College Press, Columbia University.

Hein, G. (1996), 'Constructivist Learning Theory', in G. Durbin (ed.), *Developing Museums for Lifelong Learning*, Group for Education in Museums (GEM), London: The Stationary Office.

Kolb, D. (1984), *Experiential Learning: Experience as the Source of Learning and Development*, Englewood Cliffs, NJ: Prentice-Hall.

Lave, J., and Wenger, E. (1991), *Situated Learning: Legitimate Peripheral Participation,* Cambridge: Cambridge University Press.

Mason, R., and Iwano, M. (eds) (1998), *Pupils as Makers*, London: Crafts Council.

McCullough, M. (1996), *Abstracting Craft: The Practiced Digital Hand*, London: MIT Press.

Merleau-Ponty, M. (1962), *Phenomenology of Perception*, London: Routledge & Kegan Paul.

Ofsted (2009), *Drawing Together: Art, Craft and Design in Schools*, Ofsted.

Ofsted (2012), *Making a Mark: Art, Craft and Design Education (2008–11)*, Ofsted.

Piaget, J. (1973), *Main Trends in Psychology,* London: George Allen & Unwin.

Polanyi, M. (1967), *The Tacit Dimension*, New York: Anchor.

Qualification and Curriculum Agency (2007), *New Secondary Curriculum*, <http://www.education.gov.uk/schools/teachingandlearning/curriculum/secondary>.

Read, H. (1931), *The Meaning of Art*, London: Faber & Faber.

Salmon, P. (1995), 'Learning to Teach: A Conversational Exchange', in R. Prentice (ed.), *Teaching Art and Design: Addressing Issues and Identifying Directions*, London: Cassell.

Sennett, R. (2009), *The Craftsman*, London: Penguin.

Steers, J. (2011), Letter sent to Michael Gove, 10 February, <www.nsead.org.downloads/GoveletterFebruary2011.pdf> accessed 11 February 2011.

Vygotsky, L. S. (1978), *Mind in Society: The Development of Higher Psychological Processes*, Cambridge, MA: Harvard University Press.

Wenger, E. (1998), *Communities of Practice: Learning, Meaning and Identity*, Cambridge: Cambridge University Press.

Wertsch, J. V. (1998), *Mind as Action*, New York: Oxford University Press.

Wertsch, J. V. (2007), 'Mediation', in H. Daniels, M. Cole, and J. V. Wertsch (eds), *The Cambridge Companion to Vygotsky*, Cambridge: Cambridge University Press, 178–192.

–11–

Project Dialogue: Promoting a Transdisciplinary Approach to Postgraduate Arts Pedagogy

Barbara Hawkins and Brett Wilson

INTRODUCTION

For more than fifteen years, funding initiatives for collaborative arts and science outputs from the Wellcome Trust, the Calouste Gulbenkian Foundation, NESTA and others have successfully served to stimulate increased interest, energy, and activity in multi-, inter- and transdisciplinary projects, often grouped under the broad banner of 'Sciart' (Glinkowski and Bamford 2009). Whilst such schemes have contributed significantly to a growing awareness of the benefits of collaborative relationships across the arts, sciences and humanities, there is relatively little work exploring the differential educational experience of early career artists and scientists to offer a range of tools to undertake such collaborations with confidence and understanding. However, a recent US National Science Foundation–National Endowment for the Arts workshop has sought to reformulate the way that the arts and sciences are currently being linked and to investigate how agencies might jointly promote emerging areas of research and cultural development through an 'Alt. Art Sci' approach (Malina 2011). This impetus may well help to focus our attention more closely on exploring the underlying pedagogic structures and concomitant curriculum elements in our educational system needed to support a more open transdisciplinary environment at the postgraduate level (Ox 2010). In this chapter we describe a series of teaching interventions influenced by this inclusive approach and focused towards the research-informed craft practices of postgraduate artists, designers and makers.

With factors such as these very much in mind Project Dialogue[1] was established by the authors in 2006 within the Department of Creative Industries at the University of the West of England, United Kingdom. The primary aim of Project Dialogue was, and still is, to provide a 'contemplative space' to encourage enquiry into the relationship, commonalities and differences in the underlying concepts, practices and research methodologies across the arts and sciences, with a view to informing future, more flexible, research and educational approaches in both art and science areas.

TRANSGRESSING DISCIPLINARY BOUNDARIES

'Transgressing disciplinary boundaries is a subversive undertaking since it is likely to violate the sanctuaries of accepted ways of perceiving. Among the most fortified boundaries have been those between the natural sciences and the humanities' (Greenberg 1991: 1). Artists are frequently attracted to science because of the richness of the subject matter, the evident productivity of its methodology, and the opportunity to explore other fundamental human questions in ways different from their initial training as artists. Science researchers in their turn see encounters with the arts and humanities as a way of encouraging public understanding and trust, as well as a tool for creating visually compelling expositions of scientific results. Ultimately, the creativity of both groups derives from an attitude of curiosity, of a desire to understand and explain ourselves and our universe, but this curiosity seems to have become channeled educationally into quite disparate disciplinary traditions—creating a 'methodology gap' (Arends 2003) which can be difficult to overcome. Fortunately, the present more open attitude to cooperation across the arts, humanities and sciences means we can start to negotiate the many 'fault lines' radiating from the historically-based arguments around objectivity versus subjectivity (Daston and Galison 2010: 377) and progress towards a more productive epistemological relationship. Earlier historical periods have seen a closer and more productive interaction, and so it may be hoped that the present division will prove temporary and anomalous.

Effective collaborations across disciplinary boundaries can of course vary considerably in both breadth and depth. A transdisciplinary approach to problem solving may be taken effectively to complement and extend earlier multi- and interdisciplinary ways of working (Klein 1996) in the sense that it focuses on problems that are uniquely formulated and which cannot be captured (or at times even envisaged) within existing disciplinary domains. Transdisciplinary investigators accept and adopt perspectives unique to the nature of the collaborative effort and distinct from those of the initial separate domains, offering a more holistic approach to the problem under investigation.

The subversive quality of interdisciplinary approaches referred to by Greenberg—and, by extension therefore of transdisciplinary approaches—has implications not only for researchers and practitioners but for the way in which educationalists value student endeavour that exploits such diversity. Contemplative spaces (in the broadest physical, cognitive and organizational senses) which encompass transdisciplinary discourse and discovery are vital in the study of the arts, humanities and sciences if students are to take full advantage of contemporary research cultures and play a full role in social debate and agendas. This is particularly the case at postgraduate level where students experience the accelerating influence of research and debate over direct teaching and consequently become more immediately influenced by contemporary developments.

To think and communicate effectively across disciplines students need to learn the rudiments of etiquette and language of various disciplines. An active dialogue is needed for learning how to negotiate the present space *between* current disciplines. What might this mean then for a programme of pedagogy and research training for early-career artist and scientist researcher-practitioners seeking a broader educational base? How might educators provide a tool kit and lexicon for mutual discovery and ideas? What sort of structure and timetable might prove most effective for 'unlearning' and questioning the limitations of previous attitudes?[2]

RECENT OBSTACLES TO TRANSDISCIPLINARY STUDY

Whilst the increased openness and spirit of cooperation between academics, scientists and artists has made a transdisciplinary approach to higher education much more feasible, certain factors have perhaps served to hold it back in practice. Baroness Kennedy and Professor Michael Wood, among a number of other senior academic figures speaking at the United Kingdom's 2011 Universities under Attack conference (Grove 2011), have recently expressed concern that changes to degree structures and content introduced in an era of mass education to degree level over the past twenty years or so in the United Kingdom, have been focused primarily on the shorter-term concerns of industry and commerce. As a consequence of changes to their funding arrangements, universities in the United Kingdom and elsewhere have found themselves forced to adopt a much sharper competitive relationship with one another, with many of these financial attitudes reflected by a new generation of university managers who have essentially created an internal market that mirrors the external one (Lynch 2006). These changes, reinforced by the concept of a national set of qualification standards across a range of professions, have fundamentally changed the expectations and experience of academic engagement as perceived by both staff and students. As noted by Harkavy (2005: 15): 'When Universities openly and increasingly pursue commercialization, it powerfully legitimises and reinforces the pursuit of economic self-interest by students and contributes to the widespread sense among them that they are in college solely to gain career skills and credentials'.

Judging from the direct experience of the authors and numerous colleagues in similar positions across a range of UK HE institutions, this internal market has created a climate of considerable sensitivity amongst course leaders in which externally imposed performance indicators become a 'constant point of reference for one's own work' (Lynch 2006: 7). Courses based primarily on the collating of skills, competencies and immediate market transaction are thus more likely to thrive in this environment but leave little space for reflection and collaboration in which students can experience a broader perspective on their studies. As Midgely (1997: 82) highlights, 'when the range of subsidiary subjects available to students continually narrows because of timetabling difficulties, then it becomes harder and harder for academic people to form a realistic idea of other disciplines which can compete with the stereotypes offered by current myths'. Internally the competitive environment has led to modularization of programmes of study, compartmentalizing knowledge into a series of tightly defined and prescribed areas of practice and theory. In the United Kingdom in particular, the threat of (or actual) course closures within subject areas of art, design and craft (Batty 2011; Craft Council 2011) impart a culture of compliance to develop curricula that are easier to package and assess as modular elements, and subsequently, more economical to run. Across the academy as a whole, few UK institutions invest internally in cross-faculty study in any meaningful way. A report for the United Kingdom's Higher Education Academy's Interdisciplinary Teaching and Learning Group found that 'one of the most frequently reported issues was that of deans fighting over resources and territories and not being prepared to work cooperatively to support interdisciplinary endeavours' (Thew 2007: 15). Ironically, strong support for the view that exposure to a broader and more collaborative education will enhance future postgraduate student career prospects is expressed within industry. In a keynote speech to the 3rd Arts, Social Sciences and Humanities Policy Implementation Think Tank (ASHPIT) meeting in July 2011, Peter Forbes, associate director of the Council for Industry and Higher Education, stressed the qualities of flexibility, openness to interdisciplinarity and an interest in collaboration as key skills valued by potential employers of postgraduate researchers from any disciplines (ASHPIT 2011).

TOWARDS TRANSDISCIPLINARITY

Several authors have suggested that transdisciplinary research is today a critical step in the evolution of research on complex issues (Rowe 2003; Edwards 2008). Indeed, in many areas of scientific research, the myth of the lone scientist in search of 'truth' has long been anachronistic, particularly in the investigations of large-scale, humanitarian or environmental problems. Likewise, as Barrett and Bolt suggest, 'an acknowledgement that the myth of the solitary artist attempting to solve the problems of the world is also obsolete will help to remove major barriers to understanding the philosophical dimension of artistic practice' (2007: 7). Edwards (2008), founder of Le Laboratoire, makes similar assertions regarding the significant contributions to society, industry, science and art that can be made by melding interests through the formation of groups for what he calls 'ideas translation'. Other commentators have drawn parallels between the 'culture of experiment' in both arts and science research (Punt 2000; Schwarz 2009). McQuaid (2005) offers numerous accounts of innovations in textile design and related applications brought about by combined teams of artists, designers, scientists and engineers. Eigenbrode et al. (2007) discuss the need to adjust institutional and educational structures to facilitate such work from the perspective of biological sciences, along with Frodeman and Rowland (2009) from the humanities and Dunin-Woyseth (2011) from architecture and design. The increasing opportunities available for funding research of a transdisciplinary nature can be seen most notably in the recent agreement of the major UK Research Councils on the primacy of six main overarching research themes to be conducted through transdisciplinary teams.

Certainly, there is evidence that increasing numbers of artists are working between the traditional disciplines of science and humanities in the search to create work of novelty and imagination that also engages with major contemporary issues. For example, both Pynor (2011) and Aldworth (2011) work at the intersection of science, medicine and perceptions of self, producing intriguing and challenging image-based art that has grown out of a carefully constructed dialogue with the scientific community. Within our own faculty at UWE, Southerland, Parraman and Walters are among increasing numbers of craft-oriented research-practitioners developing novel artefacts, processes and perspectives that emerge from close collaboration with colour scientists, materials technologists, robotics engineers, biologists and chemical engineers.[3] Other Project Dialogue associates, James (2012) and Platten (2012), for example create artefacts in close negotiation with the nursing and medical communities to make a distinctive contribution to and understanding of how people relate to material qualities and objects.

Vesna (2000: 11) argues that artists are in a 'semi-favourable' position in relation to the sciences—ideally placed to act as a bridge between scholars in the sciences, cultural studies and philosophy and synthesizing something unique and new from their creative work. It is evident from this that predictive and imaginal are not mutually exclusive modes of thought, but simply two very different key elements required for continual conceptual reformulation of the world we inhabit. We would argue strongly that in the broadest sense all fundamental research, irrespective of its particular background and focus, is about challenging established conceptual models in one way or another. As such, both science and the arts are intertwined forms of approaching our perceptual and cognitive worlds, with art–science projects creating new opportunities for insights from practitioners in both disciplinary areas.

However, Vesna also warns of the fairly heavy reliance of artistic research on the bibliographical references of the humanities—in particular those of postmodern philosophy. Since artist researcher-practitioners tend to look to the literary and philosophical circles for much of their underpinning discourse, it is all too easy to be strongly influenced by interpretations of the very philosophers who are perhaps themselves considered contentious by the scientific community for what are seen to be misreadings and misrepresentations (Sokal and Bricmont 1998). Whilst postmodernism has undoubtedly been extremely useful in loosening if not dislodging some of the rigid certainties in (say) philosophy of science, a postmodern approach to science often seems to alienate many mainstream scientists through its language and tone and has probably tended to widen the gap between the 'Two Cultures', rather than narrow it, especially where conceptual terms may have been misappropriated or used widely out of context.

The majority of cultural commentaries on science (as opposed to a narrower 'history of science' courses) previously presented within the educational academy have almost invariably been presented to nonscientists by cultural commentators without a working scientific background. We would argue that nowhere do we need a transdisciplinary approach more than at this particular historical interface, but it must be a considered, sensitive and symmetrical approach and not just a repeat of the antagonistic battle cries of the culture and science wars of the 1980s and 1990s (Gross and Levitt 1994). So it is vital for true transdisciplinary study that experienced scientists with broader educational interests are intimately involved alongside cultural commentaries to provide effective and direct engagement.

PROJECT DIALOGUE ART–SCIENCE SEMINAR SERIES— PREPARING STUDENTS FOR A TRANSDISCIPLINARY WORLD

Project Dialogue is a transdisciplinary research group established within the Department of Creative Industries at the University of the West of England, United Kingdom. A visiting scientist in residence regularly engages with departmental research staff to explore new sites of discourse and to stimulate novel projects, supervise doctoral research and contribute to group postgraduate teaching. By exploring some of the underlying conceptual models and metaphors within the research cultures of the arts and sciences, our pedagogic interventions aim to equip research students with some of the conceptual tools for embarking on a transdisciplinary journey. Our first symposium, Transdisciplinary Landscapes: Dialogues between Art and Science, attracted arts and science practitioners from across the United Kingdom. Since then we have held a variety of teaching seminars with postgraduate arts students and invited speakers from across a range of arts and science disciplines. Participants have included fine artists, printmakers, graphic designers, glass and ceramic artists and other craft practitioners alongside academic researchers from the physical, natural and neurological sciences. Our primary aim in these seminars has been to offer students a brief opportunity to investigate strategies by which they might better understand scientific principles, histories and conventions, in order to engage in an arts–science practice with greater creative confidence and insight. Held fortnightly, on a purely extracurricula and voluntary basis, the first series of seminars in 2010 attracted regular attendance of around twenty students, despite being scheduled for Friday afternoons. A historically based scientific narrative from the scientist in residence was interspersed with sessions led by a range of guest speakers who were actively engaged in collaborative projects. Sessions were also included for students to present work in progress for discussion and debate.

Interestingly, a number of these students could be said to be individuals who, to some extent, already had 'a foot in both camps'. These included a retired general medical practitioner studying multidisciplinary printmaking, a practicing theatre nurse on a part-time arts master's programme, a part-time fine arts student who had previously had a career as a biologist, and a doctoral student who was a graphics designer and illustrator for scientific journals. A common statement from these students was that they felt they were living a kind of split existence with the requirements and techniques relating to their 'day job' and their arts study occupying separate parts of their intellect and creativity. These participators in particular were keen to find ways of expressing and exploring a synthesis, feeling it was possible for them to create imaginative work that drew on their broader professional knowledge and experience. Yet others in the group had a more traditional arts educational background—often, having originally enjoyed aspects of science at school but then been discouraged by its seeming complexity and difficulty.

Our initial objectives with the seminar series were threefold:

1. To provide a programme of lectures tracing the historical and cultural contexts surrounding some of the major paradigm shifts in science: in deciding to include a series of semi-formal lectures on the history of scientific ideas. we were struck by John Dewey's 1934 statement that 'when an art product once attains classic status, it somehow becomes isolated from the human conditions under which it was brought into being and from the human consequences it engenders in actual life-experience' (Dewey 1934: 3).

We would assert that in the broader sweep of the history of ideas when intellectual and scientific innovations also attain 'classic status' they too can become somewhat detached and isolated from the conditions in which they had their original significance. Ideas without associated historical context can too easily be seen simply as iconic and even degenerate into mere mantra whose subsequent unthinking repetition can even inhibit fresh insights. Through our offering of a discourse which covered lectures on 'Critical Thinking: Celestial Spheres and Copernicus', 'Renaissance, Enlightenment and Paradigms', 'Back to the Future—Postmodernism and Dialogue' students were reintroduced to a broad cultural chronology of scientific discovery within its own historical period that allowed them to consider these ideas alongside the context of their own knowledge of artistic movements in similar periods. Used later, these insights would give arts students greater confidence in their future investigations and intellectual enquiry in interdisciplinary activity. Describing how what we now term 'science' often struggled to form an identity and establish a working framework for its evolving methods served to 'humanize' science to a certain degree and to make it more accessible as a historic intellectual development to those who have not experienced a long scientific apprenticeship (Broks 2008). We also referenced the often ignored craft element within science, which, especially for postgraduate students deeply involved in experimental investigations, can be a substantial component of their lab-based work through the hands-on making of original or improvised equipment (Dyson 1998).

2. To explore a shared lexicon for discussing research methods and approaches to promote transdisciplinary dialogue: traditional academic disciplines can be considered as languages; we each have our own mother tongue but can also become passably fluent in others. As Wilson (2005: 208) notes when writing about textile design, the language barrier between artists, designers, engineers and scientists was one of the most frequent stumbling blocks 'as the disparate fields tenaciously worked together to form the common vision of the group'. By examining the major research approaches across different disciplinary fields, we have been able to identify some of the fundamental commonalities that underpin successful research activities in general. In particular, by examining, abstracting and widening the usual narrow focus on 'the scientific principle', we were able to unpick and decode a number of commonly held misconceptions and illustrate in much broader terms to studio-based arts practitioners the implied parallels and similarities between traditional scientific activity and their own artistic quests. Communicable, novel, repeatable and testable were terms found to have a surprising resonance between the two communities once their usage was discussed across a broader stage. Our craft students in particular came to recognize a shared culture with laboratory practice in which tacit knowledge and personal judgment could also be important factors when solving practical problems involving physical artefacts.

Whilst accepting that some terminologies and concepts are used in highly specific ways, it was hoped that an increased awareness of a wider range of bibliographic references would help to avoid potential criticism from students (and other academics) concerning an overreliance on any particular philo- sophical approach or framework. A wide reading list was supplied, encom- passing Kuhn, Popper, Feyerabend, Sim, Elkins, Morgan and Ede. Students were consistently encouraged to follow our principle that 'you can best find good answers by asking good questions'. This is especially important for a transdisciplinary approach where good questions need careful construction to ensure commensurability across boundaries previously felt to be more or less impermeable.

3. To offer workshops and presentations in collaborative art–science projects: a number of guest speakers, including practicing artists, academic scien- tists and arts researchers, were invited to talk about their experiences and present work to give students the opportunity to discuss the nature of col- laborative enquiry. The sessions explored the difficulties and opportunities this kind of work offers, and what each party gets from the experience. Of particular interest to our craft-based student-researchers were the con- tributions of Luke Jerram, Shelley James and Carinna Parraman, each of whom described their personal learning curves from their intensive dis- course with the scientific community. It was striking how over subsequent weeks students' confidence increased in devising strategies and project ideas for working in similar ways with peers from other disciplines.

RECOMMENDATIONS AND CONCLUSIONS

It has become clear to us that developing transdisciplinary teaching packages not only benefits the students by offering a broader educational experience but also helps overturn staff misconceptions through working closely with other practitioners from dissimilar backgrounds. Our regular input over the last four years to the master's module 'Research Methods', for example, has resulted in a new language of discourse entering into discussions between staff and students about the research methods appropriated into studio practice.

Our experience has shown however that it is vital to have certain things in place to develop successful and challenging cross-curricula pedagogies:

Identify and encourage scientists within your institution who care about a transdisciplinary approach and who have a useful background in philoso- phy or history of science suitable for building into a series of postgraduate seminars.

Look for novel ways to overcome the difficulties of securing funding from within one's own institution for such transdisciplinary activities. Our semi- nars were funded from a one-off internal source for teaching innovation, but it is conceivable that staff development funds could also be accessed for this purpose. Ideally, such a project needs visibility and support at faculty level to secure funds and commitment.

Create effective publicity and access. We used our postgraduate online network to publicize the seminars, as well as recording and archiving the talks for later online access. In addition, students themselves disseminated material and new ideas through their studio environment and their usual scheduled workshops and feedback sessions.

We have been encouraged by the positive response to our seminars and the level of engagement and debate by craft and design-based students, not only from within our own institution but also further afield. For example after a recent workshop given by the authors at University Bauhaus Weimar (Hawkins and Wilson 2011), a group of practice-led doctoral students heavily involved in materials and craft-based art processes spoke up in discussion to say how they felt the transdisciplinary approach we were advocating had given them a renewed sense of validation in the trajectory of their work. At home, several of our seminar participants have subsequently developed studio works significantly enhanced by a greater confidence in exploring ideas with peers from scientific disciplines.

In the executive summary of *Making Values*, the UK Crafts Council's 2011 report, Schwarz and Yair (2011: 6) highlight the increasing numbers of makers who move from their initial training into inter- and multidisciplinary ways of working, thus 'challenging the adequacy of some of our current terms for describing work'. Undoubtedly, future innovation will be dependent on being able to equip our future researcher-practitioners with the ability to rise to this challenge. To do so will require that higher-education institutions become much more flexible in their approach to postgraduate teaching by enabling and encouraging interdepartmental cooperation to build transdisciplinary curricula.

NOTES

1. Project Dialogue is affiliated with PLaCE (<http://www.uwe.ac.uk/sca/research/place/> accessed 16 August 2012) and the Centre for Fine Print Research (<http://www.uwe.ac.uk/sca/research/cfpr/> accessed 16 August 2012) within the Department of Creative Industries, both of which also have a long history of developing practice-led research through collaboration with colleagues from scientific disciplines. These activities all support a departmental culture of postgraduate study which stimulates and encourages exploration of a transdisciplinary approach both in practical and theoretical terms. The direct experience we have gained from working with postgraduate students, staff and research colleagues associated with Project Dialogue informs much of the practical material presented in this chapter.

2. Whilst the focus of our own work is in response primarily to the pedagogic structures of Higher Education in the United Kingdom, similar concerns can be seen both in Europe (Schwartz 2009) and the United States (Crowley, Eigenbrode, O'Rourke and Wulfhorst 2010).
3. Staff in the Department of Creative Industries, <http://www.uwe.ac/cahe/creativeindustries/aboutus/staff.aspx> accessed 20 February 2013.

REFERENCES

Aldworth S. (2011), <http://www.susanaldworth.com> accessed 15 August 2011.

Arends, B. (2003), 'Experiment: Conversations in Art & Science', London: Wellcome Trust.

ASHPIT (2011), *ASHPIT Newsletter 3*, <http://ashpit.wordpress.com> accessed 10 August 2011.

Barrett, E., and Bolt, B. (eds) (2007), *Practice as Research: Approaches to Creative Arts Enquiry*, London: I. B. Tauris.

Batty, D. (2011), 'Art Schools Face Uncertain Financial Future', *The Guardian* (19 April), <http://www.guardian.co.uk/education/2011/apr/19/art-colleges-face-uncertain-financial-future> accessed 22 February 2012.

Broks, P. (2008), *Understanding Popular Science*, Berkshire: Open University Press.

Craft Council (2011), 'Craft and Higher Education: An Update', <http://www.craftscouncil.org.uk/about-us/press-room/view/craft-education-an-update?from=/about-us/press-room/list/2011/> accessed 15 February 2012.

Crowley, S., Eigenbrode, S. D., O'Rourke, M., and Wulfhorst, J. D. (2010), 'Cross-Disciplinary Localization: A Philosophical Approach', *Multilingual*, 114, <http://www.multilingual.com/downloads/114LCDR.pdf> accessed 10 October 2011.

Daston, L., and Galison, P. (2010), *Objectivity*, Cambridge, MA: Zone Books.

Dewey, J. (1934), *Art as Experience*, New York: Capricorn Books.

Dunin-Woyseth, H. (2011), 'Some Notes on Mode 1 and Mode 2: Adversaries or Dialogue Partners?' in M. Biggs and H. Karlsson (eds), *The Routledge Companion to Research in the Arts*, London: Routledge.

Dyson, F. (1998), 'Science as a Craft Industry', *Science*, 280, <http://www.sciencemag.org/content/280/5366/1014/full> accessed 10 March 2012.

Edwards, D. (2008), *ArtScience: Creativity in the Post Google Generation*, Cambridge, MA: Harvard University Press.

Eigenbrode, S. D., O'Rourke, M., Wulfhorst, J. D., Althoff, D. M., Goldberg, C. S., Merril, K., Morse, W., Nielsen-Pincus, M., Stephens, J., Winowiecki, L., and Bosque-Perez, N. (2007), 'Employing Philosophical Dialogue in Collaborative Science', *BioScience*, 57/1: 55–64.

Forbes, P. (2011), Remarks made in Q&A session at Arts, Social Sciences, Humanities Policy Implementation Think Tank (ASHPIT) meeting, 12 July, Manchester University, UK.

Frodeman, R., and Rowland, J. (2009), 'De-disciplining the Humanities', *Alif: Journal of Comparative Poetics*, 29: 1–11.

Glinkowski, P., and Bamford, A. (2009), *Insight and Exchange: An evaluation of the Wellcome Trust's Sciart Programme*, London: Wellcome Trust, <www.wellcome.ac.uk/sciartevaluation> accessed 1 March 2012.

Greenberg, V. D. (1991), *Transgressive Readings: The Texts of Franz Kafka and Max Planck*, Ann Arbor: University of Michigan Press.

Gross, P. R., and Levitt, N. (1994), *Higher Superstition: The Academic Left and Its Quarrels with Science*, Baltimore: John Hopkins University Press.

Grove, J. (2011), 'Sector Must Reject Neoliberal Business-Speak, Event Hears', *Times Higher Education Journal Online*, <http://timeshighereducation.co.uk/story.asp?storycode=418295> accessed 13 February 2012.

Harkavy, I. (2005), 'The Role of Universities in Advancing Citizenship and Social Justice in the 21st Century', paper presented at The Citizenship Education and Social Justice Conference, 25 May, Queen's University Belfast, Belfast.

Hawkins, B., and Wilson, B. (2011), 'A Transdisciplinary Approach to Research in a Postgraduate Arts Environment', workshop seminar at Practice-Based Research in Art & Design Conference, 1–3 December, University Bauhaus Weimer, Germany.

James, S. (2012), *Shelly James, Glass Artist*, <http://www.shelleyjames.co.uk/> accessed 1 March 2012.

Klein, J. T. (1996), *Crossing Boundaries: Knowledge, Disciplinarities and Interdisciplinarities*, London: University Press of Virginia.

Lynch, K. (2006), 'Neo-liberalism and Marketisation: The Implications for Higher Education', *European Educational Research Journal*, 5/1: 1–17.

Malina, R. F. (2011), 'Alt.Art-Sci: We Need New Ways of Linking Arts and Sciences', *Leonardo*, 44/1: 2.

McQuaid, M. (2005), *Extreme Textiles: Designing for High Performance*, London: Thames & Hudson.

Midgely, M. (1997), 'Visions of Embattled Science', in R. Barnett and A. Griffin (eds), *The End of Knowledge in Higher Education*, London: Cassell.

Ox, J. (2010), 'A 21st-Century Pedagogical Plan for Artists: How Should We Be Training Artists for Today?', *Leonardo*, 43/1: 2.

Platten, B. (2012), *Bronwyn Platten, Mouths and Meaning, Manchester Eating Disorders*, <http://www.bronwynplatten.com/> accessed 1 March 2012.

Punt, M. (2000), 'Not Science, or History: Post Digital Biological Art and a Distant Cousin', in R. Ascott (ed.), *Art, Technology and Consciousness*, Bristol: Intellect Press.

Pynor, H. (2011), *Helen Pynor*, <http://www.helenpynor.com> accessed 15 August 2011.

Rowe, J.W. (2003), 'Approaching Interdisciplinary Research', in F. Kessel, P. Rosenfield, and N. Anderson (eds), *Expanding the Boundaries of Health and Social Science: Case Studies in Interdisciplinary Innovation*, Oxford: Oxford University Press.

Schwarz, H. (2009), 'From Undisciplined to Transdisciplinary', in *Art and Artistic Research,* vol. 6, Zurich: Zurich Yearbook of the Arts.

Schwarz, M., and Yair, K. (2011), *Making Value: Craft and the Economic Social Contribution of Makers*, London: Crafts Council UK.

Sokal, A., and Bricmont, J. (1998), *Intellectual Impostures*, London: Profile Books.

Thew, N. (2007), *The Impact of the Internal Economy of Higher Education Institutions on Interdisciplinary Teaching and Learning*, Southampton: The Interdisciplinary Teaching and Learning Group, Subject Centre for Languages, Linguistics and Area Studies, University of Southampton, <www.heacademy. ac.uk/ourwork/networks/itlg> accessed 10 August 2011.

Vesna, V. (2000), 'Towards a Third Culture/Being in Between', in R. Ascott (ed.), *Art, Technology and Consciousness*, Bristol: Intellect Press.

Wilson, P. (2005), 'Textiles from Novel Means of Innovation', in M. McQuaid (ed.), *Extreme Textiles: Designing for High Performance*, London: Thames & Hudson.

A Question of Value: Rethinking the Mary Greg Collection

Sharon Blakey and Liz Mitchell

INTRODUCTION

Manchester Art Gallery is home to an extraordinary and little-known collection of nearly 3,000 objects of daily life, collected by one woman during the early years of the twentieth century. The Mary Greg Collection of Handicrafts of Bygone Times includes spoons, keys, tools, boxes, scissors, thimbles, clay pipes, lucky charms, toys, valentines, sundials, scales, pincushions, embroideries, stuffed animals, dollhouses, shoes and a host of other things; an extraordinary mass of artefacts ranging from the mundane to the bizarre. For the past fifty years, as with many collections in public ownership, most of it has been in storage. As museums reach hoarding capacity, the question arises: what is the value, to the museum or the public, of objects held in store?

This chapter will discuss collaborative practice between craft makers, educators and curators in the form of the project Mary Mary Quite Contrary, an investigation of a public collection in storage. A partnership between art gallery and university, the original aims of the project were modest: to invite two contemporary makers to respond to collections in the gallery stores, and to exhibit their responses alongside historic material, enabling both gallery staff and public to view the collection through fresh eyes. However, what began as a conventional guest/host relationship, developed into a more profoundly collaborative journey, which has had lasting impact on both academic and museum practice. It evolved from a standard exhibition format into a more complex and meandering organism, with multiple participants and strands of activity. This brought numerous challenges but, we would argue, resulted in more significant impact for all concerned. Our partnership has yielded new insights into curatorial, academic and creative practice, confronted long-held assumptions about the purpose and potential of museum collections and enabled the development of an alternative model for cross-disciplinary collaboration.

In this chapter, we will set out the particular context and environmental conditions that enabled our collaboration, investigate the nature of the collaboration itself and outline its impact and legacy for both individual and institutional participants.

CONTEXT

In 2006, the exhibition *Out of the Ordinary*, at Manchester Metropolitan University (MMU), showcased the work of Sharon Blakey and Hazel Jones. Both makers had been invited to select objects from MMU's Special Collections[1] as inspiration for their own work. To the surprise of curators, both were drawn to the unacknowledged objects at the back of the cupboard: a desiccated mouse, a threaded needle, an empty frame. Blakey's ceramics commemorate the ordinary: 'those everyday things we take for granted that become part of the fabric of our daily lives, remaining long after we are gone'.[2] Jones's curious metal inventions take inspiration from the small and insignificant: 'a piece of fluff, a lump of gravel, a tea leaf or some string that is too small for use'.[3] Both makers are also collectors, and the resulting exhibition included both personal and institutional collections.

Meanwhile, Manchester Art Gallery (MAG) was exploring what to do with its collections in store. In 2005, the Museums Association published *Collections for the Future*, a response to the growing crisis in collections storage (Wilkinson 2005). This report marked a conceptual shift in museum collecting, acknowledging the impossibility of keeping everything. A nationwide process of rationalization and disposal began. But how to decide what should stay and what should go? What kinds of value judgements should come into play and who should have a say?

Consequently, MAG began its own rationalization programme, as a result of which, the little-known Mary Greg Collection of Handicrafts of Bygone Times was identified as a possible candidate for disposal. Mary Greg (1850–1949) was a wealthy widow and collector of everyday things. She collected the domestic and the handcrafted, recording the histories of ordinary people through the objects they owned and used. In 1922, following the bequest of her husband's prized collection of English pottery, she gave her own extensive collection to Manchester Art Gallery. This marked the beginning of a long and influential relationship with MAG, lasting nearly thirty years until her death in 1949, and documented in an archive of several hundred letters.

By 2006, however, the collection had been in storage for many years, occupying a lowly status within the wider collections. Yet the proposal to dispose of it was surprisingly controversial, suggesting it occupied a curious limbo— not sufficiently valuable to warrant attention but too embedded in MAG's history to be easily shed (Figure 12.1).

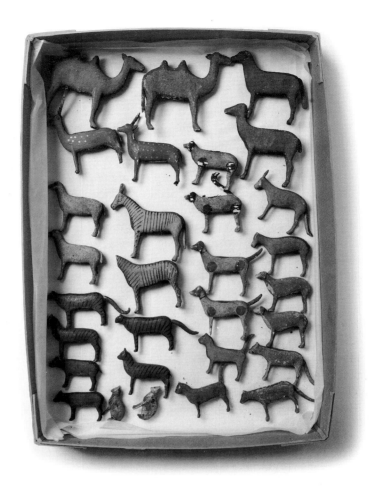

Fig. 12.1. Tray of Noah's Ark animals, painted wood, probably made in Germany, about 1840. Photograph: Ben Blackall. Courtesy The Mary Greg Collection of Handicrafts of Bygone Times, Manchester City Galleries. Accession number: 1922.486

VALUE

Museums are instrumental in establishing hierarchies of value in the material world. They decide which objects will be removed from daily life and preserved 'in perpetuity' as holders of historical narrative. In deciding what is kept (and what is not), the museum exerts considerable power over the telling of stories. In today's context, there is a further set of hierarchies at play in the competition for limited display space. Nine-tenths of the collection is hidden from view; only those parts deemed worthy are afforded the visibility of public display. Museums use vocabulary such as 'primary' and 'secondary', 'active' and 'passive' to rank their collections and identify priorities for display and further acquisition.

Suzanne Keene describes museum collections as 'stores of cultural capital' (Keene 2005: 160). Value is generated when the capital is used, that is when people come into contact with it. The notion of value located in the space between people and objects is significant. If the collection is a body of potential, it is what we *do* with it that determines value. It follows that value changes according to use and interest and that an unused collection has little or none.

For nearly ninety years, the status and value of Mary Greg's collection has been in question. From today's perspective, it sits uncomfortably within the art gallery, seemingly at odds with standard museological values—the rare, the preserved, the well-documented. It is full of highly personal things that are worn, damaged, unprovenanced and/or incomplete. Much of it is inscribed, quite literally, with the wear and tear of use and ownership. It is rich in anecdote and imagined narrative, unprovable, partial and suggestive. It doesn't behave according to the rules of good museum practice. It was also collected by a woman.

Collections amassed by women are rare in museums. Female-collecting behaviour has traditionally been dismissed as emotional, chaotic, domestic; mere accumulation, the antithesis of the rational and systematic organization of material culture which public museums were established to champion (Baudrillard 1968: 103). Mary Greg's collection subverts traditional notions of collecting in ways which have been observed in other female-collecting histories (Pearce 1995: 206–10). She is a dominant presence *within* the collection in several ways; in its focus on predominantly feminine territories (domesticity, fashion and childhood); in its blurring of the private and public through the inclusion of personal possessions (her sister's passport and an aunt's inscribed dance card) and homemade objects (embroideries and toys); and in her enduring and well-documented relationships with museum staff.

However, her energetic patronage clearly demonstrates her motivation beyond the personal. During her lifetime, she was closely involved in the display and interpretation of the collection, which enjoyed great popular appeal at MAG's historic house branch galleries, Platt Hall, Heaton Hall and Queens Park.[4] Her collection was even visited in 1927 by Queen Mary who, like Greg, was an avid collector of dollhouses. However, the primary intended audience for the collection was local and predominantly working-class families enjoying a day in the park at weekends and holidays. This was in marked contrast to the perceived visitor demographic of the main city centre art gallery, as evidenced in a letter to curator William Batho in 1930: 'I am very glad to know that the Bygones etc look so well at Queens Park & that they are enjoyed by the working class—that is just what we want—the rich can go about to see things so I feel quite satisfied that for the present anyway the things from Platt Hall are in the midst of those who work!'[5]

Mary Greg was clearly motivated by an educational and philanthropic agenda, heavily influenced by her reading of Ruskin and his belief in the educative role of museums.[6] She deliberately set out to collect objects perceived by others to be of low value and therefore at risk of being lost forever. 'I feel the work of treasuring things of the least is most important', she wrote to Eleanor Adlard, again in reference to Ruskin, in 1929 (quoted in Yates 2009).

Yet, after her death, the collection gradually disappeared from view, curatorial knowledge diminishing as institutional priorities changed. It was finally relegated to long-term off-site storage in the 1980s and acquired an anecdotal reputation amongst staff as the gallery's 'white elephant'.

CRAFT

The collection's apparently contradictory qualities, and its precarious position within MAG, prompted an invitation from Mitchell for Blakey and Jones to come and view the material in store. Their fascination with artefacts on the periphery, the overlooked, obsolete and disregarded, seemed to chime with the character, content and status of Mary Greg's collection; their focus on the valuing of ordinary things to resonate with her interest in 'things of the least'.

These initial visits quickly revealed that the contextual knowledge and material sensibilities of specialist craft practitioners was fundamental to understanding the collection, which itself evidenced many forms of craft. It includes folk craft (unselfconsciously handmade personal items such as embroideries and playing cards), guild crafts (the key maker and locksmith) and industrial crafts (hand-finished production items such as spoons and scissors). This realization provoked stimulating debate about traditional standpoints and contemporary shifts in thought and practice. The humble and personal nature of the collection and the evident wear and tear of the objects drew a parallel with Soetsu Yanagi's seminal analysis in *The Unknown Craftsman*. He argued that the highest form of craft lies not in the grand or splendid but within the ordinary things made by people for people (Yanagi 1978: 198). This resonated closely with the collection which, it could be argued, encompassed all that was laudable about handcrafted objects.

In fact, it was the objects and archive material that shaped our collaborative journey. We responded to emerging discoveries in much the same way a maker responds to material, allowing ideas and decisions to be formed by reflective observation. Hierarchical values and assumptions about objects, making and the validity of the artistic response were challenged by the discovery of two versions of a handmade toy, a leaping monkey on a stick. One displayed the fine skills of the fluent maker, the other the rudimentary work of the amateur. As an amateur maker herself (the collection includes her embroideries and homemade toys), Mary Greg believed firmly in the interconnectedness of 'head, hand and heart', and the fulfilment of making as a personal journey (as opposed to a professional pursuit). Her desire to inspire this in others is clear in a letter written to curator William Batho in 1928: 'I am glad to hear so many visitors have seen the collections. How glad I should be—we all should if we could know if any of them ever make a single thing as a result which will be a delight to themselves or their children and also those who come after. We must leave the answer to the future!'[7]

The redemptive capacity of handwork was a key theme in the recent V&A exhibition *Power of Making*.[8] Its message, articulated in the catalogue by Daniel Miller, was simple: 'go out and learn to make something. Feel for yourself that sense of achievement and exhilaration when you see before you the finished object of your own labour, and how that object has in turn made you more than you otherwise had been' (Miller 2011: 15).

The inclusion of objects by the nonprofessional within *Power of Making* serves to remind us that making is a fundamental part of the human condition, a principle that sits at the heart of the Mary Greg Collection.

In *Thinking through Craft*, Glenn Adamson argues that 'objects that are associated with craft have been unfairly undervalued since the beginnings of the modern era' (Adamson 2007: 4–5), and that, with its ethnic and feminine associations, craft has always been subordinate to art. This hierarchy is evidenced both within the art gallery and the university, where 'fine art' has traditionally enjoyed higher status than the 'decorative arts'. The Mary Greg Collection is largely made up of the artisan-made, the amateur and the anonymous. In the hierarchy of the arts, this places it at the lower end even of the decorative arts and may help to explain the collection's perceived lack of value within the contemporary art gallery.

Here was a collection that, from a historic perspective, epitomized the core qualities of craft. Yet its lowly position within the contemporary art gallery provided an interesting counterpoint. Perhaps there was more pertinence to this collection than we had originally understood. We began to see analogies between the collection's precarious existence and current perceived threats to hand making both within the school curriculum (Ofsted 2009: 6) and from digital technologies (Fraser 2012: 14). We saw potential, in the collection's rehabilitation, for analysis of the many forms of craft; of making as an investigative action, making as a human response to stimulus, making as interpretation, making as understanding. We saw an opportunity to reflect upon the shifting status of craft practitioners from the anonymous to the celebrity, to explore the multitudinous ways in which craft remains relevant to a contemporary audience, and to emphasize the continuing ability of craft to reinvent itself in the face of change.

It became clear that, whilst the collection itself might not contain the spectacular, it was nonetheless exceedingly rich. Unconstrained by dominant narrative, curatorial or institutional protectionism, its diminished merit became a positive advantage. Might its very lack of value enable us to explore the collection more freely? The parameters of the project began to shift.

COLLABORATION

Our collaboration began in a modest and informal way. Initial storeroom 'rummages' revealed a mutual and visceral connection with 'stuff', and it was clear that both maker and curator shared common ground in their passion for objects. Rummaging is neither a word nor activity that museums and galleries generally encourage; it conjures up loss of control and wayward behaviour, undermining the museum's authoritative role as guardian of material culture. But from the start, the lack of curatorial knowledge facilitated a more equitable relationship between host and guest. Investigating the collection in store as partners, it became increasingly clear that the open-ended rummage could be an intrinsically creative and serious act, comparable to the maker's playful experimentation in the studio.

This resonated with current developments in the theory and practice of museum interpretation, in particular around collaboration and co-creation.[9] Within MAG, a small team had been established, with a modest but dedicated budget, for the purpose of exploring new interpretive approaches. Operating on a kind of 'skunkworks' model,[10] the Interpretation Development Team had the freedom to experiment with small-scale projects, set apart from the mainstream of exhibition programming. The Mary Greg Collection, with its lowly 'under the radar' status, provided an opportunity for us to play.

Moreover, research into the history of the collection revealed the depth of Mary Greg's philanthropic and educational principles, prompting further reflection. In 1928, it was observed that the collection display at Platt Hall 'excites a great deal of interest and is used by the teachers in expounding the lessons of social history to the school children'.[11] Similarly, the discovery of material at Liverpool Museum revealed that Mary Greg's collections were in great demand by design and embroidery students from the College of Art.[12] This suggested that, as well as focusing on the maker's response to the collection, we might consider the development of wider educational initiatives located within both university and art gallery.

The collection became a route into investigating shared professional practice, as makers and curators, educators and interpreters, academics and researchers. Individual disciplines began to seep, one into another, as we discovered areas of common practice: the solitary nature of individual communion with material things, common to both maker and curator, balanced in contrast with the social and communicative roles of educator and interpreter. In this sense, we were experiencing the 'domain shifts' articulated by Richard Sennett in *The Craftsman* (2008: 127–9). We were developing a genuinely collaborative relationship, each team member contributing significant, relevant and alternative viewpoints, opening up a discursive space for creative thought and exploring that space between people and objects in which, according to Keene, value is generated.

But the storeroom rummage also shed light on fundamental differences of professional practice, and how the parameters of our respective fields impacted on our understanding. The creative response has become a standard model of museum and gallery interpretation in recent years; it is widely accepted that artists and makers 'create new readings, that they step outside of the authorised perception of values' (Cass 2011). The maker can explore places the museum might find difficult, exposing institutional mechanisms of power behind the supposed neutrality of museum space, challenging uncomfortable histories and offering imagined alternatives. The curator, on the other hand, operates as the institutional voice, charged with the responsibilities of factual accuracy and political sensitivity, accountable to both the legacies of past curators and the critical eye of future historians.

This was made manifest by the discovery of an envelope concealed amongst Mary Greg's letters, addressed to Samuel Crompton, inventor of the spinning mule.[13] Three small card tabs, wound with thread, fell from the envelope, on which was written 'finest cotton threads spun on the mule'. In the extraordinary moments that followed this discovery, we held the birth of the Manchester cotton boom in our hands: three tiny insignificant objects representing a pivotal moment in British history. But were they real? What was the provenance, how reliable the evidence? Sharing this moment publicly, before serious research could authenticate it, aroused concern amongst museum colleagues. The tension between historical veracity and creative imagination was palpable. The thrill of the chance encounter, the opening up of a momentary space between objects and people across 200 years of history, the frisson of uncertainty and speculation, sat in opposition to the methodical, secure, evidenced research that could confidently proclaim the material authenticity of the artefact.[14]

Our collaborative journey revealed the value of 'not-knowing', something that goes against received wisdom for the museum but is commonplace for the maker. Not knowing opens up possibility, requires participation, provokes discussion, and stimulates ideas. However, not knowing also risks getting it wrong, looking foolish and losing professional face. It requires bravery, confidence, and the ability to cope with failure as an inevitable and productive part of the process. The renegade nature of the project allowed this kind of risk to flourish. Without the certainty of destination, constraints of audience targets or deadline, we were able to become fully immersed in the process, appreciating the journey as an innately creative and stimulating act, a valuable outcome in its own right.

The inspirational nature of encounters in the stores, combined with the practical difficulties of finding time between the demands of our respective day jobs, led to the early development of a project blog.[15] The blog originated as an extension of the physical encounter in the stores, a communication device for individuals within the team to reflect on and continue discussions generated together. Every self-respecting museum now has its own blog, a glimpse 'behind the scenes at the museum'. These are usually in the form of a carefully composed curatorial monologue. The *Mary Mary Quite Contrary* blog, however, has no single primary author, but a range of voices, threads and observations. The personal and the professional have become intertwined as curatorial and artistic revelations, anxieties and vulnerabilities emerge, subverting notions of the artist or teacher or curator as authority figure. We have learnt together, getting it wrong as often as we get it right, much as a maker does in the workshop. In this respect, the blog is at the centre of the collaborative process, another space opening up in the encounter between people and objects. It has evolved into a fascinating narrative in its own right, charting the development of ideas, speculation, research findings, creative and curatorial enthusiasms and anxieties: a kind of collaborative sketchbook.

IMPACT

The impact of the project to date is visible within both institutions. For students at MMU, working within this collaborative environment has directly connected them to the world of academic research, engaging them in historic and contemporary craft perspectives. It has developed subject specific knowledge but furthermore, lateral thinking, discussion and presentation abilities, all key transferable skills. It has acquainted them with the professional world, giving greater insight into the workings of the museum and professional life of the maker.[16] Working as part of a mixed cohort across other craft disciplines and year groups facilitated shared learning and revealed more similarities than differences in approach.

The staff team embedded this approach into the second semester of the BA (Hons) Three Dimensional Design Programme, making significant impact on the curriculum. In accordance with the Mary Mary Quite Contrary model, project options now involve a diverse group of students working to live briefs with 'real' outcomes. The value of the blog as a discursive, critical and reflective tool was similarly recognized and has replaced the traditionally word-processed reflective journal. Moreover, the project was identified as an exemplar of good practice by the School of Art at MMU, and provided tangible evidence for the benefits of embedding staff research and cross-disciplinary collaboration into the curriculum, as the school introduces an innovative and award-winning Unit X module option across all of its programmes of study.[17]

Within MAG, this project has opened up a series of questions. If nobody ever opens the cupboard doors, what is the point of having all this stuff?

What constitutes risk to the value of an object, and how should we balance preservation with access? Is it possible to 'rationalize' the institution of the museum, a rarefied space full of memories and ghosts? We have found ourselves asking, paradoxically, whether the very rediscovery of the collection places it at risk. In exposing the collection to museological scrutiny, have we compromised its particular integrity? The battered and headless toy zebra from the Noah's Ark has now been meticulously put back together by conservators, at once removing all trace of the narrative we originally cherished. Is something lost when a broken object is restored? (Figures 12.2 and 12.3)

The practical and attitudinal challenges to the institution of opening up physical spaces, in the form of off-site stores, and conceptual spaces, in the letting go of interpretive authorities, are not to be underestimated. Whilst the project was 'under the radar', it was easier to manage. Once it gained critical

Fig. 12.2.   Broken spoon, brass, probably made about 1680. Photograph: Ben Blackall. Accreditation: The Mary Greg Collection of Handicrafts of Bygone Times, Manchester City Galleries. Accession number: 1922.846/3

Fig. 12.3. Chatelaine, steel and silver. Made in London, 1880. Photograph: Ben Blackall. Courtesy The Mary Greg Collection of Handicrafts of Bygone Times, Manchester City Galleries. Accession number: 1922.893

mass, it became harder to find the right shape for something that doesn't easily fit a standard model. This is perhaps, an inherent risk of working outside the mainstream. Skunkworks projects can be an effective way of trialling change but are equally easy to marginalize.

Yet the project has prompted a degree of self-analysis that is having a discernible impact on practice. Conservation and learning teams are working together to make the collection more accessible, an internal collaboration in which two apparently opposed concerns, access and preservation, are in negotiation with each other. The development of a handling box that can take accessioned items from the permanent collection into schools and other community settings is a groundbreaking development in which long-held assumptions about security, risk and value have been tested anew. The blog has revealed something of the inner workings of the organization, and the challenges it faces in managing unwieldy collections. We have recognized that the value of the collections is complex and shifting and is not determined by the institution alone.

CONCLUSION

Craft values have been at the core of our collaboration. The 'slow-burn' of the project enabled the 'what if?' observational and reflective process, so central to craft practice, to be applied to curatorial practice. In intuitively acknowledging the collection as it was discovered, and seeking to respond authentically, we were endeavouring to shape the collaboration in an unforced and organic way, subconsciously adopting the craft mantra of 'truth to material' (Pye 1968: 37–9). So the exhibition we were aiming for at the start has not happened. Instead we have facilitated a succession of participatory encounters: in the stores, on the blog, in the studio, in the gallery and in the classroom. It would perhaps be better, at present, to describe Mary Mary Quite Contrary as a series of collaborations rather than a single entity. Indeed, this process has led us to question the very notion of the exhibition as outcome.

The most engaged responses to the collection came from those afforded direct handling of real material and privileged access to the stores. These encounters demonstrate the potency of physical contact with real things, the tacit understanding that comes from being able to hold and feel and smell as well as look. They also suggest that individual agency, the ability to navigate your own path through a body of material, opens up the potential for a more profound level of engagement. Equally, sharing the speculative, multiperspective and sometimes tangential pathways that research often takes, via the blog, has yielded unexpected value. The blog format's combination of empirical research, intimate diary and open-ended dialogue was particularly sympathetic to the qualities of the collection itself: personal, informal, familiar, wide-ranging and inclusive. It proved an ideal medium for analytical reflection, reminiscence and discussion.

So what if we make the public encounter with the collection a starting point rather than a conclusion? If we could expand on the blog model, in physical space, what new readings might emerge? And what new forms of exhibition, display and interpretation would be required? These are questions we are still pursuing. In effect, we have shifted our stance from the workmanship of certainty towards the workmanship of risk (Pye 1968: 7–10).

In creative practice, risk is an essential ingredient, and it goes hand in hand with the potential for failure. Museums and galleries increasingly aspire to more experimental programming, but this is often difficult to reconcile with the perceived weight of curatorial responsibility. This project has demonstrated the potential of the Mary Greg Collection as a unique resource for collaborative learning, where student informs research, where maker challenges curator, where museum impacts on curriculum. This embedding of one discipline into another is at the core of our research and has drawn attention from the wider community as a model of good practice.[18] In her article 'Beyond the Display', Alke Gröppel-Wegener (2011) argues that the project's blend of experiential, object-based learning with electronic methodologies, provides fertile ground for learning as a complement or alternative to more conventional, academic forms of education.

Without the constraints of predetermined outcomes and target visitor figures, we were able to take the kinds of risks more closely associated with creative practice. As a result, we would argue that there is significant benefit in formalizing institutional links between university and gallery, perhaps considering the validation of joint units of study, embedding each institution within the other. This, we suggest, would not only provide mutually fertile ground for the maker, curator and educator but also, perhaps, a means of thriving in challenging economic climates.

Our final words come from Mary Greg herself: 'We owe it to those who have preceded us and have left those specimens of their painstaking and beautiful work and to those who will come after us to do likewise, to treasure good work and produce something into which we have put our best, our love, our intelligence, our power' (Greg 1922: 34).

NOTES

We would particularly like to thank the other key members of the Mary Mary Quite Contrary team, Hazel Jones and Alex Woodall, for their contribution to the project.

In addition, we would like to thank Martin Grimes, Alan Holding, Melanie Williamson, Mari Elliott, Myna Trustram, MMU students and the many others who have contributed to our research via the *Mary Mary Quite Contrary* project blog.

For more information about the project and the Mary Greg Collection of Handicrafts of Bygone Times, visit www.marymaryquitecontrary.org.uk.

1. The MMU Special Collections at Manchester School of Art dates from 1853 and is used for study by staff and students. It includes fine and decorative art, children's and artists' books and the Schmoller Collection of Decorated Papers.

2. *Out of the Ordinary* exhibition leaflet, Manchester Metropolitan University, 2006.

3. Ibid.

4. *The Guardian*, 3 October 1932, reported 159,297 visitors at Heaton Hall for the period January to September.

5. Letter from Mary Greg to William Batho, 27 June 1930, Manchester Art Gallery Archives.

6. For discussion of Ruskin's influence on Mary Greg, see Woodall, Mitchell and Blakey (2011).

7. Letter from Mary Greg to William Batho, 23 September 1928, Manchester Art Gallery Archives.

8. *Power of Making* exhibition, Victoria & Albert Museum, 6 September 2011–2 January 2012.

9. See, for example, Dr Louise Govier's project, *Leaders in Co-creation? Why and How Museums Could Develop Their Co-creative Practice with the Public, Building on Ideas from the Performing Arts and Other Non-museum Organisations*, MLA, Museums Clore Leadership Fellow 2008–9.

10. 'Skunkworks' is a term used in business to describe a small group within an organization given a high degree of autonomy to develop new untested ideas. For a discussion of the application of this principle within museums, see Nina Simon, *Museum Skunkworks: Carving Out a Place for Risk-Taking*, Museum 2.0 blog, 13 May 2008, <http://museumtwo.blogspot.com/2008/05/museum-skunkworks-carving-out-place-for.html> accessed 18 December 2012.

11. Letter from Mr Cleveland (MAG) to Mary Greg, 13 March 1928, Manchester Art Gallery Archives.

12. Liverpool Museums, Mary Greg Archive, 1935.26, 5 November 1935. We have subsequently uncovered Mary Greg material in several more museums, including Sheffield, Salford, Stevenage, the V&A Museum of Childhood, Bethnal Green and the British Museum.

13. Samuel Crompton, of Bolton in Lancashire, invented the spinning mule in 1779, so called because it was a hybrid of earlier spinning machines. It revolutionized cotton production, enabling the spinner to make different types of yarn and produce finer-quality woven cloth.

    The cotton threads were eventually selected for inclusion in the BBC project *A History of the World in 100 Objects* and can be seen at <http://www.bbc.co.uk/ahistoryoftheworld/objects/5mtwLXKHSi-vx6-rENLiFA> accessed 18 December 2012.

14. See 'Curatorial anxiety—as promised', *Mary Mary Quite Contrary*, <http://www.marymaryquitecontrary.org.uk/?s=curatorial+anxiety> accessed 18 December 2012.

15. See the project Web site <www.marymaryquitecontrary.org.uk> accessed 18 December 2012.

16. Evidenced in student feedback from appraisal questionnaires, MMU, March 2011: 'it has given me a sense of what it would be like to be a working artist. Being given the chance to talk to and present in front of curators is a really valuable experience' (Year 2 student).
17. The School of Art at MMU was awarded the Sir Misha Black Award for Innovation in Design Education in March 2012.
18. For example *Learning at the Interface* conference and publication, Brighton University/V&A, July 2010.

REFERENCES

Adamson, G. (2007), *Thinking through Craft*, London: Berg.

Baudrillard, J. (1968), *The System of Objects*, trans. J. Benedict, London: Verso Books.

Cass, N. (2011), 'What the Visitor Saw . . . Meaning Making, Artists and the Heritage Environment', Paper presented at Engaging, Creating: Arts and Maker Practitioner Residencies in Public Spaces, Victoria & Albert Museum, London, 6–8 April.

Fraser, M. (2012), *Digital Adventures in Contemporary Craft,* Lab Craft, touring exhibition [gallery guide], London: Crafts Council.

Greg, M. (1922), Preface to *The Greg Collection of Handicrafts of Bygone Times* [catalogue], Manchester: Manchester City Art Gallery.

Gröppel-Wegener, A. (2011), 'Beyond the Display—An Exploration of Collections in Art, Media and Design Teaching and Learning', *Networks*, <www.adm.heacademy.ac.uk/networks/networks-autumn-2011/features/beyond-the-display-2013-an-exploration-of-collections-in-art-media-and-design-teaching-and-learning> accessed 18 December 2012.

Keene, S. (2005), *Fragments of the World: Uses of Museum Collections*, Oxford: Butterworth-Heinemann.

Miller, D. (2011), 'The Power of Making', in D. Charny (ed.), *Power of Making*, London: V&A Publishing.

Ofsted (2009), *Drawing Together: Art, Craft and Design in Schools*, London: Ofsted.

Pearce, S. M. (1995), *On Collecting: An Investigation into Collecting in the European Tradition*, London: Routledge.

Pye, D. (1968), *The Nature and Art of Workmanship*, Cambridge: Cambridge University Press.

Sennett, R. (2009), *The Craftsman*, London: Penguin.

Wilkinson, H. (2005), *Collections for the Future: Report of a Museums Association Enquiry*, London: Museums Association.

Woodall, A., Mitchell, L., and Blakey, S. (2011), 'Mary Mary Quite Contrary', *Ruskin Review and Bulletin*, 7/1: 36–46.

Yanagi, S. (1978), *The Unknown Craftsman: A Japanese Insight into Beauty*, Tokyo: Kodansha International.

Yates, B. (2009), '"Treasury Things of the Least": Village Museums in the 1920s and 1930s', paper presented at the Social History Society conference, Warwick University, March.

PART IV

COLLABORATION IN AN EMERGING WORLD: ANOTHER WAY OF BEING?

Introduction

Alice Kettle, Helen Felcey and Amanda Ravetz

The authors in this section look at collaborations through craft as performance, as emergence, and as (his)stories of materials. They reveal how recognition of these qualities allows them to work across sites of cultural, political and aesthetic difference. Craft is discussed as a belonging, as a possession and as possessiveness of identity and a means to articulate location as local, dislocated or foreign. We see craft inhabiting the secret folds of everyday life, the domestic, the emblematic, and the functional with the stories of nationhood, power, resistance, of living and lineage. Within these chapters is a craft which both reinforces stereotypes and enables the 'gestures' of new beginnings and belongings. Through craft we are forced to question our own interaction and collaboration with the futures we create and the world we are part of, which are material, gendered and patterned by social structures and behaviours. The evidence in these chapters is of the nuanced intimacy of craft, which is both discreetly domestic and powerfully symbolic. It is also seen as audacious and demonstrative, the visible happenings and evidence of who we are and want to be.

Leemann and Stratton and Hare Duke and Theophilus are all curators. Their intentions diverge, yet both partnerships set up frameworks to view craft's potential as 'a powerful tool for thought' (Leemann and Stratton). For Leemann and Stratton the frame is contained as a theatrical platform within an art gallery. The audience watches an unfolding performance of making and building a world. Hare Duke and Theophilus move makers from one world experience into another in cultural exchanges, which are navigated through craft.

In both cases the expectation is to provoke, one with another as makers and participants and to inspire a deeper and more meaningful reflection of difference, division and dislocation. Craft is used as the language to listen with and speak through, to articulate the polarity of differing geographical positions and of cultural attitudes. The platform for Leeman and Stratton works as a productive fiction or 'relational jig'—a material imaginary that allows the contingent character of craft to remain open and live during the show as new relationships reveal themselves.

The performative nature of craft with its traditional roots and histories is also held within Smith's chapter. She describes the reenactments of battles with the associated crafts present, those which reinforce and fix powerful identities and social hierarchies. For Smith it is precisely craft's performativity that makes it a rich site for opening up these identities. Her use of craft, which she likens to the use of the theatrical prop, provides the setting for craft as representative of a persona, of a self to be debated, re-performed, rethought and possibly changed.

Hare Duke and Theophilus curate the shift and change through the experience and the dislocation of creative exchange. These exchanges also invoke identities, specifically those straddling the categories of traditional and contemporary. They reject overly simplistic binaries used to explain variation—between artists who use traditional techniques and those who don't and between traditional and contemporary craft—arguing for more nuanced understandings which emerge through the act of shared participation.

In the historical reenactments, Smith takes participation into the heart of gendered and political definitions with its roots and the primacy of craft evident within the performance. Employed as a conservative force that relies on repetition of the action, she argues that craft has a role in reproducing identities and nationalisms that work in aggressive counterpoint to everything they are not. The exposing of these contradictions occurs through craft. These contradictions are exemplified in terms of economic fairness and parity by Hare Duke and Theophilus, the differing conditions of artists with different histories made apparent through the dislocations experienced as they enter each other's environments to collaborate. This is the belonging and unbelonging.

Collaboration exposes the issue of possession, to whom authorship and ownership belongs. For O'Neill and Ravetz, it exposes questions of creativity; if to create is to bring something new into the world, is it only possible to think of this as an action carried out *on* the world? In a residency in India what begins as a simple matter of making objects which can be both given away and displayed, a question arises over exactly whose creativity should be rewarded and acknowledged. Is creativity the quality and property of an individual, transferred to the object as it is made? Or might it be a force alive in the world, ready to be tapped? The authors connect this second understanding of creativity to a way of thinking about materials that sees them not as inert stuff but as living matter always changing with associated stories. Together these understandings of materials and creativity suggest craft as a storied collaboration of many kinds of materials-in-the world. This, of course is very difficult to own. 'It' cannot be pinpointed—to say that this is the 'thing', this is the 'outcome'.

This expansive view of the nature of creativity is indicated by Hare Duke and Theophilus through the fundamentally different ways of working across cultural divides. They see the divisions as 'productive friction' which Leeman and Stratton deliberately construct as a barrier, a temporary dividing wall with small listening holes for craft communication. The work, which they describe as a 'gesture of resistance', knowingly acknowledges the opposing places and difficulties of relationships in a material world. It equally serves as a demonstration of craft's power to provoke thought in regard to social relations. The use of resistance in this foundational piece is common to the work by all the artists. For O'Neill and Ravetz the contrast is in the cross-fertilization of ideas invested in an object and in making, collaborating and material forms, which are predominately dispersed and emergent.

All the authors believe in craft's forward-moving potential. It is a 'searching, researching, learning, teaching, knowing, endeavouring, discovering, failing and thriving' power (Leemann and Stratton). Yet they present no utopian vision. Contrary to what some others have argued, craft in their experience is not straightforwardly democratic. They point to the tensions and flashpoints of performative craft. Smith reminds us of craft's deeply conservative tendencies, of how objects have the power to (re)generate rupture—of civil war, of family, of history/time. Hare Duke and Theophilus witness fellow travellers' complaints at being shown 'traditional' crafts during a visit to Pakistan, and the frustrated response of a host worn down by South Asian craft only being viewed through a modernist lens. The audiences of Stratton and Leemann's show struggle to respond to the open risk of an exhibition that does not instruct viewers how to look; O'Neill and Ravetz worry whether and how the tension between two different understandings of creativity can be resolved.

What is clear is how craft flows across cultural and temporal borders, that craft incites heated debate, that *it matters* (Venkatesan 2009). It can lead us to question our understanding of the past, our cultural interactions and our emergent futures. Neither a marker of unchanging tradition, nor a badge of pure innovation, forward-moving craft of the kind discussed here is freighted with knowledge born of the everyday, of the past and of the future. Craft provides a lens, a 'view', which offers an extraordinary depth of field.

Modernity, says Giddens, is a society that lives in the future rather than the past (1998: 94). When the future is what matters, progress becomes synonymous with the new—new ideas, new objects, new projects (Leach 2007: 106). It has also been said that with modernity, comes the rise of possessive individualism—that what was once commonly inherited and shared is appropriated by people acting for themselves (Leach 2007: 106). Consider the many categories applied to craft—ethnographic, bygone, world, traditional, folk—and ponder how things that fail the 'future-new test' are marginalized and demoted. Once the future alone becomes the proper destination for humankind, shared inheritance is pressured. As opposed to possessive individualism, here we see craft revealing an ardent plurality. We see craft revealing the inseparable nature of things; as opposed to defining objects, ideas and projects, we see it examining the spaces in between; as opposed to recognizing the one creator to be credited, we are forced to recognize a view that is harder to fix or grasp on to.

Not all societies privilege the future; speakers of Amarya for example conceptualize the past as ahead and the future as behind (Núñez and Cornejo 2012). We might propose that emergent craft faces what has unfolded while 'walking backwards' into the future—and that this constitutes its own form of progress. These chapters question our definitions of progress—they highlight the limitations of these definitions. They are not solely rooted in the past, nor focused solely on the future. They are only 'true', only really seen, as they happen. Their 'life' is not contained within one graspable object to be kept and admired but in what emerges from the actions of many.

REFERENCES

Giddens, A. (1998), *The Third Way: The Renewal of Social Democracy*, Cambridge: Polity.

Leach, J. (2007), 'Creativity, Subjectivity and the Dynamic of Possessive Individualism', in E. Hallam and T. Ingold (eds), *Creativity and Cultural Improvisation*, Oxford: Berg, 99–116.

Núñez, R., and Cornejo, C. (2012), 'Facing the Sunrise: Cultural Worldview Underlying Intrinsic-Based Encoding of Absolute Frames of Reference in Aymara', *Cognitive Science*, 36/6: 1–27.

Venkatesan, S. (2009), *Craft Matter: Artisans, Development and the Indian Nation*, New Delhi: Orient Blackswan.

–13–

Expanded Battlefields:
Craft as a Different Sort of Reenactment

Allison Smith

As a contributor to the final section of this volume on craft and collaboration, I am actually going to share some thoughts on craft and conflict. This is not a text on the war between art and craft, nor is it about the old guard versus the new wave of craft. To echo the words of Glenn Adamson, 'I would like to see craft set free of both its embattled mentality [. . .] and its presumption of moral superiority' (Rauch 2009). The trajectory of my work has not advanced in relation to the American studio craft movement, nor is it especially aligned with do-it-yourself (Levine and Heimerl 2008) or craftivism movements (Bryan-Wilson 2008: 78–83; Halper and Douglas 2009: 296–300; Adamson 2010: 620–28). Rather, I have arrived at my approach to craft through a critical inquiry of historical reenactment, or Living History, a cultural phenomenon and popular pastime in which dedicated history buffs dress up in period costumes and fight mock battles using meticulously crafted reproductions of uniforms, weapons and other props. Living History is founded on the idea that historical events gain meaning and relevance when performed live in an open-air, interactive setting. Here, performing the 'art' of war has everything to do with crafting objects in such historically accurate detail that they can actually facilitate time travel.

In 1995, I began investigating American Civil War reenactment (Ward et al. 1992; Horwitz 1998), which for many in the United States carries overtones of right-wing conservatism as well as racism because the war signifies a massive division in the country over states' rights in connection with the abolition of slavery. Considering that the reverberations of this cultural conflict are still being felt 150 years later, I was fascinated by the apparent need to replay the Civil War over and over as a material-based hands-on practice. This collaborative form of history *in-the-making* became a pivotal focus of my work, offering a rich set of activities and objects that I bring into association with contemporary art. These endeavors have evolved out of the concept of 'sculpture in the expanded field' (Krauss 1979), alongside emergent theoretical discourses on relational aesthetics (Bourriaud [1998] 2002; Bishop 2004), dialogical art

(Kester 2004), social practices, material culture studies, and thing theory (Brown 2001). My work is research- and project-based and it owes something to conceptual art; however, the ideas that most interest me concern 'craft' and the social histories of making (Matthews 2005: 6–14; Rauch 2009).

I came of age in the era of so-called post-studio art (Jacob and Grabner 2010: 30–36) and the 'post-medium' condition (Krauss 2000), therefore like many artists of my generation, rather than committing to a primary medium, I negotiate which materials and methods are best suited to the work at hand, knowing that even my choices and actions in this regard are citational and carry meaning. In my practice I move freely between variously skilled, deskilled and reskilled modes of production, which I employ consciously. I make many things with my own hands; I also hire fabricators and learn from artisans. Rather than accepting a singular idea of authorship, I believe that all art is collaborative but that we often blind ourselves to the many hands that go into artworks, from the harvesting and processing of materials before they even reach the art supply or hardware store, to the final 'product' and its need for at least one viewer to recognize and complete it as art. Rather than embracing a singular definition of craft, I see myself often acting as a mediator between various ideological camps. I would never privilege or celebrate one form of craftsmanship over another; when I look at art I consider the way something is made in relation to historical methods, and I ask what motivated those decisions on behalf of the maker. In my opinion, craft is not something that can be defined but is rather something with which people identify. To some, my craftsmanship is seen as fanatical; to others, I may be considered a dilettante. However, intrinsic to my praxis is the destabilizing of master narratives (and notions of mastery), and I'm comfortable playing the role of jack-of-all-trades, master-of-none in my efforts to create conversations between and across disciplines. In truth, I share a deep love for the 'traditions' commonly associated with craft and have definitely spent more than 'ten thousand hours' (Gladwell 2008; Sennett 2008) honing various skills. I identify with craft; it figures into my personal myth (Jung 1961: 3), and I return to it over and over. But I am not a champion of craft in and of itself; in fact, I implicate myself within a conservative use of craft. To me, craft is indeed 'a problem to be thought through again and again' (Adamson 2007: 168).

As a student in early 1990s New York City, artists associated with institutional critique, feminist art, and identity politics inspired me. While pursuing undergraduate degrees in art and psychology simultaneously, I sought practical training in art therapy and immersed myself in art criticism informed by psychoanalytic thought and social theory. I was deeply influenced by the writings of post-structuralist philosopher Judith Butler, who famously theorized the performativity of gender, sex and sexuality. Arguing that the ground of identity, tenuously constituted in time, is instituted through the stylized repetition of acts, Butler discusses how identities are socially and culturally constructed within regulative discourses, frameworks of intelligibility, and/or disciplinary regimes though a ritualized production—not a conscious performance *per se*, but everyday acts that appear naturalized because they are constantly being repeated. Importantly, she proposes the possibility of *a different sort of repeating*, in the breaking or subversive repetition of style (Butler 1990, 1993: 95; Adamson 2010: 458; Sennett 2008: 294). My senior thesis paper attempted to reconcile the psychological *self* (as psychic organizing ground) and the socially situated *subject* (as political possibility), through a form of 'critical autobiography'. Connected to the second-wave feminist assertion that 'the personal is political', the term suggests that the autobiographical can also complicate the theoretical (Smith 1995). Charged by much contemporary art of that time, I felt personally called to self-reflexively consider my own subject position (Segrest 1994; Alison 2002). Butler says that identity is not what one is but what one does. In my formulation, perhaps craft is what one does and, through repeated performance, constructs who one is (Brown 2001: 1–22; Butler 1993: 250).

I grew up in the Northern Virginia suburbs of Washington, DC. My mother is an early American crafts enthusiast and Martha Stewart acolyte; she gave me my first exposure to art through more than fifteen different kinds of 'women's work', including numerous forms of needlework, from patchwork quilting to crewel work embroidery, as well as decorative stenciling, Bauernmalerei, and tole painting. Our home was furnished with historical reproductions, like a stage set for reenactment in the everyday, and these mother–daughter rituals provided a portal through which the nineteenth-century values of Protestant morality, Victorian etiquette and Southern hospitality were passed down and kept alive. For my mother, craft was a way of Living™ and of loving. But my father is also crafty. In perhaps humorously gendered complement to my mother, he is an electrical engineer, computer geek and tinkerer. He made model airplanes, boats, and steam engines and is a prolific kite maker. Although I didn't know this as a child, he works for the US Central Intelligence Agency and is involved in *tradecraft*, or the art of international espionage, designing secret spy gadgets and objects known as *concealments*: things that look like something familiar but in fact have a hidden function. For my father, craft was a form of escape as well as a vehicle for transmitting and receiving secret knowledge. The things he made had multiple, elusive identities—like himself. While many of the domestic arts I practiced with my mother were inflected with a spirit of American patriotism and wholesome femininity, my father's crafts had a wilder, darker side, and I was filled with a deep sense of anxiety and inner conflict over his role in events on a world scale. In the words of Richard Sennett, 'The craftsman's skills, if natural, are never innocent' (Sennett 2008: 294; Adamson 2009; Heidegger 1971).

Almost every year we would go to both Colonial Williamsburg, a quasi-fictional town in which interpreters dress and work as colonists did in the eighteenth-century capital of Virginia, and the Waterford Fair, a juried crafts exhibition in which 'heritage craftspeople' provide hands-on demonstrations in period costume.[1] In these pedagogical spaces of consumption, nationalism is performed through embodied forms of making such as linen weaving, gunsmithing and all sorts of other pre-modern trades that figure prominently in the mythology of America's founding. In 1976 the United States celebrated its bicentennial, sparking a boom in reenactment as a national pastime and boosting the popularity of traditional handcrafts on a massive scale. Books like *With These Hands They Built a Nation* (Lazarus 1971) described the skills—weaving, carpentry, candle making, metalworking and others—that allegedly enabled the early American colonists to start life from scratch in the New World. People on both sides of my family have been preoccupied with genealogy, and with ancestors having come to America from England, Ireland and Scotland in the 1700s, these experiences offer an opportunity to walk in their footsteps. I am from one of many families in the southern United States for whom the American Civil War never really ended. My ancestors owned cotton plantations off the coast of Charleston, South Carolina, and two of them signed the original Ordinance of Secession that sparked the war. This moment of rupture is one that my family returns to again and again, particularly through (finely crafted) objects that tell the story of our forebears' wealth, accomplishments and ultimate ruin. Through reenactment, whether as a theatrical form of public spectacle, or a private or even subconscious daily ritual, history is revealed as an active, participatory and collaborative process. Nationhood is one kind of imagined community, and across nations and communities of all kinds, crafts are used to shore up a sense of cohesive identity, especially in troubled times. I am interested in the charged role of craft in these constructions of identity, whether for the creation of personal mythology or political propaganda.

As history-making institutions, I have always wanted to subject forms of Living History to institutional critique. With my background in psychology, I am struck by its seeming connections to trauma, dissociation and object relations theory. I wondered what motivated reenactors, and I began conducting my own ethnography of the Civil War reenactment community (Smith 1997; Foster 1996; Clifford 1997) much like an indigenous anthropologist studying my home society. I've always been fascinated by groups of people who demonstrate an intense investment in history through hands-on, material-based practices. It is like a parallel art world and a useful reminder that history itself is a contestable field. To my mind, all uses of history are political, many are conservative, and some are pernicious. Art offers a way to revise, replay, restage, redo, re-craft, and reclaim one's position in the so-called master narrative. Art is a great place for holding things that cannot and perhaps should not be easily resolved, and through my work I have tried to propose craft as a way of literally taking history into your own hands: consider craft a form of direct democracy in the struggle for meaning.

Through his idea of social sculpture, Joseph Beuys wanted to 'extend the concept of art in a radical way, and make it an anthropological one—taking the starting point for creativity as inherent in thinking, which in turn is capable of creating forms in the world' (Beuys and Volker 2004). In other words, if everyone is inherently capable of creativity, then everyone collaborates in shaping society. Recall that Beuys himself was a German pilot whose plane was shot down and crashed over the Crimea. As the story goes, he was saved by nomadic Tartar tribesmen who wrapped him in felt and fat. This is a trauma he reenacts through the materials, processes, and forms of his sculptures, ritualistic performances, lectures and other demonstrations. His own reenactment impulse is revealed in this quote: 'I have never thought that contemporary civilization should be judged as something negative. It's true I do turn back, go back, try and expand what exists by breaking through it in a forward-looking way. In this way ancient, mythical content comes to have contemporary relevance' (Beuys and Volker 2004). Just as imaginative portrayals of the future in science fiction novels and films reveal the fears and aspirations of the time in which they are created, it is important to remember that historical reenactment is always about the present. When people ask me about the role of nostalgia in my work, I invoke the original definition of the term, as a medical diagnosis for soldiers suffering from homesickness.

Early in my research on Civil War reenactment, I went to visit the site of my ancestors' cotton plantations on Edisto Island and slept in a house that once belonged to Confederate kin. While there I photographed some graffiti left on the walls of the summer kitchen by northern troops who occupied the house during the war. I later transformed these drawings, many of which took the form of boats, into a repeat pattern suggestive of a masculine drawing room interior, which I hand painted onto a large wall using a traditional stenciling technique. Working with a professional photographer, I invited Bill Max (a reenactor I had met on the Internet) to pose for a formal portrait in front of the wall. While we were taking his photograph, he played the role of an informant, schooling me on every kind of boat depicted in the graffiti and its function during the war, as well as the name of the occupying regiment—until then unknown to my family. Our conversation segued into a story about him being chosen to read the names of fallen soldiers at a commemorative wreath-laying ceremony and while recounting this experience, he cried. Ironically, his own ancestors had emigrated to the United States from Eastern Europe during the early twentieth century, but he felt sure that if they *had* been in the country during the war, they would have fought for the North. In addition to the Civil War, Bill had also participated in Revolutionary War and Second World War reenactment; he was also a Vietnam War veteran. This encounter offered an intimate and surprising view of the ways gender, heritage and personal experience motivate reenactors. The installation *Edisto* consisted of this painted wall and Bill's full-color framed portrait placed onto it.

From 2004 to 2006, I organized a series of large-scale public art events in which I invoked the aesthetic vernacular of American Civil War battle reenactment as a stage set for a polyphonic marshalling of voices in my artistic and intellectual communities. Instead of pitting two sides against each other, I organized these events around the question, What are you fighting for? and called the project *The Muster*, a military term meaning a gathering of the troops for the purposes of inspection, critique, exercise and display. In 2005, the project took form in a creative encampment at Fort Jay, on Governors Island, New York Harbor, in which approximately 125 enlisted participants fashioned uniforms, built campsites and declared their causes publicly to an audience of more than 2,000 spectators. I saw this as creating a literal platform for free expression, complete with banners and flags. I directed but did not script the event, so that its outcome was only revealed at The Muster itself. One of the most exciting aspects of this project was that it brought together an incredibly wide range of participants and spectators, from feminist and genderqueer artists and tourists to actual Civil War reenactors and former military residents of Governors Island (Eccles et al. 2007). On a grand scale, this project created an opportunity to enact the aesthetic and performative qualities of reenactment culture in countless ways, repeating it differently and opening it up to myriad interpretations.

Soon after *The Muster* I created the performative sculpture *Hobby Horse* (2006) while on a residency in San Antonio, Texas. This piece was originally inspired by a small, hand-carved rocking horse that I found at a country fair in England. I wanted to monumentalize the toy in homage to its anonymous maker, as well as to physically 'enter' equestrian statuary, the best-known form of war memorial sculpture. The title *Hobby Horse* refers to the notion of craft as 'merely' a hobby as well as to history as a fixation. At the exhibition opening, I rode the horse in costume, singing a song set to the tune of the patriotic Civil War ballad 'When Johnny Comes Marching Home', which was in fact based on an older Irish folk song. The Civil War version is a call to welcome home the heroic soldier, while the other is a sad lament on the horrors of any war, wherein Johnny returns a broken man. In my own version, I asked when or if soldiers ever can 'come home', rocking in place as a way of gesturing towards a contemporary state of cultural impasse. Many of my sculptures over the past decade have taken the form of toys that refer to 'official' forms of sculpture, suggesting both socialization and play (Figure 13.1).

I have done several works inspired by the writings of Samuel Clemens, also known as Mark Twain (McGregor 2007; Berger 2011) (Figure 13.2). What most interests me in Twain's writing is his use of time travel as a way of holding the past up to the present, explaining in a sense 'how we got here' but also reminding us that we make our world. Twain takes extra care in describing the costumes, 'props' and interiors in which the action of each story plays out. There are also many references throughout his work to trades, crafts and

Fig. 13.1. *Hobby Horse*. 2006. Allison Smith. Photograph: Todd Johnson. Commissioned by Artpace San Antonio

the pleasures of manual labor. Twain delights in role-play and provides many an object lesson on the performativity of identity, and especially the way masculinity and nationalism are performed. As the saying goes, 'the clothes make the man', and Twain's stories are filled with accounts of mistaken identity and the use of disguise. These performative accounts serve to elucidate deeper concerns: walking in the shoes of others in order to understand injustice, or exploring feelings toward war and the role one plays in it, for example. Twain's protagonists navigate through complex social realities in playfully mischievous ways, often doing the 'wrong' thing in order to do the right thing. In his stories, he often creates a sticky situation, or a test, asking the reader to grapple with questions that don't resolve into a single easy answer. In one episode

Fig. 13.2. *By the by and by and by*. 2007. Allison Smith. Photograph: Stefan Hagen. Commissioned by Wave Hill

of *Adventures of Huckleberry Finn*, Huck and Jim see a house floating down the flooded Mississippi and raid it for supplies. Jim finds and quickly covers a dead body, which is later revealed to be Huck's abusive father. Huck looks away from the corpse and instead takes a detailed inventory of the objects in the house, perhaps to avoid thinking about the murdered man to whom they might have belonged. For *A Good Haul* (2010), I gathered and created 'historical reproductions' of the objects of Huck's careful attention, based on Twain's textual descriptions, in part while travelling up the Mississippi River from New Orleans to Chicago. The work, like Twain's novel, treads the line between fiction and faithful retelling, research and re-creation, describing the old and constructing new fables and artefacts (Figure 13.2).

Another project that involved my own form of historical reproduction was Needle Work (2010) which emerged from a series of photographs of early cloth gas masks that I had been taking in European and American military history museums. I was struck by the haunting, almost ghoulish quality of these masks and their visual equivalence to other kinds of masks, hoods, costumes and veils. I was also attracted to their handmade quality, which seemed to suggest a simultaneous loving care and functional inadequacy. I saw these remnants as an as-yet unwritten history of needlework (Smith 2010). The repeated thought that 'someone made this' compelled me to recreate many of the masks and to expand my search to kindred forms found on the Internet. I used these out-of-focus, poorly lit and pixilated images to inspire my own flawed 'authentic reproductions', using materials from local fabric/craft retail stores and recycling centers. I invited others to work with me at making our own versions of the masks: plainly stitched, unspoiled, stain-free and ready to be used. I was thinking of this process as a kind of quilting bee, akin to that of the seamstresses who supply the material culture for the field of Living History. This form of making-as-performance in the studio was then followed by the performance of the articles in a series of staged portraits in which I invited others to 'perform' the masks, using this idea of handle-ability or materiality-as-process to demonstrate acts of survival, cruelty, modesty, disguise or fetish. As part of this project I also collaborated with my father on the creation of a series of silk parachutes that were printed with images of the masks from my research. The title Needle Work was meant to suggest a creative process that literally gets under the skin.

Fancy Work (2010) is an installation that looked to an exuberant early-nineteenth-century decorative arts movement known as American Fancy to trace an alternate lineage for modernist abstraction and psychedelic light shows—a wartime art form made using military surplus materials that represents both escape and consciousness-raising. Drawing from patchwork quilts by Rebecca Scattergood Savery and others that were inspired by the 1815 invention of the kaleidoscope, I gathered a group of local makers to create a vibrant, dizzying quilt top composed of more than 2,400 screen-printed, cut, and sewn linen diamonds. The design is a variation of the traditional Star of Bethlehem quilt pattern, which Scattergood innovatively took to the edges of her quilts like shockwaves that could not be contained. This monumental quilt top then served as the projection screen for a mirrored colonial wall sconce and a large electrified candle. The form of the sconce was like an inverted disco ball scaled up to the size of a giant satellite dish. Viewers navigated the space with punched tinwork lanterns, creating moving patterns of light and shadow, while a series of musicians played the musical saw. I invited a number of speakers to activate the space between the quilt and sconce, including historian Sumpter Priddy III on American Fancy, media arts scholar Robin Oppenheimer on West Coast light shows of the 1960s and '70s, light show pioneer Bill Ham on light shows as a forgotten folk art form, American quilt historian Roderick Kiracofe on his collection of eccentric improvisational quilts, and activist and NAMES Project AIDS Memorial Quilt founder Cleve Jones on AIDS activists' strategy of turning a symbol of American family values on its head: quilt as battlefield and mass grave (Figure 13.3). Subsequently, the scraps from *Fancy Work* became a braided rug at the Museum of Contemporary Art Denver, co-created with museum-goers and which served as a platform upon which to reflect on the connections between domestic handicrafts and handmade militaria.

As you can see in these examples, many of my works have engaged with early American material culture. For *Jugs, Pitchers, Bottles, and Crocks, Household Linens and Yardage in Stock* (2008), I worked with Pittsburgh, Pennsylvania, potter Bernard Jakub to make a series of stoneware vessels adorned with

Fig. 13.3. *Fancy Work (Crazy Quilting)*. 2010. Allison Smith. Photograph: Allison Smith. Commissioned by SFMOMA

cobalt blue imagery and text. These were inspired by rare examples of early American utilitarian ceramics that commemorate important dates, battles, political figures and movements, though the significance of this information is mostly lost to history. The images and slogans with which I decorated these 'vessels of anxiety' relate to contemporary wars and catastrophic events, terrorism and religious fundamentalism. *Stockpile* (2011) is a large structure comprising objects and materials suggesting early-American colonial craft re-enactment and reproduction. Made from craft kits purchased on the Internet, I included such familiar forms as crates, barrels, and baskets, pieces of unfinished wood furniture for domestic interiors and campsites, a spinning wheel, flags, drums, canteens, wooden guns, and many other items held together precariously like a stockpile of raw materials poised at a tipping point. This work is akin to a campsite or period room turned in on itself, in which objects for the home and battlefield form a collected pile of loot, held in reserve for use at a time of shortage. Consisting primarily of unfinished wood, this sculpture suggests a campfire or funeral pyre, and a blank canvas upon which to project imagery. The objects appear to be new and ready to be used, like props for a reenactment, but in their massive piling suggest anxiety or obsession. Many of the items were made in Thailand, Malaysia, Vietnam, India, Brazil and China, bringing these colonial reproductions full circle from their historical referent to current issues of American mass consumption and outsourced labor. I think of this work as a collaboration with the factory workers in other places who began the process of making the objects for me the American consumer to finish—so that I could fulfil a fantasy of craftsmanship, reenacting the role of the early American craftsperson in the twenty-first century.

Finally, ARTS & SKILLS Service is an ongoing project that re-stages a Second World War era collaboration between the American Red Cross and the San Francisco Museum of Modern Art in which hundreds of Bay Area artists and craftspeople were enlisted to teach hands-on workshops to returning GIs. Quoting from promotional materials from that time, 'Here in San Francisco over fifteen hundred men a month are being sent out from our three military hospitals with a new weapon in their hands: a skill or craft with which to fight discouragement or boredom'.[2] This project has evolved into a series of interactive installations, public conversations, workshops and other exchanges with Bay Area makers, veterans, art students and art therapists. In 2011, I began partnering with Swords to Plowshares, a San Francisco–based nonpartisan veteran service organization whose program SHOUT! for Women Veterans was inspired by the notion that the arts encourage expression and healing.

Throughout my practice, I engage craft as a different sort of reenactment, using it implicate myself and others in processes of identity formation, nationhood construction and collective myth-making. I use craft to expose the limits of conflicting arenas of traditional public sculpture, socially engaged art and performance. My work presents an uneasy relationship to authorship, avoiding a definitive stance and at times offering a polyphony of viewpoints. I use craft in a strategic way, allowing it to act as a civic catalyst in the public sphere. While studio craft and social practices in contemporary art don't often merge, both share the desire for an intimate and direct mode of engagement. One privileges the material object, exchanged 'hand to hand' while the other may forego the object altogether in favor of direct actions or conversations. I make sculptures that are large-scale conversation pieces, artefacts that facilitate and witness occasions to engage in conversation and conflict. Positioned between utopian and critical discourses, these works craft backwards and forwards.

NOTES

1. See Waterford Fair: Saving the Best to Last, <http://www.waterfordfoundation.org/waterford-fair> accessed 20 March 2013.
2. Sophie Morris Kent, 15 June 1944. San Francisco Museum of Modern Art (SFMOMA) Archives.

REFERENCES

Adamson, G. (2007), *Thinking through Craft*, London: Berg and the Victoria and Albert Museum.

Adamson, G. (2009), 'Craft in the 21st Century: Directions and Displacements', lecture, Museum of Craft, Portland, Oregon, February.

Adamson, G. (2010), *The Craft Reader*, Oxford: Berg.

Alison, D. (2002), *Trash*, New York: Plume Books.

Berger, M. (2011), *Huckleberry Finn*, San Francisco: CCA Wattis Institute for Contemporary Arts.

Beuys, J., and Volker, H. (2004), *What Is Art? Conversations with Joseph Beuys*, London: Clairview Books.

Bishop, C. (2004), 'Antagonism and Relational Aesthetics', *October*, 110 (Autumn): 51–79.

Bourriaud, N. (1998), *Relational Aesthetics*, France: Les Presses du réel.

Brown, B. (2001), 'Thing Theory', *Critical Inquiry*, 8/1 (Autumn): 1–22.

Bryan-Wilson, J. (2008), 'The Politics of Craft: A Roundtable', *Modern Painters* (February).

Butler, J. (1990), *Gender Trouble*, New York: Routledge.

Butler, J. (1993), *Bodies That Matter: On the Discursive Limits of 'Sex'*, New York: Routledge.

Clifford, J. (1997), *Routes: Travel and Translation in the Late Twentieth Century*, Cambridge, MA: Harvard University Press.

Collins, L., Gschwandtner, S., Mazza, C., and Smith, A., moderated by Julia Bryan-Wilson (2008), 'Crafting Protest' panel discussion, Vera List Center for Art and Politics, The New School, New York, 26 January.

Eccles, T., Smith, A., Trainor, J., and Wehr, A. (2007), *Allison Smith: The Muster: What Are You Fighting For?* New York: Public Art Fund.

Foster, H. (1996), 'The Artist as Ethnographer', in *The Return of the Real: The Avante-Garde at the End of the Century*, Cambridge, MA: MIT Press.

Gladwell, M. (2008), *Outliers: The Story of Success*, New York: Little, Brown and Company.

Halper, V., and Douglas, D. (eds) (2009), *Choosing Craft: The Artist's Viewpoint*, Chapel Hill: University of North Carolina Press.

Heidegger, M. (1971), 'The Thing', in *Poetry, Language, Thought*, New York: HarperCollins.

Horwitz, T. (1998), *Confederates in the Attic: Dispatches from the Unfinished Civil War*, New York: Vintage Books.

Jacob, M. J., and Grabner, M. (2010), *The Studio Reader: On the Space of Artists*, Chicago: University of Chicago Press and the School of the Art Institute of Chicago.

Jung, C. G. (1961), *Memories, Dreams, Reflections*, London: Collins, Fount Paperbacks.

Kester, G. H. (2004), *Conversation Pieces: Community and Communication in Modern Art*, Berkeley: University of California Press.

Krauss, R. (1979), 'Sculpture in the Expanded Field', *October*, 8 (Spring).

Krauss, R. (2000), *A Voyage on the North Sea: Art in the Age of the Post-medium Condition*, London: Thames & Hudson.

Lazarus, L. (1971), *With These Hands They Built a Nation: The Story of Colonial Arts and Crafts*, New York: J. Messner Publishers.

Levine, F., and Heimerl, C. (2008), *Handmade Nation: The Rise of DIY, Art, Craft, and Design*, New York: Princeton Architectural Press.

Matthews, L. (2005), 'Homespun Ideas: Reinterpreting Craft in Contemporary Culture', in C. Fink (ed.), *Practice Makes Perfect: Bay Area Conceptual Craft*, San Francisco: Southern Exposure.

McGregor, J. (2007), *Twain and Poe Projects: Simon Leung/Allison Smith/ Amy Yoes*, Bronx: Wave Hill.

Morris, K. S. (1944), *Arts & Skills* [promotional materials], American Red Cross and the San Francisco Museum of Modern Art.

Rauch, A. (2009), 'An Interview with Glenn Adamson', *PORT: Portland art + news + reviews* (17 February), <http://www.portlandart.net/archives/2009/02/glenn_adamson_t.html> accessed 29 August 2012.

Robleto, D. (2005), conversation with Allison Smith.

Segrest, M. (1994), *Memoir of a Race Traitor*, Cambridge: South End Press.

Sennett, R. (2008), *The Craftsman*, New Haven, CT: Yale University Press.

Smith, A. (1995), 'Cultivating the Self and Subject through Art,' Senior thesis paper, Parsons School of Design/Eugene Lang College, The New School for Social Research, New York.

Smith, A. (1997), 'Springing to the Call or Chasing Camp: An Ethnography of Living History', written for Brian Wallis's Critical Issues seminar, Yale University School of Art, MFA sculpture program, December.

Smith, A. (2010), *Allison Smith: Needle Work*, St. Louis, MO: Mildred Lane Kemper Art Museum, Washington University in St. Louis.

Smith, P. H. (2006), *The Body of the Artisan: Art and Experience in the Scientific Revolution*, Chicago: University of Chicago Press.

Ward, G. C., Burns, R., and Burns, K. (1992), *The Civil War: An Illustrated History*, New York: Knopf.

14

Crafts and the Contemporary in South Asia—A Collaborative Journey

Barney Hare Duke and Jeremy Theophilus

INTRODUCTION

. . . in which we outline our practice, our fields of production, and where we identify some of the issues we have encountered.

We have been working together as A Fine Line: Cultural Practice a partner-ship of creative producers, for the past eight years, developing and delivering a programme of international artists' residencies. Our mission is the explora-tion and expression of contemporary crafts practice, that is to say craft pro-duced by makers living and working in the twenty-first century, whether or not they are working within what can be described as a traditional craft format. Jyotindra Jain has talked about 'the endless contemporary in tradition', and for us there is no dividing line here,[1] nor should there be a binary distinction between the two categories. The challenge is mediating the differences and exposing the potential for new forms of craft.

As A Fine Line: Cultural Practice we are intrigued by national and cultural difference and challenged by the distinction within international crafts be-tween the realities of making to live, rather than making to please. By this we are highlighting the comparative luxuries of Western makers for whom there is a choice whether to be a maker or not, as opposed to those in South Asia for many of whom it is a necessity to make in order to survive. For both, the mo-tivation to continue is finely balanced between the creative and the economic. Unpicking the aesthetic awareness in each category of maker is an uneven exercise. For example, a Warli painter[2] appreciates the skill of telling a story in a number of different ways, but it is very difficult to provoke from them an opinion on the sense of quality that differentiates one piece from another.

Inasmuch as difference implies a pair of states, we have found ourselves working as pairs between cultures, exploring the possibilities for connections rather than similarities. Indeed we delight in the difference between, that space where one looks in both directions to fix one's own fluid state. In other words, by observing and absorbing the different practices, we can take a fix on our own somewhat disturbed position as mediators and enablers. That fluidity is a positive state within which we seek to find new solutions to age-old questions.

However, this anxiety about working in a middle ground has manifested itself more as we have developed each programme, to the point where we designed and pursued a research enquiry between ourselves, called Craft: Who Cares? With funding from the Crafts Council we were able to buy time out from the round of creative productions for critical reflection. The questions we asked ourselves interrogated the likely direction for craft practice, whether the crafts are enjoying a critical global renaissance or becoming an endangered species, the role of value attached to the craft object and ultimately, who cares, to whom does it matter, and why? This forced us to take a more objective view of our activities and to evaluate our achievements, as well as to allow us to share ideas with makers and curators within the sector.

This chapter summarizes our practice and draws on the direct experiences of those whom we have worked and supported through their residencies to identify themes that have become central to our thinking forward on contemporary craft as it is practised across the two cultures in the United Kingdom and in South Asia. In so doing it acknowledges what we learned from Craft: Who Cares? and re-applies it to the initiatives we plan and the makers and their practice with whom we continue to work, culminating in a possible definition of the state of this kind of transitionary craft practice, together with some signposts to further enquiry.

THE PROGRAMME: EXCHANGE AND INVESTMENT

. . . being the foundational aims upon which we have based our activities.

Our ethos is built on the necessity for exchange between cultures, a balancing act with the ambition to move artists between countries in a perfectly equable motion of fairness. This means equal fees, accommodation, subsistence and support. To avoid the potential danger of our practice being perceived in the context of faded colonial footprints,[3] we have tried to walk at a different pace, but by no means with the success which we would have liked to achieve. Perhaps the greatest problem is that of creating a structure from the United Kingdom that tries to anticipate the difficulties without having the appropriate degree of onshore input. We are now reshaping projects that take this into account but still face the task of attracting investment from South Asia, something that would help to provide a necessary balance.

We have developed a programme with three interrelated strands that offer different ways of facilitating this process of engagement and that reflect our

Fig. 14.1.   Arts Reverie, Ahmedabad, India, 2011. Photograph: Helen Felcey

own increasingly deepening relationship with India in particular. Their relationship is based on a continuing development as projects grow from each other, and as new partners bring their own expectations and requirements to bear on each programme. These are the International Exchange Residency linking artists and arts organizations and academic institutions; our shared ownership of Arts Reverie as a special house for artists in Ahmedabad, India; and the current programme, Material Response, facilitating makers responding to museums, their collections and their audiences. Each is dependent on developing new partnerships, creating a 'family' of networks and participants. These include the selected artists, host organizations and museum staff, local artists' networks, regional nongovernmental organizations, interest-specific groups and agencies and, to an increasingly lesser extent, stakeholders and funders (Figure 14.1).

HAT: HERE AND THERE

We started this journey in 2002 with a project called HAT: Here and There[4]— a structured programme of international exchange residencies for the crafts that has, over the past ten years, linked England with Australia, China, the Caribbean and, most especially, with South Asia. We have worked in a number of collaborative ways: with artists, craftspeople and artisans; between cultures, disciplines, economies and hierarchies; in museums, galleries, academic institutions, agencies and art centres.

The exchange residency links two artists and two institutions for a period of three months for each artist whilst they undertake personal research in a state of displacement. It forms part of a programme of several such exchanges, at whose completion all those involved come together for a week of discussion, workshops and networking. A Web site documents the programme with opportunities for each artist to upload diaries and images, and short films are commissioned as a means of creatively analysing the residency experience.

Exchange was built into our initial planning for HAT and became a core component: we wanted to enable artists from each country to experience one another's working environments on the same financial basis and with the same opportunities, based on UK fees and country-specific subsistence rates. We wanted to see what might transpire as outcomes in both directions: that this was not to be one-way curatorial tourism but to explore ways in which meaningful legacies might be exchanged. We are not interested in making a curatorial invasion of an *other*'s culture to then try and represent those spoils in the United Kingdom within a false environment. Instead we want to try and establish meaningful opportunities for artists and makers in each partner country.

HAT was about cultural trade with a number of specific objectives. It was to support the development of individuals' creative practice, to promote an increase in mutual understanding, awareness and appreciation across cultural boundaries and to facilitate a greater communication and collaboration between artists and the movement of ideas and creative product between countries.

HAT grew out of an initial collaboration between North West Arts Board (now Arts Council England, North West) and the Object Gallery in Sydney. In February 2001, NWAB took *Make Me . . .* an exhibition of contemporary craft and design from Manchester, to the Object Gallery, presenting work from a cohort of new fresh designer-makers closely associated with (re-branding) Manchester's confident, cool independent creative industries sector. The wider cultural context for the North West at this time included Manchester's hosting of the 2002 Commonwealth Games (to be succeeded by Melbourne), and Liverpool's bid for Capital of Culture. Timed to coincide with the exhibition, Claire Norcross, one of the exhibitors, worked for three months as artist-in-residence at the Pyrmont Jewellery Workshop in Sydney. This residency, from which a Habitat[5] best-selling lampshade was born, served as the initial pilot residency for the HAT Project. It offered a different way of looking at exhibition making by foregrounding the artist as producer whose work would shape the nature of the final presentation.

The success of the project and interest generated by the combination of residency and exhibition stimulated the request from other promoting agencies to be involved. Working with four host regions in England and five states in Australia, seventeen jewellers were selected to undertake three-month residencies in 2003. The culmination of the residencies was the HAT conference in Manchester, affectionately dubbed the "cHAT Week". It not only provided all the artists with their only chance to be together in one place but also became the point of curatorial decision making for the content of the exhibition, as each artist brought their own research material for inclusion. Through openly examining the individual experiences of the residencies and exploring some of the common themes of dislocation and the familiar, what were revealed were not only their professional working practices but also the layers of the emotional experience. The person, the process and the work became the subject matter for the exhibition in a way that had not necessarily been anticipated at the start of the programme.

An award-winning publication documented the programme, with each artist designing the content for their own page, and this accompanied the exhibition that toured over two years in both Australia and England.[6] The artist/film-maker Johnny Magee provided still and moving images as documentation of the residencies, as well as developing and managing the Web site. His approach to documentation added considerably to the visitor's understanding of a residency and its associated displacement for the artist, and has become an integral part of each successive programme. The Web site became an opportunity for artists to document their residencies, although this was, in the main, significantly underutilized.

The exhibition was designed as a series of workstations, with visitors encouraged to sit down and absorb the research material assembled by each artist. For some it was completed work, for others simply a set of files of photographs: each reflected the way in which they dealt with the challenge of residencies. The collective content of the residencies could be broken down into distinct but often overlapping categories of research: the response to the size and colours of the landscape and environment; an interest in the details of the natural world; experiment with materials and techniques; research and development of work through museum collections; the social uses of jewellery. It was one of the artists themselves who most clearly summarized the differences between the two groups as being that of 'inside and outside'. The British were overwhelmed by the environment, its scale, and the exoticism of its flora and fauna. By contrast the Australians tended to focus on a more internal, documentary form of research through public collections and personal histories.

A striking example of an artist's adaptation to the unfamiliar, indeed the uncanny, was Liz Rattigan, who found that 'environment had the largest impact on me during my residency in Sydney, as noise in many forms caused anxiety and lack of sleep'. Unable to hear birdsong as anything other than human distress, this was further compounded by a murder in the park outside her flat. She found solace in earplugs and then, fascinated by their diversity, embarked on a collection of work that utilized their raw properties, calling it 'displacement behaviour'.

These two quotations from participating artists highlight some of the generic responses to the residency experience:

> A wonderful aspect of the Here and There residencies was being able to immerse yourself solely in the creative process. There was no expectation to produce finished pieces while away. The familiarity of a jeweller's bench, surrounded by your own tools can keep you closed in an environment that you already know and feel safe in. It is not easy but essential to leave it behind. (Mah Rana, London, resident in Melbourne, whose page in the publication was two shades of UK and Australian battleship grey entitled 'Little Differences')

> Inspiring everything so that even the usual has another flavour, I have meetings with objects and experiences that I would not have found on the other side of the world. I let my mind roam over observations, dreaming up connections between things, weaving my own story of how the world fits together. I'm given glimpses into other peoples' lives and minds, indulging in the ever explicating connections of the journey. (Sheridan Kennedy, Sydney, resident in Birmingham, who took the journal style of 'discovering' Europeans in Australia as the model for her page, listing museums visited and purchases made)

The success of this first programme, measured as a model that worked for artists and with a public outcome that went some way to explaining creative process in a fresh and accessible way, led to the development of HAT2, which took South Asia as its focus whilst retaining a link with Australia. The reasons for this included a need to move the HAT model to a different culture, the established links already in place through Barney Hare Duke's work with British South Asian artists and organizations in the North West, and early indications of interest in this area from potential UK host organizations.

One of the failings of the first HAT programme was the lack of engagement with indigenous Australians and their craft practice: we didn't push hard enough against the unwillingness of partners to open those doors. This was quite literal in certain cases where we were not taken into the studios where indigenous students were being taught. With HAT2 we were determined to explore traditional craft practices in South Asia as well as its contemporary practice, across all forms of craft. In so doing we opened up an opportunity to challenge perceptions, both of ourselves and of those of the second network of newly selected artists.

The HAT2 Asia/UK programme involved up to twenty individual research residencies with partner countries, including India, Pakistan, Bangladesh, Sri Lanka and Australia, taking place in 2006 and 2007. The residency programme in the United Kingdom was centred on the north west of England with up to four of the international artists being based with hosts and partner organizations across the region in Liverpool, Manchester and Carlisle. Partnership with three other regions in the United Kingdom (East Midlands, South East and South West) supported a further twelve residencies, with each region hosting two international residencies and supporting two artists from their regions to take up the reciprocal residencies abroad. Artists were nominated from within the widest definition of craft practice, ranging from traditional weavers from Kachchh in north-west India, through art school trained artists in Pakistan who revisited traditional techniques such as miniature painting, to paper and ceramic artists from the United Kingdom.

HAT2 was a far more complex model to manage and it culminated in a second cHAT Week held in New Delhi in March 2007 together with an associated exhibition at the British Council Gallery. Sessions of show-and-tell were interspersed with visits to studios, evenings of traditional Indian dance and guest speakers. To allow the artists who described their techniques as traditional an opportunity to explain their work, workshops were run for participants to engage with techniques and to communicate on a one-to-one basis.

The broad research theme, which was common to all residencies, was to continue the exploration of displacement and to examine the ways in which new work is developed in response to new cultural contexts, both in South Asia and the United Kingdom. For the UK artists their residencies allowed for a broad range of enquiry into their new temporary cultural contexts and an understanding of the differing economic and social environments that affected the survival of traditional and contemporary practice. Tom Coles, a UK furniture designer, saw the problems faced by Kachchh-based woodworkers seeking a sustainable living:

One thing is clear—the craftspeople (I have met) can only respond to a market. If a market for their products or skills exists, then the crafts will prosper. But keeping that market alive is tricky. To rely on a market that buys craftwork as a historical souvenir or a symbol of a romantic ideal, is short sighted. The long-term survival of the crafts depends on the craftspeople's ability to develop new products and ways of presenting their skills. One of the problems facing the organizations and designers working with the craftspeople is communication. For example it is not possible to simply give the lacquer-workers a working drawing of a component and expect them to make it. They are more artists than engineers; their manufacturing process is not attuned to the repeat manufacture of precision components. The challenge for the designer is to allow for tolerances and visual differentiation between components. Surely though, this is the potentially exciting aspect of working with the traditional craftspeople.

Jaimini Patel, an artist from the United Kingdom who was based in Sri Lanka, incisively described the difficulties of encounter and understanding:

> I knew that I did not want to be an observer that collates to take back in order to make sense at a later stage. Once you leave a place what you have of it changes—I wanted to make here with all that that entails, because it is this experience that determines what happens. All the activities that involve living in a place, cooking, shopping, travelling become part of understanding the wider issues of history, politics, language, trade. There is also the gradual process of absorbing these through relationships with people and the exchange of books, films, music and personal stories. My research was not an academic activity that I could quantify. I did not get as much from museums and institutions as I did from talking to people. I learnt about shared cultural beliefs, myths, legends and language. Most people assumed I was Sri Lankan until I opened my mouth. It was my first time to spend a significant amount of time in an Asian country and I felt aware that I was from both east and west but not entirely of either. A case of—'here nor there'! Being surrounded by artists that make predominantly issue-based work however did make me much more sure of my own position—that I wanted to see if it is possible to make work that does not need language or culture to validate it or give it meaning. The intention of the artist when displaced requires explanation or translation; I wanted to ask if there is such a thing as a visual language that can transcend difference. Meaning is processed through thought and I am interested in that which comes before this: an experience of the work that doesn't come from intelligence. I want to see what this experience might be when the work is displaced.

Artists from South Asia used their residencies in the United Kingdom in apparently much more straightforward ways. For the traditional crafts practitioners, it was to learn about new markets, to make and sell work, and for some to improve the economic status of their families and communities back home. Artists took the opportunity to learn new skills available in art school departments, to make new contacts and to visit galleries and museums. Through this period there was a growing awareness of the developing art market in India in particular, and so there was perhaps a more even sense of 'trade' between the two cultures.

Self-documentation using the HAT Web site blog was not a comfortable mechanism for the visitors to the United Kingdom, primarily because so few had direct experience with computers and/or were uncertain about their command of written English. This of course is an area that we could have addressed more appropriately given more time.

ARTS REVERIE

That A Fine Line: Cultural Practice should become a part owner of a town house in Ahmedabad was never in our original vision for the partnership, but the need to secure accommodation for two UK designers after their original host failed to deliver, found us joining forces with our Indian partner, Anupa Mehta, and taking on the running of what became a guest house for artists. However we realised that having such a base in India would encourage further projects and partnerships that could move beyond the HAT model as well as making it clear that we were serious about our commitment to South Asia. For A Fine Line: Cultural Practice the house would meet a number of objectives. It would primarily (and commercially) serve as a base for artists' residencies from which inter/national artists could explore their own practice and in so doing become a creative house that could facilitate interdisciplinary and inter-cultural dialogue. More strategically we saw Arts Reverie as a specialist na-tional centre—for the exploration of emerging new crafts practice; a centre for an ongoing partnership of exchange between the United Kingdom and India and a catalyst for the re-activation of the historical cultural and commercial connection between Manchester and Ahmedabad.

Arts Reverie is a 100-year-old *haveli* (town house) in the middle of the Old City of Ahmedabad in the state of Gujarat with accommodation for six guests with a large, top-floor multipurpose space. The house's role is a focal point for activity both within the immediate neighbourhood and across and beyond the city, where visiting artists can build their own relationships with craftspeople, agencies and communities. Through this process partnerships are created that can result in new product and new uses for traditional techniques.

Examples of projects that have developed out of Arts Reverie include Making Space Sensing Place, a residency and exhibition project with the Victoria & Albert Museum of Childhood and The Harley Gallery; the Warli project, an exhibition/residency/commissioning programme based around a particular tribal painting from Western India; a research base for MMU MIRIAD staff; and the current Cot-ton Exchange project with museums in north-west England (Figure 14.2).

Tanvi Kant is a British artist with family roots in Gujarat, who was awarded an Arts Reverie subsidized residency in March 2008. There follows extracts from her blog that honestly describe the tension and uncertainty of displacement:

> I have a meeting late in the evening which runs close to midnight with our de-signer friend, Lokesh Ghai. I discuss my work and show samples made while I have been here, as well as existing work. There are two options in the ways in which we could work together, I am hopeful, but also a bit wary. Clear and con-sistent communication is key and also firm decision making. I will try my best. I think I may need to talk with people back home for thoughts too . . . I have always wanted to collaborate with designers or craftspeople here, but having actually discussed it seriously, I'm quite nervous. Having too much choice is maybe just

Fig. 14.2. *Painted Bedford Truck*, Luton Museums, 2011. Photograph: Jeremy Theophilus

as difficult as not having a choice sometimes although, I prefer having too much choice. Some people have no choice in what they want to do, where they want to go or how—like many of the people I have met here, most yearn for a better life without realizing what they have is actually pretty special.

Arts Reverie has allowed us to develop other forms of residency and interaction with a culture; it has also provided a foundation that indicates a serious desire to develop longer-term relationships with the city and beyond. However our inability to devote more time to being out there and working on the ground has meant that projects have taken much longer to produce.

EXPANDING THE PRACTICE: CONCLUSIONS

Throughout the development of these projects we were responding initially to an expressed desire from UK artists in what was regarded as a critically neglected field as compared with the fine art academy, for the opportunity to explore and extend their experience of practice between location and dislocation. We set up the framework within which this could take place and invited artists to participate based on their own lines of enquiry, some of which were inevitably quite vague and unresolved, some of which remained so until well after the residency experience.

In the research, developing, delivering and reviewing of these programme strands, we have accumulated many more questions than answers and have been asked many questions we have found it difficult to answer. One such question was posed by Salima Hashmi in Pakistan, who asked us: 'Is it not possible to look at the contemporary without using the lens of modernism?' This elegant and very restrained retort to some rather clumsy positioning by fellow travellers on an earlier curatorial trip to Lahore has rung in our ears ever since. Our colleagues came with fixed ideas about what they wanted to see, that is studio craft similar to that being practiced in the United Kingdom. The growing irritation amongst our Pakistani hosts with what they viewed as a Western-centred, blinkered view of how contemporary craft in South Asia might be encountered and understood was artfully condensed by Salima, and indeed her question continues to underpin our own ongoing encounters in this area. It is a difference that shouldn't be neutered by a more globalized reading of contemporary craft, particularly when the term 'contemporary' cannot be used freely without challenging its meaning within a given cultural context. It serves as a warning to those who harbour preconceptions without the balance of an open mind, as well as reminding us of the radically differing approaches to the practice of art in the face of global creep.

This is the stuff of international collaboration, but these misperceptions, whether wilful or ignorant, are pertinent, sharpened by the ferocity with which global events can affect so many people's lives simultaneously. We have made many journeys, both physical and conceptual, marking that particular circular trajectory from theory through practice and experience back to theory, which we continue to follow in some bewilderment, convinced we remain far from the answers we seek. However, we feel confident that we now have a meaningful position from which we can continue to collaboratively interrogate and inform contemporary craft practice.

The movements we initiate depend on recognizing the importance of, and respect for, difference: how then should we behave when that difference becomes eroded through a culture's development so as to make the journey less meaningful, to be mirrored by the 'excesses' of one's own culture, to see what is a reminder of one's own lost cultural practices being similarly neutered and discarded? And why do we continue to do it?

The departure points for enquiry are as numerous as the individuals involved: the residual legacy of experience from the journey, as evidenced in both what is left behind and in what is packed in baggage to carry home, becomes the measurement of outcomes and impacts. These can be broadly located in four areas: economic, social, ethical and cultural. The terms under which artists enter these programmes will implicate them in being provoked, in being challenged in their place in the world, in confronting forgotten nostalgias and in being forced to take moral and ethical decisions. Given the inescapable fact that we cannot change economic disparities, is our ambition for fair and equable exchange somewhat naïve?

Furthermore, in a society that is increasingly multicultural and diasporic, values are an integral part of an intercultural exchange that can be misunderstood or misinterpreted. How therefore is value (economic or cultural) sustained and communicated across cultures? Within the global superstore of made objects, craft, through its many guises, represents the mark of the hand, known or unknown: the value attached to that imprint varies hugely.

Interest has led us by way of engagement in the field to intervention. Through partnership and collaboration we have found ourselves pursuing several pathways—in the quest to construct an understanding of the contemporary across craft practice in South Asia and the United Kingdom, and to mark out an area where we can continue to explore its value and significance within decentred cultural, social and economic contexts. In our use of the term 'contemporary' we are identifying what is being made today in individual cultures, without making any value judgements with regard to levels of development. We are interested in the here and now, wherever that may be taking place, but also in the way in which it can relate to cultural tradition.

We have arrived at a staging post on our journey at which to establish further collaborative enquiry: to test what part we can play in being meaningful contributors in locating what we would define as 'expanded/ing crafts practice' in new and unfamiliar contexts.

Expanded and extended craft practice is that area of art making, creating and imagining that sits in a space between disciplines, between notions of the traditional and the contemporary, a meeting place of artists and artisan, where the gaps are narrowed and the edges of design and art loose validity, where conservation and preservation give way to change in perception and process, where everything is on the move: producers, markets, uses and promoters.

Drawing on case studies from ten years' experience, we will emphasize key factors that support our enquiry into locating this territory and identify proposals for the direction of further travel with our partners within it.

NOTES

1. Jyotindra Jain was the director of the National Crafts Museum, New Delhi, and is now professor at the School of Arts and Aesthetics at Jawaharlal Nehru University, Delhi. Video presentation to CAS National Network Conference, Liverpool, 2010.
2. The Warlis are an indigenous tribe living in mountainous and coastal areas of Maharashtra-Gujarat border, India.
3. Noting here the significance of key postcolonial commentators to our research approach, such as Edward Said (1979), Homi Bhaba (1994), Rasheed Araeen (Araeen et al. 2002) and Kobena Mercer (2005), to name a few.
4. HAT International Research Fellowships, 2002, <www.hat.mmu.ac.uk> accessed 18 March 2013.
5. Habitat, a retailer of household furnishings in Europe, was founded by Terence Conran in 1964.
6. Glorious Creative Manchester, 2004, <www.gloriouscreative.co.uk/portfolio/the-hat-project> accessed 18 March 2013.

REFERENCES AND FURTHER READING

Araeen, R., Cubitt, S., and Sardar, Z. (2002), *The Third Text Reader on Art, Culture and Theory: On Art, Culture, and Theory,* London: Continuum International Publishing Group.

Bhaba, H. (1994), *The Location of Culture*, Oxon: Routledge.

Crawford, M. (2009), *The Case for Working with Your Hands*, London: Viking/Penguin.

Flusser, V. (1999), *The Shape of Things: A Philosophy of Design*, London: Reaktion Books.

Haapala, A. (2005), 'On the Aesthetics of the Everyday: Familiarity, Strangeness and the Meaning of Place', in A. Light and J. M. Smith (eds), *The Aesthetics of Everyday Life*, New York: Columbia University Press.

Malouf, A. (1996), *On Identity*, London: Harvill Press.

Mercer, K. (2005), *Cosmopolitan Modernists*, Cambridge, MA: MIT Press.

Said, E. (1979), *Orientalism*, London: Penguin.

Saurma-Jeltsch, L. E., and Eisenbeiâ, A. (eds) (2010), *The Power of Things and the Flow of Cultural Transformations: Art and Culture between Europe and Asia,* Berlin/Munich: Deutscher Kunstverlag.

Sen, A. (2005), *The Argumentative Indian*, London: Penguin.

Venkatesan, S. (2009), *Craft Matters Artisans, Development and the Indian Nation*, Hyderabad: Orient Black Swan.

15

Circling Back into That Thing We Cast Forward: A Closing Read on *Gestures of Resistance*

Judith Leemann and Shannon Stratton

INTRODUCTION

The exhibition *Gestures of Resistance* came to life in January 2010 at the Museum of Contemporary Craft in Portland, Oregon. Its first, nascent appearance had been in Dallas, Texas, at the 2008 College Art Association Conference. Between a panel discussion and an exhibition at local artist-run space Grey Matters, the first exploration had set a tone for discovery: what was the relationship between the slow movement (slow cities, slow food, etc.) and the popular interest in craft as a methodology? Why were artists returning to craft to express political positions—from responses to war, to queer identity, to awareness-raising around labour practices? What was powerful about craft as a site for these positions?

As curators of *Gestures of Resistance* we were interested from the beginning, in investigating practices that used craft performatively—placing emphasis on making visible the labour of craft, a live engagement with materials and/or public encounters both in and outside of traditional art institutions. The invitation to mount the exhibition at the Museum of Contemporary Craft gave us the opportunity to approach the exhibition design in a way that mirrored the interrelated nature of craft, performance, dialogue and encounter with the aim of nurturing interaction, conversation or participation, between the artists, the artists and the city, the museum's visitors and the institution.

We started with the premise of physically building a meeting place—a site for conversation that would serve as studio for each of the participating artists' residencies at the museum and as a literal and figurative platform for other undertakings—roundtables, workshops—as the need arose. This 'platform' was the possibility of an open, dialogical, exhibition—a kind of exploded frame where studio, exhibition, conversation and performance could all take place and bleed into one another.

The design of the platform was generated as a residency/performance/ sculpture with artists Sara Black and John Preus. Black and Preus discussed each of the subsequent resident artists' needs with them—seats, ironing board, places to hang materials, and so on—and then set about designing and building a site-within-the-site. As long-time collaborators, this project became an opportunity for Black and Preus to 'perform' the collaborative relationship—a live build-out where they separated themselves with a temporary wall and then, via verbal communication only, each replicated the craft decisions the other was making on their side. At the close of their two-week residency, Black and Preus removed the wall and revealed a stunning structure—the differences between the two sides both subtle and significant, with beautiful indications of the nuances of interpretation. Preus for example had built a cube out of 'scraps'—for him, this cube was assembled patchwork from pieces left over from the build-out. Black's cube was made from scraps as well, but she carefully sanded and finished its surface. Nuanced treatment of the materials differentiated each artist's work, but what was remarkable was the apparent richness of their collaborative relationship, made manifest in a structure that was balanced, yet not completely identical.

Black and Preus were followed by 'residents' Anthea Black, Carole Lung, Mung Lar Lam, Cat Mazza, Ehren Tool and Theaster Gates. Each artist spent from three days to two weeks in Portland, working on-site in the structure built by Black and Preus and off-site throughout Portland. Each artist was invited to make themselves at home in the structure and to leave behind their mark and materials as they saw fit, positioning themselves in relationship to one another, installing their work on the walls that surrounded the platform and reinterpreting materials that were left behind (Figure 15.1).

At the end of the exhibition, Theaster Gates performed *A Good Whitewashing*, covering Black and Preus's structure, and all of the artwork and materials positioned on it, in porcelain slip. As the slip dried, the site was transformed from a liminal space—a site for work and dialogue in flux—to a calcified relic. The slip had a way of defining edges, accentuating textures and holding impressions that invited another viewing, another consideration of the project. We noticed Ehren Tool's plastic army men hiding in the eaves of Black and Preus's work, clay marks over Anthea Black's silk-screen prints made for secondary readings, Gates donned one of Carole Lung's plastic bag windbreakers. After having to watch the site transform in fits and starts (neither of us live close to Portland where the exhibition unfolded), taking it all in at once, and after a final passionate performance by Gates, was a moment for attentive looking.

Our intention in writing this chapter is to use our privileged position as collaborating curators of an exhibition of performative craft to address the anthology's paired interest in craft and collaboration from *within*, as subjects of and subject to the structure we created for our exhibition. To do this, we

Fig. 15.1. Ehren Tool, *Occupation*. 2010. Photograph: Heather Zinger. Courtesy of Museum of Contemporary Craft, Portland, OR

oscillate between retracing the ways our (here we intentionally lump the exhibition's artists and ourselves into one *us*) thinking was made material and the ways that the material evidence of various processes set us to thinking in new ways. Through this oscillating perspective we hope to draw out how craft can function as a communicative force—open, in flux, a powerful tool for thought.

A few terms bear introducing at the outset, among them those we used as tools in thinking the exhibition forward, and those we use now as tools to read the exhibition backward. The notions of gesture and of resistance allowed us to organize our earliest thinking together, and our sense of the latter in particular was much enhanced by the publication of Richard Sennett's *The Craftsman* (2008), with his nuanced rendering of the role resistance plays in problem solving and problem finding. Sennett writes, 'Resistance always has a context', and we would say the same of gesture; context and action are both already enfolded in the two terms. A gesture derives its meaning for the maker, the receiver, and any witness in large part from how it runs counter to the prevailing efficiencies of any setting. Resistance we found most useful when we let blur slightly the distinction between material and social resistances.

Reading the exhibition backwards, two adapted terms prove useful as formal descriptors of behaviours operating at various scales within the exhibition. We introduce the notion of a 'productive fiction' to mean an invented story presented as if already true, that through its canny deployment actually becomes the cause of its own predicted effect. A second invented term, that of the 'relational jig', attempts to render spatially what productive fiction renders temporally. We use the term as a conceptual lever for better understanding how the exhibition's artists use the mechanics of their material practices to engineer new kinds of social relations.

ON EXHIBITING DIALOGUE

For the opening event of the exhibition, we were asked by the museum's curator Namita Wiggers to give a curator's talk to an audience of a hundred people. The talk was to be videotaped for the museum Web site, but we were asked not to prepare a formal slide talk, rather, to just arrive and have a conversation. This presented us with a dilemma: how to speak coherently to an audience anticipating a presentation prepared with care and at the same time to stay in the spirit of ongoing dialogue? It seemed impossible and a bit of a set-up for all involved, until we hit upon an elegant solution: to perform a live dialogue in this situation, we would need to accelerate *past* the real and over-structure or hyper-perform dialogue. We devised a set of beginnings—writing questions for one another. We devised a set of endings—bringing out into the open the very weak spot of our collaboration, a tendency to cut one another off, and accelerated that tendency by bringing in a bell with which we could each signal the moment when we felt the other had said enough. The bell, its function established, became, any time we gestured towards it, a way to tease one another and to let the audience in on the game; it kept us all lively. We met the situation with a structure that allowed what flowed through to be 'more than real', and in this way remained able, in front of an audience, to experience the kind of moving thought that was the stuff of our working conversations; the presentation had became another moment of working our way forward together, not a static representation of the already figured out.

We emphasize this moment because now, reading it backwards, we recognize the dilemma we faced in giving the talk as close cousin to the question that set the show itself in motion. How does one devise structures that allow audiences to encounter living process without resorting to the kind of retroactive performance of past liveness, which affectively cannot ever pass for live itself? How not to ignore the expectation attending contexts of lecture or exhibition that some eloquent thought, some finely wrought object be delivered, but rather to use that expectation as another element to be intelligently worked with? The craft artists whose work we wanted to bring into the exhibition were already messing with habitual punctuations of process and object, of studio and public. What structure could we as curators devise that would allow them to further those experiments while feeding our own curiosities about generous/generative exhibition design? (Figure 15.2)

Fig. 15.2. *Gestures of Resistance*, after final performance by Theaster Gates. 2010. Photograph: Nathan Henry-Silva. Courtesy of Museum of Contemporary Craft, Portland, OR

The open, changing platform that anchored *Gestures of Resistance* operated practically, as a work site, as well as metaphorically, as an 'open platform', connecting to both contemporary ideas of collaborative communities (Wiki, open source) and more traditional ones (atelier, town square). It suggested a broad understanding of dialogue by situating the artists in conversation with the institution, the audience, each other, the curators and everything in-between. The platform was a hub from which multiple conversations radiated. Because only the structure was predetermined, not the way in which artists would engage it, there was no set and repeatable form for how to 'use' the exhibition. This caused some discomfort. We received feedback that visitors were confused by the show (despite, perhaps, too many didactics),[1] because not only was the overall exhibition different with every artist's residency, but more important (we surmise) because this audience was most comfortable with the existing script for museums: stand back, don't touch, observe silently. Furthermore, nearly all museum-users expect the institution to be arbiter. With only the open invitation to inhabit and explore and make value that was personal rather than predetermined, these museum-users might have felt at loose ends.

Gestures of Resistance proposed that by presenting practice and inviting participation, artists can create a physical form of discourse (both a platform for discourse and evidence of discourse) that makes manifest the nature of craft—the struggle, commitment, endurance, dialogue, collaboration and care. Attempting a framework for multiple styles of exchange, *Gestures* hoped to engage, on the part of the museum's audience, an analysis of craft as communicative force—an active form that is open, in flux and something to think with.

As Umberto Eco writes in *The Poetics of Open Work*:

> the Poetics of 'work in movement' . . . sets in motion a new cycle of relations between the artist and his audience, a new mechanics of aesthetic perception, a different status for the artistic product in society. It opens a new page in sociology and in pedagogy, as well as a new chapter in the history of art. It poses new practical problems by organizing new communicative situations. In short it installs a new relationship between the contemplation and the utilization of a work of art. (Eco 2006: 39)

ON CRAFT AS VERB

We want to pull into the conversation the distinction David Pye brought into early critical craft discourse, between the workmanship of risk and the workmanship of certainty. His distinction cut squarely across the prevailing one pitting the handmade against the industrial. For Pye, the workmanship of risk meant 'workmanship using any kind of technique or apparatus, in which the quality of the result is not predetermined, but depends on the judgment, dexterity and care which the maker exercises as he works. The essential idea is that the quality of the result is continually at risk during the process of making' (Pye 1968: 20). He continues: 'In the *workmanship of certainty* the result of every operation during production has been predetermined and is outside the control of the operative once production starts. In the *workmanship of risk* the result of every operation during production is determined by the workman as he works and its outcome depends wholly or largely on his care, judgment and dexterity' (Pye 1968: 52).

What becomes visible when we overlay Pye's distinction on our own cu-ratorial undertaking, when we ask what a workmanship of risk looks like in the arena of exhibition design? Let's say that the handmade versus indus-trial distinction Pye was writing across translates for us to the prevailing habit of valuing the action in craft versus the object of craft, as if this were the key opposition. And while it may have appeared in this exhibition that we were looking primarily to champion the action half of that division (in a context more accustomed to valuing objects), what actually feels far more important now was the attempt to devise a structure (physical, temporal, re-lational, fiscal) that would allow each of our makers to keep everything in a state of live risk for as long as possible, to keep everything facing forward and moving towards, to allow the artists to perform their practice not know-ing.[2] Pye was not opposed to the use of technique or apparatus to support the achievement of particular ends; what mattered was whether the quality of the result was at risk or was guaranteed. The question arises then: in the context of a museum-based craft exhibition, how do institution and audi-ence become more fully engaged in participating in such risky undertakings? There is something wonderfully perverse about the audience that values deeply the risks taken in handcrafting but wants to be shown only the pol-ished outcome of that undertaking; like steak lovers averse to knowing too much about butchering.

Craft is a transitive verb: to make or to produce with care, skill or ingenuity. Transitive verbs show action, and it is through this idea of an active, mean-ingful gesture that 'acts upon', implying movement, change, passage and transmission that we see the importance of craft as a way of being in its own right. Craft is something we do. It is active, it is acting, it does. As a choice of presence and action, craft has important meaning in addition to the sym-bolic qualities of an object's apparent materiality or construction. *Gestures of Resistance* was an exercise in exploring that presence and action by bringing to the fore and making central the 'doing'. Resulting 'objects' were not dis-missed, but their treatment (how they were displayed or circulated, finished or destroyed), was in the hands of each participating artist.

The power of craft as an endeavour is at the heart of Richard Sennett's *The Craftsman.* Sennett details the way thinking and acting like a craftsman can have a 'sharp social edge' (Sennett 2008: 44), where practice, embod-ied knowledge and relational thinking are the skills needed for world-making: 'Both the difficulties and the possibilities of making things well apply to mak-ing human relationships. Material challenges like working with resistance or managing ambiguity are instructive to understanding the resistances people harbour to one another or the uncertain boundaries between people' (Sennett 2008: 289).

As something we do, craft begins to wield itself as a powerful gesture. Sen-nett sees in the 'craft of making physical things', insight into how to relate to others, calling for, in his conclusion, 'the value of experience understood as a craft' (Sennett 2008: 289).

As index, craft is (among other things) a reminder of functionality, commodity, amateur labour, pleasure, pain, leisure, the personal, the domestic, tradition and community, but as a way of acting, it is also searching, researching, learning, teaching, knowing, endeavouring, discovering, failing and thriving. To move beyond craft as merely an index, and to go deeper into the wealth of tacit knowing that craft carries, the kind of knowing that although valuable, escapes language or picturing, craft needs to be practiced 'out-loud'. *Gestures of Resistance* was a framework for that audible craft, designating it 'performing craft'—a public enactment of making and exchange (both of objects—as in Tool's free cups—and dialogue, as proposed by the exhibition's design). Artists working at the intersection of craft and performance take craft outside of the settings that have institutionalized it, whether the domestic sphere or the museum,[3] and show craft as a powerful site of connection and communication.

Craft as an operation of care, ingenuity and skill makes it a fluent site for discourse on such current issues as sustainability and globalism as they affect communities of real hungry, sick, struggling or labouring bodies. James Sanders in 'Moving beyond the Binary' points out that, through embodied knowing, craft/art viewers may come to appreciate the humanity we share and embrace the plurality of expressions that surround us as well as the traditions from which they emerge. Craft, with its 'rich experience of human need and desire' is the subjective intimacy needed now (Sanders 2004: 102). The millennial body in performative craft refixes the body, its labour and actions and trades on the meaning implied in 'the doing' of craft, on labour and skill-building as sites for meaning. Performance, social practice and craft begin to bleed together as artists visualize labour, social intercourse and participation as a means to address consequence: what are the results and effects of human action and through what forms might responsibility and engagement be tested and modelled?

RELATIONAL JIGS

Theaster Gates, whose porcelain-slip whitewashing of the galleries served to close our exhibition, is a master of performing what Brian Massumi calls 'virtual events of foretracing'. Our own notion of a productive fiction tracks closely with this 'foretracing', running a path in advance of a thing such that the effects of the running cause the thing to then advance along the tracks left by the speculative telling. Massumi delineates a particular kind of politicality, one less invested in making statements than in availing itself of 'imaginative powers', by which he means the 'ability to marshal powers of the false, not in order to designate the way things are but to catalyze what's to come, emergently, inventively, un-preprogrammed and reflective of no past model' (Massumi 2011: 173). We understand Massumi to mean that, while language can and does get used to make statements about what is, of greater value is its power to invoke, to compel, to falsify first, if need be, the thing one wishes into being.

Theaster Gates tells the story of the potter Shoji Yamaguchi, fleeing post-Hiroshima Japan and settling in Mississippi where he marries May, a black civil rights activist and begins making 'ceramic plate ware specifically for the foods of Black people'. As Gates tells it: 'The Yamaguchis invited people of all kinds to their dinner table, which table quickly became a place where people from all over the country came to openly discuss issues of race, political difference and inequalities of all sorts' (Gates 2008). Through a series of events, Gates becomes caretaker of the Yamaguchi collection, and in this role he continues their work. He hosts a series of Plate Convergences in which his South Side Chicago neighbours and members of the art community are invited to eat a meal served on genuine Yamaguchi wares and to continue the conversations that animated the Yamaguchis' dinner table. Everyone involved knows that the story Gates tells is a fiction, but what gets generated is real. The fiction cast backwards becomes the utterly convincing reason for a series of gatherings that without it could not have struck the affective note they did. At the same time, the story invents perfect ancestors for Gates's own complex practice.

In developing *Gestures*, we found ourselves using the term 'productive fiction' as a kind of shorthand for those stories we invent to 'foretrace' that thing that the story, once floated, will then require of us. We float some fiction and build for it just enough of a material substrate that others can choose to suspend disbelief and join in. Gates's own pottery influenced by his ceramic study in Japan, easily passed for that of Yamaguchi. That being asked to participate in a self-confessing fiction should so often trigger delight as well as real engagement indicates the great political potential of such operations. That the retelling of the move at both temporal and geographical distances leaves its humour and intelligence undiminished suggests that there is something of the portability of fables in its construction.

If we trace the kinds of moves that characterize the work of the artists folding themselves one by one into the exhibition, we may discern several distinct strategies by which craft, as context, is brought into active play. We are most familiar with play undertaken *within* the context of craft: the traditional disciplinary boundaries of a particular craft are claimed, and the demands of contemporary art or other disciplines external to that craft are held at bay. The craftsman says, 'I am a potter' and inflects the traditional choices of the potter—form, glaze, function—in ways that posit a new set of relations *within* the field. To play *within* the context of craft is to emphasize relations within the category, not to engage the category itself. By contrast, to play *with* the context of craft is to treat craft and all its attendant expectations, norms, affordances, as a kind of found object, or unearthed material. To cut into it, reform(ulate) it. To play *with* the context of craft is not to try to unmake the distinction of craft, but rather to see all that can be done with this particular distinction: to deploy its lowness, to meet its respect for tradition and lineage with something else entirely. It is too simple to read this contextual mischief as 'against craft', so intimately does it know craft and so often, at least in this exhibition, do these operations come from artists of long engagement in a craft discipline.

If the notion of a productive fiction lets us articulate temporally and narratively some of what took place in this exhibition, we need still some device by which to see things spatially, architecturally. To this end, we want to consider that there could be such a thing as a relational jig. A jig, in manufacturing, is 'a device for accurately guiding and positioning a drill or other tool in relation to the work-piece, or for positioning the parts of an object during assembly. . . . A name variously applied in different trades to mechanical contrivances and simple machines for performing acts or processes' (*OED*). So a jig is already relational in that it positions one thing with respect to another to achieve a particular end. If we consider a jig in the context of communication, and use our felt sense of its mechanics, might we open a new way of reading the work in the exhibition? If what you care about is the social, if your lineage anchors you in a particular craft, if you have the mind, hands and courage to think these things all together, what do you devise?

In our early thinking together we talked about a gesture as being an essentially contextual creature, standing out against the background of other actions by how it runs counter to prevailing expectations and habits. Across the show there were recurrent moments where the artists made things more difficult for themselves, less efficient, less autonomous, less likely to succeed. For us, understanding the material and relational logic of introducing increased resistances is an important part of what we're after here. We see these resistances—made, met, moved through—as central to how the work in this show works.

In the children's game Telephone, a phrase is whispered from person to person through a group, arriving at the end an utterly changed thing. The title of Sara Black and John Preus's project Rebuilding Mayfield is lifted from the *Guinness Book of World Records*' longest game of Telephone, beginning with a whispered, 'They inherited the world and then the army came and scorched it' and ending as 'Mayfield College' (Black and Preus 2010). Charged with both constructing a platform for the artists to follow and performing their collaboration, Black and Preus devised an elegant procedure, setting out to build a thing that would, after its completion, continuously broadcast both the attempt and the failure of their undertaking.

What did Black and Preus do? They began by gathering inherited lumber and setting out the basic parameters of what the artists to follow them would need and then built a twenty-four-foot wall down the middle of the gallery, making densely material the space across which they would need to communicate. Over the course of seven days, alternating who led and who listened, they attempted to communicate construction plans through small listening holes drilled in the wall. Building their way down the wall, they attempted to render exactly the instructions received at the start of each day. When they were finished and had sawed out and removed that resistance, what remained was a structure whose intended symmetry was evident. But what spoke out over the symmetry were the breaks, where communication had failed, and *sent* did not equal *received.*

So what? Don't we already know that constant small breakdowns in communication inhabit (inhibit) all working together? What is gained by introducing a material that catches these breakdowns and puts them on display? Or do we look too far? Is it enough to read into the photograph of Preus leaning his forehead against the wall to see what kind of machine this was? Eyes closed, forehead to wall directly across from where Black speaks her instructions to him, we see his attention in this image, his focus on the other side of the wall, all of him tuned to listening.

In another photograph, this time of Carole Lung a.k.a. Frau Fiber out in Portland on her bike-powered sewing machine, there is again this sense of seeing captured the extension of attention. The volunteer who has agreed to pedal looks over her shoulder, eyes on Lung's hands as she works. Lung has a series of commands, power on, power off, to signal to the human provider of the machine's drive what is needed. But to see the gaze of the pedaler, intent on Lung's hands, is to see an attunement in excess of simple verbal commands. The rider is entirely tuned to the task, beyond herself, moving with Lung, anticipating the command before it is even spoken.

Lung's instructions to the intern working with her were precise: no recruiting, only respond to those who approach. Having set herself an ambitious daily production schedule (a productive fiction buoyed by clipboards and timecards), what is gained by then putting herself at the mercy of others' willingness to participate? If the constellation that is sewing machine grafted onto bike plus the alter ego that is Frau Fiber plus production schedule plus public space is a relational jig, then what is Lung engineering?

Several days into Ehren Tool's residency word gets out that the museum is giving away free cups. Two women stand before Tool's cups while he works away inside his bunker. (Tool had built himself a bunker out of one ton of bagged clay and had set himself the task of throwing all of it into cups to be fired, glazed and given away by the end of his weeklong residency.) Having confirmed with Tool that they could indeed take a cup, they start to shop. 'I don't know, maybe this one? This one is edgier, and I think I'm kind of edgy. What do you think?' The Gulf War veteran whose cups are emblazoned with images of fallen soldiers, dismembered children and trophies of war lets them shop.

What kind of jig is this that allows itself to be so misread? After they leave, one of us asks Tool what it was like for him to hear that exchange. And he is quite clear that what matters is that the cups go out into the world, that they are lived with daily so that in the homes where they find themselves, they may one day, within some set of circumstances not in his control, be seen for what they are.

The deployment of slowness that was of such interest to us in the first iteration of *Gestures* makes its presence felt again here. Tool knows that delivering a statement against war in the handing over of the cup can only diminish what the cup itself, given time, might trigger. He cannot state; he can only make and distribute in the deceptively soft affective register that is *giving away*. Everything at risk. So it was for us with Mung Lar Lam's minimal ironings gracing the walls of the museum after her residency. Nothing she said to us or let creep through into any museum didactics spoke of war or the care of soldiers. All the more stunning in the last week of the show to suddenly register the perfectly pressed repeating chevrons, the muted green-grey tans of the shirting material and the affective charge of almost having missed the very thing animating these ironings.

We began *Gestures* with an interest in how the story or the rumour behind the thing acts productively (and, in choosing the word 'gesture' were most interested in how *productive* needn't be grand, but could be small, temporary, and low-key by comparison to that which is normally thought effective, 'gesture' for us carrying an affective charge.) The strategy for the structure we presented Black and Preus was meant to stimulate exchange, but in closing, in circling back we see it, too, of course, as a jig, as a productive fiction. We imagined its end, talked about its purpose, but left its story up to the artists to tell. Although we asked each artist what they might need on site, none of them could predetermine how they would react to being in Portland, being before or after another artist, who they might meet. The 'show' was dependent on this jig—was this jig—and in fact, in hindsight, is the story of the 'show'. A 'show' that is always different, depending on which artist, which visitor, which volunteer, which staff member, which 'curator' is telling the story.

CONCLUSION: SOME THOUGHTS ON CIRCULARITY

This is an exhibition animated by a circular logic: knowing there will be eyes on it at every stage, it starts to use that in such a way that, at the end, reason and result have spun eddies into one another. This is an exhibition animated by a circulating dialogue: generated between any two (co-curators, collaborating carpenters, artist and cloth, artist and subsequent artist) and positioning itself in open relation to an audience so as to invite the circulation to continue. Such a moment came midway through the show when the artist Tracey Cockrell contacted us to ask whether she might in downtimes between artists in residence bring her poemophones[4] into the museum to play musical translations of our study centre texts. In this way she extended the exhibition and moved it forward, meeting its needs with her own and modelling a rare and beautiful will to become the very audience for whom this show might have been designed.

If performing a living dialogue was the problem of that first curator's talk, then we reach here the equally compelling problem of this written chapter. We are well aware of deep habits that expect reason to precede result in ways tidy, linear and critically defensible. But in making and witnessing the unfolding of this exhibition, it is the very beautiful slips and transpositions of reason and result that stand out. We believe them worth tracing out for what they might reveal of the complexity of thought that characterize deep engagement in both craft and collaborative practice. One aim of this essay has been to diagram this circular, recursive approach to making and showing that uses *everything at hand* to trick new sets of relations into being, and to ask whether this approach has a privileged relation to craft as we have understood it and craft as we are coming to understand it. We also wanted to lay out the critical thinking alongside which we designed this exhibition, trusting the reader to hold to the notion 'alongside' and to inhibit casting the exhibition as an attempt to prove or disprove anything. It simply wasn't that kind of undertaking.

NOTES

The authors wish to acknowledge the staff of the Museum of Contemporary Craft for their support of this undertaking, in particular Namita Wiggers, curator, Kat Perez, exhibition coordinator, and the interns and volunteers whose work let us stage this exhibition from a distance. More on both versions of the exhibition, including extensive images, can be found at www.performingcraft.com.

1. The museum's two-level architecture lent itself to staging two very different kinds of encounter with the artists' work. On the first floor, where visitors entered, we staged simple plywood signs with basic descriptive information about each artist's project. These didactics were stored, visible, on a side-wall and moved into the space during each artist's residency. All interpretive and overtly didactic language was housed on the second floor, in a study centre populated by artefacts of past projects by each of the artists and generous amounts of background information. This was information we wanted to make available but only after visitors had navigated the live performance space on their own.

2. That this way of working produced remarkably beautiful forms, surfaces, arrangements should in no way be seen as contradictory to our valuation of the live risk. In the hands of skilled makers, would we expect the engagement in extended and live risk to produce anything less than compelling objects? Certainly, Black and Preus in how they designed for the needs of subsequent artists and in their choice of materials and methods set a precedent for beautiful workmanship.

3. Both in the exhibition and in the original conference panel we co-chaired, our interest was in playing with the affordances of each institutional context, not so much a rejection of institutional habits as an experiment in surfing them.

4. Cockrell's poemophones are lamellophones housed inside old typewriter cases.

REFERENCES

Black, S., and Preus, J. (2010), Rebuilding Mayfield, <http://blackpreus.org/projects/rebuilding-mayfield> accessed 30 December 2011.

Eco, U. (2006), 'The Poetics of Open Work', in C. Bishop (ed.), *Participation*, London: White Chapel and MIT Press.

Gates, T. (2008), *Yamaguchi Story*, <http://theastergates.com/artwork/239815_Yamaguchi_Story.html> accessed 30 December 2011.

Massumi, B. (2011), *Semblance and Event: Activist Philosophy and the Occurent Arts*, Cambridge, MA: MIT Press.

Pye, D. (1968), *The Nature and Art of Workmanship*, Cambridge: Cambridge University Press.

Sennett, R. (2008), *The Craftsman*, New Haven, CT: Yale University Press.

Sanders, J.H. (2004), 'Moving beyond the Binary', in M. A. Fariello and P. Owen (eds), *Objects and Meaning: New Perspectives on Art and Craft*, Lanham, MD: Scarecrow Press.

–16–

Expanded Craft, Dispersed Creativity: A South Asian Residency

Cj O'Neill and Amanda Ravetz

INTRODUCTION

This chapter discusses a collaboration that emerged during a month-long residency at Arts Reverie, an artists' house in the old city of Ahmedabad, India, in 2010.[1] The residency brought together three UK researchers (including the authors of this chapter), two Indian partners and a number of local people in a cross-disciplinary and cross-cultural project.[2] The outputs from the collaboration included workshops, an event, a film and a number of ceramic pieces. But there were also less tangible outcomes—working relationships between collaborators and questions about what collaboration through craft requires or demands of researchers, producers, makers and participants.

The word 'collaboration' evokes the difficulties, as well as the pleasures, of working with others. The extremes of experience common to collaboration are often explained through reference to the differences between the knowledge and practices being combined. It is not easy, we tell ourselves, to bring difference together without friction, without sometimes falling out. The urge towards collaboration in spite of its well-rehearsed pitfalls, provokes the first of two questions we address in this chapter: what is it about collaboration that we and others value so much?

The second question grows out of the value we give collaboration and our argument that it may rest on the power we find in combination, which in turn invokes a mode of creativity that the anthropologist James Leach has called 'dispersed' (2004). Dispersed creativity links in important ways to understandings of craft that suggest we approach it as an *activity*, a way of thinking and being in the world (Adamson 2007: 167). How do expanded ideas of craft and dispersed ideas of creativity challenge the established practices of makers and anthropologists and those who become involved in their work?

THE COLLABORATION

The residency was based at Arts Reverie, an artists' house in Dhal ni Pol, one of approximately 600 'pols' found on the east side of Ahmedabad. Pols are high-density neighbourhoods that were once homogeneous communities associated with different castes but are today increasingly heterogeneous. Historically, pols would have had 'only one, or at the most two entrances (apart from secret ones), one main street with crooked lanes branching off either side, and walls and gates (now removed) which were barred at night' (Gillion 1968). Today, the narrow streets, the outdated services and the dilapidated state of many buildings are contributing to out-migration from the east to the west side of the city—'modern' Ahmedabad—which boasts newer dwellings and infrastructure.

Our residency was the result of a PAL lab held at Arts Reverie in February 2010 where representatives from different agencies had come together to discuss ways for artists, environmentalists and residents of Dhal ni Pol to tackle a number of local environmental issues.[3] Our initial ambition was to pilot this vision of artists collaborating with environmentalists. However, a few weeks before the project was due to start, the environmental partners were forced to pull out due to a clash with another project. In their absence, we decided to take as our brief the topic of the festival where our work was due to be shown. *Making Beauty*, the title of the Ahmedabad International Arts Festival (AIAF), became the theme of our work.

Given that the original emphasis of the lab had been on community participation we wanted to engage with people living near Arts Reverie. We were joined by two Indian researchers to help us with this. The artist Lokesh Ghai took the role of project manager and communications graduate Palak Chitaliya who had consulted with local people about environmental conditions on previous occasions became our translator and helped run several community workshops. Something that allowed us to develop relationships with local residents in Dhal ni Pol was the timing of our visit, which coincided with Navratri, a festival of dancing lasting nine nights. Each night we were invited by neighbours to join in the dancing in the streets around the house.

Although all of those involved in the residency had envisaged supporting one another as a team, for us, the authors, this cooperation went beyond discussing ideas or sharing resources. As we traced how our collaboration developed, it was difficult to remember who came up with an idea or did what. Part of the explanation for our close collaboration has to do with shared interests, for example we are both intrigued by the relationship of people to materials. But there are differences too, since we have different skills, media and ways of theorizing.

In our first week in Dhal ni Pol, we focused on developing relationships with people, thinking about the objects people were using and observing the built environment.[4] What we noticed depended on what we were surrounded by as well as the preoccupations we brought with us—with Cj thinking as a ceramicist and designer and Amanda, as a filmmaker and visual anthropologist. We noticed for example the everyday ceramics, the architectural details and the social importance of the liminal spaces of the otlas—wide steps outside houses where people socialize and how people were very insistent that we take photographic portraits of them posing formally in their doorways. Our ideas for work began to crystallize when we saw that the camera was a powerful way to create introductions to people as well as to document things we wanted to think about more. The work we eventually made came about through Cj's wanting to find visual stories with which to decorate chai ceramics and Amanda's wanting to develop links with her current preoccupations with reverie and play. Through various discussions and permutations, we arrived at an idea for an event which would take place over one day—a doorway, reflecting the liminal space of the otlas, would be set up in a public space and people would be invited to interact with it while Amanda recorded video from a fixed point and Cj took photographic portraits (Figure 16.1).

On the auspicious day of Dushera, the festival that ends Navratri, after negotiating with Mayur Fadiya, a moped mechanic in Dhal ni Pol, we set up the doorway in the courtyard-cum-street outside his house and video recorded people's interactions with it, each other and ourselves. Cj took still shots,

Fig. 16.1. Neet/Community, 2010. A still photograph made during the filming of *Entry* in Dhal ni Pol, Ahmedabad, India. Photograph: Cj O'Neill

Fig. 16.2. The Pol Project, 2010. Neet/Community. Ceramic cup and saucer with hand-cut silhouette decoration in black taken from a still photograph made during the filming of *Entry* in Dhal ni Pol, Ahmedabad, India. Photograph: Cj O'Neill

inviting people to pose in the doorway. The video recording was edited into a fifteen-minute film entitled *Entry*[5] and shown one week later to a large crowd in the same space where it had been filmed. For Cj the event provided a narrative around which to build a series of ceramic pieces using hand-cut transfers. These pieces were then shown at Arts Reverie and the British Council Library[6] (Figure 16.2).

All in all what each of us could have done separately was enhanced and extended by working together, pooling ideas and resources so that we eventually made an event that served both our needs and changed our understanding in the process, while also allowing us to produce two quite distinctive outcomes and objects.

DILEMMAS AND DIFFICULTIES

The collaboration was not without its difficulties, and these can be summed up using three brief examples. On Amanda's last night, after screening the film, someone who had played a large part in the filming was angry that he had not been given a DVD with everything she had filmed on it—all the rushes. Instead, she had given him a copy of the finished film. What this moment of tension suggested was that, at the point of finishing and leaving, we seemed to be appropriating something that had not until this moment been a matter of dispute.[7]

A child who had decorated a cup and saucer during a workshop was asked if she would like these to be included in an exhibition at the British Council Library. A prestigious event in some people's eyes, she told Cj that it wouldn't be possible to lend the ceramics as her father drank tea from that cup every day now. He wouldn't be very happy if he had to use something else, even for a few days, so it was not possible to include her work in the exhibition.

Parshottam, the chai walla who we came to know during our stay in Dhal ni Pol and who sold tea at the three-day event in which the ceramics and film were shown, was given a series of gold spot cups by Cj to use on his stall, or at home, as was Mayur Fadiya, who allowed us to set up the doorway outside his house and who encouraged his friends and family to join in the filming; a tea service was gifted to the British Council Library in Ahmedabad to have on display; each child who decorated a cup in the workshop took a cup home; and Devi Singh, Mohan and Mohanlil who work at Arts Reverie each received a cup. But not everyone we worked with or met were given a cup and saucer— there were not enough to go around.

Each of these stories highlights issues obscured in the account of the collaboration we gave above, notably the contributions and roles of people living in Dhal ni Pol, their reactions to the objects and their feelings about the ownership of the objects. Thinking about these and other reactions we wonder who the authors of the film and ceramics are and what else, apart from the objects and questions of authorship, might be at stake here?

ASSIGNING VALUE IN COLLABORATIONS

Explaining what makes cross-disciplinary collaborations such as ours a success often involves pointing out the differences and the affinities between the collaborating agents, the understanding being that it is through *cross-fertilization* that innovation and novelty occur. Indeed, the growing dialogue between our two fields, craft and anthropology, referred to as the 'ethnographic turn' in the arts and the 'artistic turn' in academic research, is underpinned by ideas of cross-fertilization through which comes new knowledge.[8]

But evaluating the success of collaborations using notions of cross-fertilization in the arts is not without its critics. Writing in 1991, Rogoff was concerned with the way artistic collaborations that were justified through 'cross fertilization' quickly reverted to tropes of heroic individualism with singular figures being celebrated, rather than more collective forms of authorship being acknowledged. There are two ways this critique is pertinent to the account we have given of our collaboration so far. Having invoked cross-cultural and cross-disciplinary potential, we also restricted our descriptions of novelty to ourselves, failing to mention other elements that went into the creativity we were involved in. To verify this creativity, we pointed to the objects—the outputs—as if it were only in them that we might find the proof of our creative efforts.

Is it possible then to think about collaboration differently? Are there other ways of valuing what happened? Or can we only point to the objects made and the changes made to our understanding?

Working in Papua New Guinea (PNG), anthropologist James Leach has long been concerned with questions of ownership.[9] PNG is recognized by anthropologists as exemplifying different understandings of ownership and personhood from our own. As an anthropologist comparing PNG and Euro-American ways of thinking, Leach suggests that questions about authorship, ownership, intellectual property rights and collaboration are underpinned by some fundamental assumptions we tend to make about creativity which link to our ways of assigning ownership and authorship in, for example, intellectual property rights (IPR). Leach identifies three elements that permeate what he calls dominant Euro-American ways of thinking about creativity. First, we tend to recognize creativity where combinations of things or ideas are apparent. Second, we expect that this process of combination has been directed by a will or an intent. Third, we deduce creativity using evidence of novelty of form or outcome.

Leach explains that purposeful, intended collaborations seem to evoke all three of these elements. In describing our collaboration, we emphasized combination of skills, people, subject areas and cultures. We highlighted will and intent through a narrative about deliberately setting out to use our creativity to make something happen; and we drew attention to novelty, arguing that the film and ceramics were unique to our cross-fertilization, with the bonus being that each of our practices was changed/reformed by the experience.

But Leach insists that, although this is a dominant model of creativity in Euro-American thinking, there is another mode we are also aware of, although we are less likely to articulate it or to assign value to it. In this mode, creativity is immanent in all moments; it is distributed through creation, and it is not the preserve or property of a particular institution or deity.

Leach's observations about distributive creativity are illustrated through his fieldwork with people of Reite in PNG. He tells us that Reite people do 'appropriate from nature, produce objects, and own them, *but they understand this as the creation of persons*' (2004: 170; our emphasis).

He goes on to describe how for Reite people models of ownership are not based on an appropriative creativity but on a distributed creativity. Humanity is defined by the necessity of embodying and acting creatively, and it is people themselves who are valuable rather than the emphasis put on objects. Accordingly, Reite people let ritual objects (such as *Torr* posts used in rituals) rot away in the bush. This 'demotion' of objects is reflected, says Leach, in 'creativity' being understood as something distributed throughout existence.

By contrast, in dominant Euro-American ways of thinking about creativity, 'IPR has the effect of concentrating creativity in particular individuals, and then in individual kinds of mental operation which amount to forms of appropriation by the subject' (Leach 2004: 171).

Roy Wagner another anthropologist of PNG has remarked on the degree to which Westerners value the objects, the outcomes of creativity. 'We keep the ideas, the quotations, the memoirs, the creations and let the people go. Our attics . . . [and] museums are full of this kind of culture' (Wagner 1975: 26, quoted in Leach 2004). A common solution to tensions in collaborations around objects has been the instigation of a more democratic and participatory approach to the production and subsequent ownership of the objects. In a project like ours this could involve films being made by participants, exhibited alongside artists' work—or work being produced by a collective. But while this may well be desirable for a number of reasons, it would not necessarily get to the more fundamental issues that seem to be at stake in what Leach and Wagner tell us about the 'effects' of creativity being registered in objects, rather than in persons.

Thinking about the demotion of objects Leach speaks of in PNG, we wonder now about the value of the work others did 'in us' in Ahmedabad—how people lent themselves not only to our project but also as an effect of this, to the success that would register in us as persons—in our careers, our earning potential and so on. This consideration of whose creativity has registered its effects in us, raises a further question too; how to demarcate who did work in us and who did not. Should we include the people we danced with each night but whose names we did not know? Or those we saw more often and knew by name? Or was the valuable work only properly registered by those who we are still in touch with?

OBSCURING CONNECTIONS

This uncertainty relates to what another anthropologist of Papua New Guinea, Stuart Kirsch, has talked of as short and long networks. Kirsch argues that Papuans who claimed against the Lihir Mining Corporation about the death of some pigs on the island of Lihir, east of Papua New Guinea, brought 'long networks' of social relations into view. The Papuans argued that a series of events linked the mine to the death of the pigs, including the original construction of the mine which had forced people to relocate (Kirsch 2004: 82). By contrast the counter-claims of the corporation attempted to cut the networks short—arguing it was not their (social and ethical) responsibility that the pigs had died, and this could not be proved to be a direct result of their actions in taking over the land. The Euro-American approach, Kirsch suggests, tried to obscure the social relations between the people, the pigs and the mine.

Kirsch's contrast of long and short networks helps us understand the difficulties we had in working out where to draw the line around our collaboration in Ahmedabad. Put bluntly, we recognize in Kirsch's description a tendency to avoid too many entanglements that might result in obligations beyond those we were prepared to meet. The word entanglement gives us an additional clue to how long and short networks might tie into the idea that we tend to register creativity through objects. Anthropologist Tim Ingold makes the point that, whereas networks are created by drawing straight lines between objects—which are then referred to as material culture—meshworks suggest something deceptively similar but actually very different:

> The meshwork consists not of interconnected points but of interwoven lines. Every line is a relation, but the relation is not *between* one thing and another—between, say, an artefact here and a person there, or between one person or artefact and another. Rather, the relation is a line *along* which materials flow, mix and mutate. Persons and things, then, are formed in the meshwork as knots or bundles of such relations. It is not, then, that things are entangled in relations; rather every thing is itself an entanglement, and is thus linked to other things by way of the flows of materials that make it up. So while the material world might be depicted as it is in the weblog logo, as a network of interconnected objects, the world of materials would be better described as a meshwork of interwoven substances. (Ingold 2007: 35)

Ingold's preference for meshworks over networks and materials over materialities suggests two things in relation to what we have been talking about. First, that the idea of demarcating who is inside and outside a collaboration seems to belong to the idea of networks rather than of than meshworks. Such demarcation suggests distance—either conceptual or spatial or temporal—and possibly after the fact. But in our experience decisions about how to work with others and what reciprocities and ethical questions mattered were taken in the midst of life's entanglements. These decisions were worked through with varying degrees of success. But they were made not from blue print but by feel and practice. As long as we were immersed in the meshwork of the pol we managed this tolerably well. It was only once we were about to leave and ours and other people's foci moved from our unfolding relationships to objects that we encountered problems. Cutting things short, we suggest, is connected to the distancing of (our)selves from experience and is made possible in part through talk of networks. Second, what appears to be happening when we focus on objects and on what is now routinely called material culture is that we are in danger of ignoring the materials themselves (Bunn 1999). Discussions about skill, technology and so forth can easily lose sense of the maker's feel for materials, the push and pull, frictions, properties and so on. With this development comes an impoverishment in our understanding of what Ingold simply calls 'being alive' (2011).

We want to suggest that, as it is for the maker and materials, feeling their way, becoming more practiced the more hours they put in, so it is for collaborators more widely—practice, materials, tension and friction all figure, and the successful collaborator like the successful maker is attuned to the materials, whether working with or against their properties—for it would be naïve to suggest there could be all flow and no resistance. Fariello, quoting Richards (2011: 25), talks of the way materials tell us how they have been worked. The clay that cracks in the kiln is articulating its story. People also change, are changed, by whom and by what they work with, where and how.

CONCLUSION

To return to the first question with which we began this chapter—what is it about collaboration that we and others value so much? We have argued, following Leach, that the assigning of value to collaboration depends on more than one understanding of creativity. Novelty can be registered outside the relationships that produced it, but creation can also be seen as immanent, always available, so that value is about the work each of us does in others. Pivotal to these two perspectives are ways of understanding people, places and things as either relations formed between ourselves and separate objects in which we make individual ownership claims, or as meshworks in which claims are made around the work done in others. The first perspective depends on highlighting and celebrating the combinations that led to the outcomes and the outcomes themselves. The second involves assigning value to forms of creativity that remain dispersed between agents. Attempting this, as Leach reminds us, challenges our tendencies to detach creativity from its generative conditions in order to register its effects in external objects. It means valuing modes of creativity seen for example in the way work done by one person registers in the changes and growth of another.

Having established this we then questioned the consequences for makers and those who work with them, when what is valued about craft shifts from a concern with the object and the studio to action and site. We want to conclude this chapter by suggesting a tentative answer to this second question: rethinking craft as something that leaves the studio and goes out into the world also requires rethinking the way we understand 'materials'—what can be included within the category of material and what working with materials therefore means. Instead of seeing the makers' materials as substances with certain discrete attributes to be worked in studio conditions—wood, glass, clay—we might think about materials-in-the-world. Following Ingold's view of materials as having (hi)stories, this would mean keeping in view the huge range of different states materials assume. At certain points in the making process, though not necessarily all, our relationship with materials gives us clear glimpses of a border zone where boundaries between self and other, medium and substance dissolve. To think of materials-in-the-world we suggest, is to include people as part of the world in which and with which makers collaborate. Collaboration through craft then allows for an alignment of human and nonhuman materials, so that craft knowledge incorporates the material movements of human life—the practiced flow between substance and medium.

This is not to deny that objects presented in the context of for example an academic institution appear as *mine/ours*. Bringing the film and the ceramic pieces back to the United Kingdom they were viewed as *outputs*, and we described them as such. But this language, while it helps us to explain some things, also obscures others, the long view of materials—human and nonhuman—their stories. The subjects, objects, origin of the cups; the clay, the glazes, the firing of the transfer; the translation, advice, conversation, filming, placement and testing; the sounds, smells and sights of the Pol that contributed.

Keeping this in view is complex, especially in academic environments. But we believe there are further explorations to be carried out around ways to make and unmake the boundaries between different modes of creativity and different understandings of materials, and to craft collaborations with materials-in-the-world that might then be valued in plural ways.

NOTES

We gratefully acknowledge financial and other support we received from A Fine Line: Cultural Practice, The British Council and MIRIAD. Steve Dixon, Palak Chitaliya, Lokesh Ghai, Mayur Fadiya and residents of Dhal ni Pol, Barney Hare Duke, John Hyatt, Anupa Mehta and many other people helped us and contributed to the success of the project.

1. For information about Arts Reverie, see <http://www.artsreverie.com/last> accessed December 2011; and Chapter 14, this volume.
2. The researchers and participants were Cj O'Neill, Amanda Ravetz, Steve Dixon, Lokesh Ghai, Palak Chitaliya, Mayur Fadiya and residents of Dhal ni Pol.
3. For more information about the PAL lab, see <http://www.pallabs.org/portfolio/timeline/here_and_there_lab_10_02/> accessed December 2011.
4. Observations and experiences undertaken as part of the research included dancing, visiting neighbours, interviewing professionals, visiting the children's library, photographing people when requested to, noting chai ceramics, flowers, bicycles; khadkis (house groups), framed and/or liminal spaces of the *otla*—wide steps outside houses; the public squares and the *chubutaras* (bird feeders). During the project the team ran three workshops, attended by more than 100 children. We gave people copies

of their portraits and of the film, and we were invited by several people to come back and work in a school in the Pol and take part in the kite festival.

5. *Entry* can be seen at <https://vimeo.com/19328902> accessed 16 August 2012.
6. The work was shown at the British Council Library and at Arts Reverie as part of the Ahmedabad International Arts Festival 2010.
7. On a return visit in April 2012, Amanda discussed this with Naitik Fadiya who told her that the man who became angry had thought the aim was to make a box office hit.
8. As a result of cross-fertilization, we might argue, anthropology, has moved towards more performative understandings of both the world and itself and art has begun to make its knowledge and the contexts for its operation explicit, whether through social contextualization of its practices, or by engaging with social and critical theory to confront its own 'ways of knowing'.
9. The ideas about dispersed creativity we use in this chapter come from Leach (2004).

REFERENCES

Adamson, G. (2007), *Thinking through Craft*, Oxford: Berg.

Bunn, S. (1999), 'The Importance of Materials', *Journal of Museum Ethnography*, 11: 15–28.

Gillion, K. L. (1968), *Ahmedabad: A Study in Indian Urban History,* Berkeley: University of California Press.

Ingold, T. (2007), *Lines: A Brief History*, London: Routledge.

Ingold, T. (2011), *Being Alive,* London: Routledge.

Kirsch, S. (2004), 'Keeping the Network in View: Compensation Claims, Property and Social Relations in Melanesia', in L. Kalinoe and J. Leach (eds), *Rationales of Ownership: Transactions and Claims to Ownership in Contemporary Papua New Guinea*, Wantage: Sean Kingston.

Leach, J. (2004), 'Modes of Creativity', in E. Hirsch and M. Strathern (eds), *Transactions and Creations,* New York: Berghahn, 151–75.

Richards, M. C. (1962), *Centering in Pottery, Poetry, and the Person*, Middletown, CT: Wesleyan University Press.

Wagner, R. (1975), *The Invention of Culture,* Englewood Cliffs, NJ: Prentice-Hall.

EPILOGUE

A Response: The Limits of Collaboration

Glenn Adamson

Lewis Hyde, in his influential book *The Gift* (1983), offers the following, initially perplexing example of generosity. Two Frenchmen, strangers to each other, sit at a café table. The first silently pours wine for the second. The second recip-rocates. Both drink. Nothing of value seems to have been created in this quiet moment. Each man gets as much wine (more or less) as he would have other-wise. There has been no sharing of ideas or sentiments, not even a word was spoken. Nonetheless, Hyde claims that it is in such exchanges that 'society' is created. By such apparently marginal, even meaningless acts people distin-guish themselves from purely self-interested actors. The very pointlessness of the exercise—that is to say its disconnection with any motive of profit—is what makes it significant. Only through the 'gift economy' can we enter into a truly productive social contract with one another.

It's an idea to warm the heart, to be sure. But there are counter-arguments to consider. Perhaps gift-giving is actually a thinly disguised form of mutually advantageous trade. After all, those Frenchmen might meet in the market-place some days hence. So their friendliness, which requires no investment in any case, might just pay off. Taking matters somewhat further, it is clear that what initially seems to be generosity can be a form of outright aggres-sion. Think of the medieval custom of honorific presents, in which courts vied to humble one another with freely given masterpieces or the Native American tradition of the potlatch, in which tribes competed to see who could be most lavish in the display of largesse. And finally, a real pessimist might point out that the inclusivity of gift-giving is always partial—and therefore, always a way of excluding others. Though one would like to think that our imagined French-men would pour for a visiting Algerian, would they in practice? In Japan, it is considered deeply impolite to pour *sake* into your own cup. That sounds very civilized, until you ignorantly trespass on the custom, marking you straight-away as an outsider. Viewed from this perspective, the act which Hyde pres-ents as social adhesive comes to seem more like a mild but effective form of community enforcement.

It may seem cynical to do so but similar questions must be asked of the present volume. What is the point of celebrating the custom of artistic collaboration? The authors in this book, who effectively function as anthropologists of creativity, offer as many possible answers to that question as they offer models of collaboration itself. In these pages, we read of partnerships between two equals; instances of dispersed authorship, where a single artist brought a range of others into their vision; discursively rich 'threeing', in which decision-making occurs in an ongoing cascade; and dispersed 'meshworks' activated through interactive technology. There is talk of 'co-confusion', 'non-didacticism' and 'shared lexicons'. Artists collaborate with scientists, pattern cutters with plastic surgeons, a writer with a stitcher with a furniture maker. In one striking example, two curators commission a timber platform for their gallery. This stage is successively occupied by one artist after another, in a process of accumulative overlay, until the resulting palimpsest is finally given 'a good whitewashing' by artist Theaster Gates.

Clearly, these various instances of interchange, elaboration and cancellation bring many kinds of complication to bear, and none are reducible to the simple act of gift-giving. Yet at heart, each offers the hope that relinquishing control will produce better, more holistic results. This optimistic view is perhaps connected to the fact that, for the contributors to this volume, craft lies at the heart of the collaborative process. It functions as the mechanism that ensures mutual respect. Skill is the wine in the bottle, if you like. Through craft, a collaborator can part with his or her own time, energy, and hard-won knowledge, and always have more to give. Hyde theorizes art precisely along these lines. It is like an inexhaustible gift, there in a radically open way for anyone who chooses to receive it. Though it may well be commoditized, the artwork yields its 'true' value freely, independent of any consideration of ownership.

Yet there are also, scattered throughout this volume, indications of the limits of collaboration. Allison Smith for example professes her wish to be a 'jack of all trades, master of none'. In her account, it seems that a surplus of craft know-how would be a wall rather than an open door. She retains the posture of an interested amateur, rather than a master dispensing her skills. Stephen Knott goes so far as to argue that the most salutary aspect of cross-disciplinary art school experience is the discovery of basic incompetencies—a 'strategy of discomfort', in which a fashion designer comes clean by making a mess at a potter's wheel. And Lesley Millar, in a moment of disarming frankness, asks a question so fundamental that Hyde (like most in the art world) doesn't dare consider it: 'What do we, the practitioners, think about the role of curator as interpreter? Is this what we want?' Here she recognizes an obvious truth: sole authorship, and sole ownership, are the norm in art for good reason. Each partner in any joint project must give away part of his or her own authorship. For anyone wanting to maintain professional standards or to treat artwork as a repository of value, collaboration is always going to present challenges.

What all these moments of doubt have in common is the theme of *friction*. This is a good craft word—you can't do anything without the resistance of materials, but that resistance also limits possibility. So it is with collaborations: in an ideal (and perhaps idealistic) world, agency would flow effortlessly from one hand to another. But in reality, collaboration profits from resistance, just as woodcarving and silversmithing do. When this sense of one vision rubbing up against another is lost, so is the spark of invention. Two plus two can well make three, instead of five. It is notable that most really successful collaborations tend to involve long-term partnerships, such as between Picasso and Braque, Gilbert and George or the Guerrilla Girls, so that the sense of multiple distinct agencies is eroded over time.

More transient artistic collaborations—like most of those addressed in this book—tend to be valuable, instead, for the friction, the intelligent disruption, that they bring about. I think that this is what Smith, Knott and Millar are recognizing in their different ways. As in the case of Hyde's Frenchmen, we must understand the collaborative act as a break within a broader pattern, not as an isolated event. Most artists, when they put their heads together, will learn a lot about themselves. But the real benefit of their experience will hardly ever be immediate. Probably, it will not be clear until they return to their own way of practicing, their own 'discipline'—a word that is currently undervalued but deserves respect in all of its registers of meaning, especially when matters of craft are at stake. Following a collaborative encounter, artists may well find new directions to pursue. Their work will, at best, be inflected in ways they find meaningful. In this respect, working in pairs, trios and teams can be crucial. But even (and perhaps especially) in a world as thoroughly networked as our own, it is only by taking ownership of those new vectors that most artists will really make the collaboration worthwhile. What all art requires is a sense of responsibility. And even in the best of all possible worlds that is not something you can give away.

REFERENCE

Hyde, L. (1983), *The Gift: Imagination and the Erotic Life of Property,* New York: Random House.

Index

Adamson, Glenn, 2, 4, 6, 132, 175, 193
aesthetic qualities of creations, 95
    form and beauty, 88
aesthetics of waste, 88–90
    developing collaboration, 90–2
A Fine Line: Cultural Practice, 206
animals, re-animation, 61–2
anthropology, 2–3, 197, 237, 243n8,
    248
archaeology, 2–3
architecture, 79
    benefits of collaboration, 87
    transdisciplinarity, 161
    use of textiles, 77
artist-curators, 27–8
Arts Reverie (Gujarat), 214–16, 233–42,
    242n1
    challenges, 236–7
    community participation, 234–5
    cross-cultural work, 233, 237
    cross-disciplinary work, 233, 237
    Making Beauty, 234
    Material Response, 208
    value of collaboration, 233, 241
        assigning value, 237–9, 241
assumptions for collaboration, 35–7
Ave, Masayo, 27

Belford, Trish, 73–5
Beuys, Joseph, 197
Binns, David, 74
Black, Anthea, 220
Black, Sara, 220, 228
Blakey, Sharon, 12, 171
Boswell, James, 103
Bould, Trish, 23–4
Bourriaud, Nicolas, 132–3, 193
bowdlerization, 109
Brass Art, 59–68
Bremner, Alasdair, 91–2, 97, 98n2

Brick Project, 91
bricolage, 133–6
Broadhead, Caroline, 142, 149
burn-out see devoré

Carnac, Helen, 11, 19–20
Carter, Paul, 25, 27–8
Catalytic Clothing, 77–8, 79–82
Catt, Oron, 115
ceramics (recycled), 88–9
chemical processes (impact), 77–8
    see also environmental issues
Chitaliya, Palak, 234
choice, 214–5
choreography, 42
circularity, 230–1
civic culture, 12, 193–203
Claxton, Guy, 145
Cleverly, Jason, 11, 74, 100–2, 107–8
    interdisciplinarity, 105
    new media, 105
Coates, Caroline, 78
co-confusion, 35–7
collaboration, 34, 248
    benefits of collaboration, 86
    challenges, 248–9
    communicative practices in
        collaborative art, 47
    contingent nature, 37, 41
    cultural diversity, 206
        cross-territory collaboration, 209–11
        expanding practice, 216–17
        international collaboration, 216
    defined, 34
    design sensitivity, 110
    impact on content, 110
    individual practices versus, 38–9
    interaction, 47
    interdisciplinary collaborations, 100,
        158–9

international collaboration, 216–17
limits, 247–9
participants, 240
practice of collaboration, 46–8
  case studies, 47–54
  conversations, 46–7, 54–6
  generally, 45–6
  identities, 48
process of collaboration, 34, 248
transdisciplinary collaboration,
  158–9
vocational learning, 142–9
see also collaboration through craft;
  institutional collaborations
collaboration through craft, 1–2, 247–9
certitude, 5–6, 224
collaborative expertise, 1
conversation, importance of, 11, 34,
  41
cultural factors, 12
deterritorialization, 6
focusing through materials, 5
generally, 20–1
historical factors, 12
impact on expressive powers of the
  individual, 9
movement, importance of, 7, 11
new contexts, 45–6
reasons for, 19, 23–4
remembering, 41–2
risk, 5–6
sociality of craft, 2–4, 235, 247
teamwork distinguished, 24–6
tensions, 19
territory, challenges of, 6
theories, 4
time, investment of, 7
transience, 65, 249
value, 13–14, 248–9
workmanship of certainty, 224
workmanship of risk, 224
see also collaboration; institutional
  collaborations
collaborative enterprise, 94–6
collaborative expertise, 1, 8–10, 75,
  86, 92
challenge to individualism, 22, 23–4
curatorial collaboration, 26–7
role of the expert, 128–9
teamwork, 24–6

collective voice, 59–65
communication *see* conversations
computer-aided design/manufacturing
  (CAD/CAM), 107
computer simulations, 101
concrete and textiles, 77–8, 82–6,
  98n2
conditions for collaboration, 5, 35–7
Condorelli, Celine, 131
contingency, 1, 3, 9
  contingent nature of collaboration,
    37, 41
  contingent nature of craft, 189–90
conversations, 31, 34–5, 38, 41, 219,
  229
  cross-disciplinary, 127, 194
  importance, 11
  material conversations, 3
  reflective conversation, 3
  see also participation
craft, 2–3, 132, 225–6
  application of skills, 75
  association with practical knowledge, 2
  civic culture, 12
  collaborations, experience of, 1
  collaborative potential, 3
  conflict and, 193
  contemporary practice, 33–4
  contingent nature, 189–90
  historical re-enactment, 193
  history of idea of craft, 2
  industrial production, 74
  integration, 75
  living history, 193
  material conversations, 3
  performative nature, 190
  political expression, 219, 227
  power to expose ideas, 12
  practice, 19
  problematic of collaboration, 10
  schools, 142–3
  sense of place, 74, 103–4
  sociality of craft, 2–4
  teaching, 12
  traditional perception, 10
  United States, 195–6
craft knowledge, 6, 94, 147–9
  textiles and, 82–3
craft of discomfort, 136–9
Craft: Who Cares?, 207

creative collaboration, 24, 26–7, 29
creative practitioners, 32–3
cross-collaborative projects, 78
cross-fertilization, 2, 10, 73, 238,
 243n8
 of ideas, 191, 237
cultural diversity, 206
 cross-territory collaboration, 209–11
 expanding practice, 216–17
 international collaboration, 216
culture of craft, 95
curatorial collaboration, 26–7, 60
Cunningham, Ward, 103

dance, 149
Davies, Siobhan, 32, 37, 42
Department 21, 12, 128, 130–9,
 140n1
 artistic freedoms, 132–3, 136, 139
 beginnings, 130–2
 interdisciplinarity, 131–2
design
 design principles of wiki, 103–4
 design sensitivity, 110
 schools, 143
 teaching, 12, 142–4
design qualities, 95
 form and beauty, 88
devoré, 78, 80
Dewey, John, 147, 163
Dialogue, 31
digital bookmarking, 105
dispersed creativity, 233–42, 243n9
Dormer, Peter, 5, 6, 7, 133
 craft knowledge, 148–9
 knowledge distribution, 6
dynamic changes
 collaboration and, 31–2
 conversations, 41
 remembering, 41–2

eco-responsible practices, 75
 see also environmental issues
Edelkoort, Li, 74, 88
educational psychology
 cognitive development, 147
Eglin, Phil, 142
Eisner, Elliot, 147–8
Elzenbaumer, Bianca, 130, 140n1
embodied experience, 66

enhancement of the self, 114
 possession of property, 9
 possessiveness, 9–10
 reconstruction of the self, 114
 status, 9
environmental issues, 11–12, 160,
 210, 234
 environmental responsibility, 73, 75
 recycling waste, 88–97
 impact on the environment, 97
 sustainable practices, 75
 sustainable resources, 95
exhibition curation, 22, 24
 balancing responsibilities, 110
 creative collaboration, 24, 26–7
 moderators' roles, 109
 performative crafts, 219, 220
 technical constraints, 110
 transition of influence, 109
 visitors' engagement, 109–10

face masks, 115
facial reconstruction, 115
fashion surgery, 119–20
fossilization of textiles, techniques,
 84–5
Fox, Shelley, 115
Franz, Fabio, 130, 140n1
funding, 92–3
furniture, 106
 relationship to sculpture, 45
 relationship to space, 45

Galloway, Anne, 37
Gates, David, 10, 20
Gates, Theaster, 220, 226–7
Gauntlett, David, 3
generative power of craft
 merging of materials, 73
 science and technology, 73
Gestures of Resistance, 219–31
 audience engagement, 225
 productive fiction, 227–8
 workmanships of risk and certainty,
 224
Ghai, Lokesh, 234
Giddens, Anthony, 191
Gillies, Harold, 115, 118, 121n5
glass, 95
 recycling, 95

Gonzalez-Torres, Felix, 132
Gormley, Antony, 22
grain, 115, 121n6, 121n7, 122n8
    direction of, 115–16
    of skin, 116
grants, 92–3
Green, Charles, 59
Greenhalgh, Paul, 2, 75
Gröppel-Wegener, Alke, 182

hand-making, 7, 59–60, 66, 134,
        174–5, 200, 224
    industrial versus, 224–5
Hare Duke, Barney, 13, 189–90
Hartley, Paddy, 115
HAT: Here and There, 208–13
Hawkins, Barbara, 12, 127
history, 189–92
    material culture, 45
    re-enactments, 193, 196–8
Horn, Andy, 33
House of Words exhibition *see* Johnson,
        Samuel (Dr.)
Hunter, Polly, 139, 141n14
Hyde, Lewis, 247

improvisatory collaborative projects, 42
individualism, 248–9
    limitations of individual authorship,
        133, 136, 203
    reliance on others, 136
industrial production, 74, 97
    sustainability, 74
Ingold, Tim, 3, 4, 7, 13, 240, 241
institutional collaborations, 127
    expertise, 128
    experts' roles, 128
    exploring research issues, 129
    material preservation, 128
    projects
        Department 21, 130–9
        Mary Greg Collection, 170–82
        Project Dialogue, 157–66
        Skills in the Making, 142–54
interactive design, 105, 110
    see also computer simulations;
        virtual realities
interconnectedness, 20, 37, 174–5
interdisciplinarity, 131–2
    Barthes, Roland, 133–4
    collaborative design projects, 101

House of Words, 100–11
    use of emerging technologies,
        101–3
    interactive interfaces, 103–4
international collaboration, 216–17

Jain, Jyotindra, 206, 218n1
Johnson, Samuel (Dr.)
    house, 100
        design and construction, 106–7
        design process, 105–8
        visitor engagement, 109–10
joint working, 8
    loss of specialist knowledge, 8
Jones, Hazel, 171

Kant, Tanvi, 214
Keene, Suzanne, 173
Kesseler, Rob, 146
Kester, Grant, 9–10
Kettle, Alice, 10, 20
Kirsch, Stuart, 239–40
Knott, Stephen, 12, 127, 248
knowledge, 74, 76n1
    artists' knowledge, 28–9
    material conversations, 3
    tacit knowledge, 3
    textile knowledge, 77–8

Langer, Karl, 116
    Langer's lines, 116
language, evolution of, 102
Lar Lam, Mung, 220
Lash, Scott, 8
Leach, Bernard, 88
Leach, James, 13, 238–9, 241, 243n9
Leemann, Judith, 189, 190
Levi-Strauss, Claude, 133–4
Limberg, Alexander, 11, 119, 120
Lind, Maria, 34, 42
Living History, 193, 196, 201
locatedness, 104
loss of self, 9, 21, 59, 66
Lucas, Bill, 145
Lung, Carole, 220, 229

McCabe, Richard, 93–4
makers and making
    history of craft, 47–8
    human nature and, 175–6
    knowledge, 84

language of making, 24, 120, 149
luxury or necessity, 206
performative craft, 189
sociality of making, 3
tacit knowledge, 149
transdisciplinarity, 114, 118
vocational learning, 142
Malone, Kate, 142, 148–9
Mary Greg Collection, 12, 128, 170–82
collaboration, 176–8
impact, 178–81
museum collecting, 171
representation of craft, 174–6
Massumi, Brian, 226–7
material conversations, 3
material culture, 45
United States, 201–3
materials, 241–2
analysis, 94
generating new materials, 73
grain of cloth, 116
materiality of skin, 115
personalization, 117
qualities, 4–5
transformative ability, 5
Mazza, Cat, 220
memories, 33, 41, 46
Merleau–Ponty, Maurice, 148
Millar, Lesley, 248
Miller, Daniel, 175
Mitchell, Liz, 12
modernity, 4, 8, 175, 191–2, 216
Mori, Junko, 142, 146
Morrow, Ruth, 74, 77, 79, 82–4
multiculturalism, 217
museums, 28, 100, 105, 239
interactive designs, 110
museum collecting, 171
value of collections, 170–4
visitor engagement, 110

O'Neill, Cj, 13, 190, 191
open source technologies, 104, 223
Orlan, 115
otherness, 133
ownership, 190, 238–9, 241, 248–9
see also enhancement of the self

Pairings project, 45, 46–7, 57n1
Pantling, Simon, 65
participation, 102, 106–8, 224

Art Reverie (Gujarat), 234
community participation, 234
conversation, 219, 224
procedures of participation, 106–11
see also visitor experiences
Patel, Jaimini, 213
Payne, Rachel, 12, 127
pedagogy and the crafts, 127–9,
144–5, 167n2, 224
performative crafts, 189–90, 198–203
Living History, 193, 196, 201
practices, 219
transience, 65
place, sense of, 74
plastic surgery
craft techniques, geometry and constructive considerations, 118
models for planning, 119
Orlan, 115
pattern cutting and, 114, 120n1
aesthetic qualities of skin, 116–17
collaboration, 120, 121
function and form, 120
grain, 116
planning processes, 117, 120
postmodernism, 162, 164
power of artists, 28–9, 29n4, 189–90
pre-collaboration, 108
Preus, John, 220, 228–9
processes, contingent nature, 37
productive fiction, 227–8
professional development, 142–4
approaches to learning, 144–5
practical experience, 147–9
teachers, 142
value of working with practitioners,
145–7
Project Dialogue, 157–8, 162–5,
166n1
interdisciplinary collaborations, 158–9
relationship between arts and science,
157
transdisciplinary collaboration,
160–2
benefits, 165
obstacles, 159–60
Pye, David, 5, 141n13, 224–5

Ravetz, Amanda, 13, 190, 191
Read, Herbert, 148
reconstruction of the self, 114

recycled waste, 89, 92–4
    generating new materials, 97
    see also environmental issues; glass
Recyling Lives, 94–7, 97n4
relational aesthetics, 132–3, 137, 139
    subjective interaction with other-
        ness, 133
relationship between art and science,
        73, 78–9
    collaborative relationships, 157–8
    obstacles, 159–60
    Project Dialogue, 162–5
    textiles and science, 79–82
    transdisciplinarity, 160–2
    transgressing boundaries, 158–9
remembering, 41–2
    see also memories
resistance, 191, 221–2, 225, 249
Rider, Paul, 119–20
Risatti, Howard, 8
risk, 1
    certitude and, 5–6, 224
    risk assessments, 107
rituals and ritual objects, 61, 195–7,
        238–9
Roberts, David, 89
Roberts, Spencer, 65
Rogoff, Irit, 67, 237
Ryan, Paul, 48, 55
Ryan, Tony, 79–80, 82, 85

Schön, Donald, 3
Schwab, Marios, 115
Sennett, Richard, 22, 149
    philosophy of pragmatism, 133
    power of craft, 225–6
    resistance, 221–2
sensitive fabrication, 74, 105–6
shadow-play, 59–60, 62–5
    collective void, 65
    imagination, 65
Shear, Tim, 11, 74, 107–8, 110–11
simulations see computer simulations
skin
    aesthetic qualities, 116–7
    direction of grain, 116
    material qualities, 115
sKINship, 119–20, 121n3
    introduction, 114–5
Smith, Allison, 12, 190, 248

sociality of craft, 2–4, 132
    Hyde, Lewis, 247
    Ingold, Tim, 3
    social role of furniture, 45
Solomon, Rhian, 11, 74, 75
South Asia, 206–17
    Art Reverie (Gujarat), 214–16, 233–42
    cross-territory collaboration, 209–11
    cultural diversity, 206
    HAT: Here and There, 208–14
    traditional craft practices, 211–12
space, 61, 65
spatial awareness, 148
Storey, Helen, 74, 77–82, 86
Stratton, Shannon, 189
sustainability, 74–5
    design style, 74
    eco-responsibility, 75
    quality, 74
    sustainable practices, 75
    see also environmental issues

Tactility Factory, 74, 77–9, 82–6
talk as a component of creative
        practice, 34
    see also conversations
taste and style, 75, 117, 121
Taylor, Simon, 12, 127, 142
teacher training, 149–54
teaching craft and design, 142
    Skills in the Making, 142
        development of the project, 154–5
        professional development for
            teachers, 142–4
    vocational learning, 145–7
teamwork
    collaboration distinguished, 24–6
    contingent nature, 37
technologies, 147
    digital bookmarking, 105
    incorporating new technologies, 79
    interactive interfaces, 103–4
    PDAs, 105
    use of emerging technologies, 101–3
    Web 2.0 technologies, 103–4
textiles
    applications of textile processes,
        87
    architecture, 77
    concrete and, 82–6

materiality of skin, 115
science and, 79–82
textile knowledge, 77
Theophilus, Jeremy, 13, 189–90
Thompson, Paul, 130
time passing, 62
transience, 65
Tiravanija, Rirkrit, 132–3
tissue engineering, 80
Tool, Ehren, 220, 229
traditional techniques, new technologies
    and, 45, 101, 105
see also technologies

United States, 193–203
American Fancy, 201–2

value in collaborations, 237–9
value of collections, 171–4, 180–1
value of objects, 239
Versalius, Andreas, 115
virtual realities, 101
see also computer simulations
visitor experiences, 102
engagement, 104, 109, 132

impact of new technologies, 105
see also participation
vocational learning
cognitive development, 147–9
teachers, 145–7

Wagner, Roy, 239
Walking, Talking, Making, 35–7
waste (recycling), 89, 92–4
environmental impact, 97
see also environmental issues;
    recycled waste
Web 2.0, 108
collaboration, 104–5, 110
interfaces, 108
Webb, Jane, 10, 20
Web sites see World Wide Web
Wentworth, Richard, 131
Wiki, 103–4, 110
Wilson, Anne, 4
Wilson, Brett, 12, 127
Wise, R. J., 119
wonderment, 62–4
World Wide Web, 59–60, 108–9, 110,
    222